To my friend Don with all my best always Clyde B.: 5-09-03"

60 Years an Alcoholic
50 Years Without a Drink

Freeman Carpenter Clyde B. June 20, 1946

Freeman Carpenter (pseudonym)

‖|‖|‖‖‖|‖|‖‖|‖‖‖‖‖|‖‖|‖
☑ W9-BMQ-313

First Edition

Unique Educational Services Newtown, PA

60 Years an Alcoholic
50 Years Without a Drink

By Freeman Carpenter (pseudonym)

Published By:
Unique Educational Services
P O Box 341
Newtown, PA 18940 U.S.A.

Copyright 1996 by Freeman Carpenter (pseudonym)
First Printing 1996
Printed in the United States of America

Library of Congress Catalog Card Number 96-90221
Carpenter, Freeman
    60 Years an Alcoholic: 50 Years Without a Drink
  by Freeman Carpenter. - 1st ed.
    ISBN 0-9651618-4-6

"Sadness, pain, despair, hope, joy, recovery, serenity...the steps from addiction to life, told with a voice so eloquent that you almost hear the Irish brogue as you read. The road to recovery is excitingly spiced with historic tidbits while it invites you to follow Freeman Carpenter through his joyous journey from fear to faith. A great book for anyone in the field of addiction or someone who recognizes these steps as their own."

Janet Jensen, M.H.S.,C.A.C. Diplomate,CCJS

"This is a very poignant account of one man's descent into the bottle and into hell, his struggles with recovery, and the steps to a new life. His story details the twists of emotion that alcoholics experience as they hopelessly descend into the gutter of the street or the mind and the frustrations of those, ignorant of the effects of the disease, as they try to convince an alcoholic that they are in need of help. A 'must read' for those interested in understanding the emotional battle all alcoholics face and for understanding how a seeming 'normal and rational' person can cause himself so much pain and cause so much misery to those that love him."

Ann Porter, J.D.

"I lost several nights sleep engrossed in the continual chaotic and unpredictable events of Freeman's life and the progression of his disease of alcoholism. I was truly fascinated by his life, from the insanity of his childhood to the progressively addictive, uncontrollable allergy that compels us down a destructive road to hell, ultimate despair and hopelessness. My faith in God and His loving grace, expressed through Alcoholics Anonymous, was strengthened as I explored Freeman's surrender to this disease and his fifty years of continuous sobriety. I recommend this book to any recovering alcoholic and to those still suffering from this disease, unconvinced that a solution exists or are unwilling to reach out for help."

Jim B., a recovering alcoholic with more than four years of continuous sobriety.

"It's all here --- a dysfunctional family background, a tortured young man seriously considering suicide, his life almost ruined by alcoholism --- and then, just in the nick of time, the young man's encounter with Alcoholics Anonymous. This story so parallels mine that it gives me hope for continued sobriety and growth.

I am sure that you will find this book as helpful as I did."

Steve T., A.A.C.11 --- the primary therapist in a rehabilitation center.

"Everyone whose life has been touched by addiction should read this book.

The distinction between alcohol and drugs is somewhat artificial and while this book concentrates on alcoholism, the story is relevant across the board.

Someone has said that fiction has to adhere to probability while real life does not have such constraints. The breadth and depth of pain produced by alcohol on the Carpenter family would not be credible if presented in a novel. Nor would it be credible that such a recovery could occur in a life so affected by alcohol.

This is a book about addiction to alcohol and the pain produced by it. But it is also about how one of the great discoveries of this century --- the twelve step recovery program of Alcoholics Anonymous --- can salvage lives.

I have experienced the pains of alcoholism at first hand, as have others of my family. I have seen that those who where fortunate enough to be affected by the program of A.A. had a much more fortunate future than those who did not.

This book chronicles a history all to familiar to those in recovery. And to those not familiar with the program, this story will point to 'How It Works'."

Richard J.

THE MONSTER LEGEND

During my years as a member of Alcoholics Anonymous, I have been asked to speak about my alcoholism on numerous occasions.

Those talks had to be designed to answer the challenge A.A. put forth --- to share our experiences, strength and hope with each other.

In other words, I was to tell what it used to be like; what happened that directed me to A.A.; and finally, what it's been like living sober.

The purpose behind all that sharing was twofold:
1) To help me stay sober myself, and
2) To help the suffering alcoholic in
   the audience to stay sober as well.

Much to my own surprise, my oral description of my alcoholism as being a monster that had me trapped, impressed many an alcoholic enough so that they were able to identify with us. A few of them, both men and women, told me how that description matched exactly how they had felt for years but they had never been able to put it into words.

Because we have all heard that a picture is worth a thousand words, I was curious to see if that adage would hold true in this case --- and so my ogre Al-R-G was born.

When I showed the pictures to my friends they loved the representation immediately and many newcomers were profoundly moved by them.

And so I decided to keep Al-R-G as a teaching guide. Over a long period of time he has become indispensable.

I know that no barroom closed
when I stopped my drinking but
I think that one of our local
breweries laid off the night shift.

TABLE OF CONTENTS

Part One
Inside A Dysfunctional Family

Table of Contents Continued

Part Two
My Introduction To Alcohol

Table of Contents Continued

Table of Contents Continued

Part Three:
The Birth Of A Miracle

ACKNOWLEDGMENTS

I want to acknowledge the valuable influence that Alcoholics Anonymous has had in my life. Then too, I wish to express my gratitude for the many individuals---alcoholics and non-alcoholics alike---who gave me encouragement and support along the way when I was in desperate need.

I want to acknowledge the valuable contributions my children made in my recovery. And there is an apology needed here before I can go any further. I was able, with the help of God, to give my five children a comfortable life up to a point. I gave them food, clothing, an education and a roof over their heads, but that was about all. I didn't give them any emotional love---I didn't have any to give.

I sometimes think that I didn't raise my children, they raised me. By that I mean, being responsible for their welfare, and wanting to do a good job, I was forced to grow up. However, during the growing, one could say that emotionally I was an absent father.

Not that I wanted to be, I just didn't know any other way. I was so engrossed in overcoming my alcoholism and earning a livelihood that I was unaware of just how beautiful children could be. By the time I was able to recognize how important my children were they were all grown and married. I am sorry that I had to miss so much of their childhood.

I want to say "Thank you" to my first wife, Irene. She saw me through those last three horrible years of my active alcoholism---worse, she lived with me during the early years of my recovery when I was so difficult to live with and impossible to understand.

And last, but very important, I want to acknowledge Megan, my present wife. She not only encouraged me to get my manuscript out of mothballs and get it finished, she helped me do it. She worked long hours on editing. "Thank you, Megan, for all of your involvement."

I did not stop my drinking
because I saw the light ---
I stopped because I felt
the heat.

PREFACE

The book you are about to read was written by a seventy-five year old man. It is a unique account in many ways, in that the author was fortunate enough to become a member of Alcoholics Anonymous when he was just twenty-six. From that day until this, he has not had a drink of alcohol in any form. Hopefully, this story will be helpful in carrying the A.A. message to alcoholics everywhere.

The writer has used a pseudonym in keeping with the eleventh tradition of Alcoholics Anonymous which states: "Our public relations policy is based on attraction rather than promotion; we need always maintain personal anonymity at the level of press, radio and films".

The thoughts and ideas expressed throughout the book are the author's alone and do not necessarily reflect the thinking of Alcoholics Anonymous as an organization. Each member of A.A. is free to interpret the meaning of the twelve suggested steps of recovery in his or her own individual way. With this generous freedom, the author comfortably takes license and shares his thoughts.

I look forward to this book reaching a large audience of interested people. It is my hope that many professionals will read these pages and give credence to my observations and my conclusions. Any person having alcoholism in his family could look here for constructive ideas.

I dedicate this book to the members of Alcoholics Anonymous the world over. Their unselfish giving of themselves as they carry the A.A. message of recovery to the still active alcoholic has always been, to me at least, incredible. These wonderful men and women saved me from an early alcoholic death or permanent insanity.

By the time I was twenty-six, I had experienced ten years of uncontrollable drunken binges. Try as I would, I could not control my drinking once I started; neither could I stop altogether. I knew nothing of alcoholism at the time. Insanity seemed the only sensible explanation for my erratic behavior. Time after time I would go into a bar to have just a couple of drinks; I ended up drunk every time, quite often in jail.

Slowly but steadily I became mentally and physically exhausted. Eventually I no longer had the strength to keep up the struggle. I began to be seriously worried about my future, or if I even had one. What was I to do? Was I destined to live on skid row with the rest of the drunks? The prospect of that life was so objectionable though, I began to consider suicide as the only way out. Several times I planned a way to kill myself but discarded each one because I was a coward. Apparently I could not even use this avenue of escape. I was a complete failure in everything I tried to do, or at least I thought I was.

Nevertheless, through all those confusing years, I was able to maintain a bold front. After all, I thought, a real man does not let anyone know he is up against a problem he can't solve. Especially one he seems to be deliberately creating for himself. Even a close observer could not guess the turmoil raging inside and I surely was not about to tell him. As I became more desperate, I knew it was just a matter of time before I conquered my fear of death and took the plunge one way or another. I could not keep living like I was; I knew the end was near. At that critical point I was directed to Alcoholics Anonymous and not a moment too soon.

I give credit to the fellowship of Alcoholics Anonymous for most of the changes I had to effect to become the person I am today. The A.A. fellowship taught me that theirs was a program of action. Members warned me --- no one was going to do the work for me. My recovery from alcoholism was entirely my personal responsibility. Alcoholics Anonymous could only show me the path to take; it was up to me to take it. Members further cautioned that every bit of gain would bring emotional pain. It was firmly suggested I take the chip off my shoulder and relax. I quickly learned that anger, hatred and resentments were luxuries I could not afford. They were like a cancer, eating at my heart and mind. I was asked to "resign from the debating society" and listen to other people for a change. I so desperately wanted to get sober and stay that way I went to work with enthusiasm; in doing so I found that all my A.A. friends were right. I am still sober fifty years later.

Unquestionably, the people I met in Alcoholics Anonymous were responsible for the beginning of a learning process that allowed everything else to happen. However, I received assistance along the precarious road to sanity and sobriety from many other sources. Often I was helped over some tough hurdles by a friendly psychiatrist. A book written by a concerned psychologist became a constant source of direction and comfort. Many a clergyman gave freely of his time when he could sense my needs better than I knew them. People who I felt for years were my bitter enemies became helpful once they knew I was working at being sober. Even police officers and creditors became kinder than I ever thought they would. Only a small handful of these people were recovering alcoholics. The rest of them were just good people wanting to help another human being.

From the beginning of Alcoholics Anonymous in 1935, non-alcoholic people unstintingly contributed their time and effort to the cause. Without their involvement and patience, I doubt whether Alcoholics Anonymous could have survived its first few years. I sincerely thank every one of them, not only for their early contributions, but for the multitude of alcoholics whom they have befriended over the years. To me, the help I received from knowledgeable non-alcoholic men and women along the way, has been as vital to my recovery as Alcoholics Anonymous has been on a daily basis. It has been my special privilege to have known them.

One by one the fallacies of the past are being abandoned as new knowledge becomes ours. For example, there was a time, not too many years ago, when the thinking of most people concerning alcoholism and the alcoholic was that you had to wait until the alcoholic asked for help before he could be helped. The result of this thinking was that thousands of alcoholics died in their alcoholism. Many others died driving automobiles while drunk. Still others took their own lives in their desperation. A good number of these people died without ever realizing their problem was alcoholism, or at the very least, alcohol abuse. We now know how dangerous to the alcoholic that thinking was. We said we could accept the fact that alcoholism is a disease, that the alcoholic is a sick person. But then we were also saying we could do nothing unless the alcoholic asked us for help. We have learned many things we can do to coerce the sick person to face his moment of truth. Yes, thousands of alcoholics who asked for help responded favorably to the help offered. However, for many others, even when they asked for help, it was too late. Records now show the ratio of success and failure is the same whether the alcoholic walks in off the street looking for help or is forced into treatment by his employer, spouse or the courts. I have heard several alcoholics publicly express their gratitude for an employer who insisted they go into a treatment center or lose their jobs. They said it was the beginning of their recovery from a malady they did not know they had. Again I have heard others say the same about their loving wives or husbands who would no longer tolerate their drinking, but stood by them when they went for help.

It has been estimated that approximately 3% of all alcoholics are on skid row and exposed to public scrutiny. And once on skid row, the road back, although not impossible, is most difficult and painful. Many of these people were drinking alcoholically, without knowing it, for several years before they became a resident of skid row. If the estimate is correct it means the other 97% are scattered throughout our society and appear, at least

16

publicly, to be living normal, productive lives. Even
at that, the residents on skid row usually represent
the male alcoholic only.

Public censure toward the female problem drinker
is stronger than it is for any man. As a result, a
woman who begins to have a problem with the way she
drinks, learns to hide her drinking very early. As a
woman's drinking progresses, she may become what is
known as a closet drinker. For many others, their
bedroom becomes their refuge from an apparently cruel
world. In either case they have created a skid row
environment right in their own homes. Their condition
was, and still is, more desperate than that of the men
on skid row, as they could not even experience the
company of others as miserable as themselves. These
women usually suffer in silence, shame, and loneliness
for a very long time before they become frantic enough
to respond to any offers of help.

It has always been possible to recognize an
alcoholic in the last throes of his disease. What is
revolutionary today is the knowledge we have that
allows us to identify alcoholism in its earlier
stages, before it has taken its heavy toll. As with
any disease, the earlier it is detected the easier it
is for the victim to respond to treatment. The
practice of sitting back not knowing what to do while
people destroy each other and themselves is in the
past. Where it may have been understandable some
years ago to hear a person say, "I don't know what
more I could have done", it is not so today.
Alcoholics themselves say that an alcoholic is a
person who has a physical allergy to alcohol coupled
with a mental obsession he can't live without it. I
have no argument with this definition. In fact it
fitted me perfectly when I presented myself to
Alcoholics Anonymous. However, I found many an
alcoholic, including myself, who could identify with
other definitions as well. For example, here is
another that described my dilemma: An alcoholic is a
person who, once he starts to drink, experiences an
insatiable craving for more and more alcohol. Such a
person is no longer able to predict how much he will
drink, how long he will be drinking, or what will

happen to him during the drinking episode. He may or
may not experience a phenomenon known as a blackout, a
period of time when the drinking person functions
normally to a casual observer but remembers nothing
the next day. There are several other definitions,
all accurate, that can identify particular types of
alcoholics. It is not the purpose of this book to
discuss them all.

One thing is absolutely certain. Whether
alcoholism comes on the victim suddenly, as it did
with me, or takes years to develop to the point where
it is obvious, once you have it you have it.
Alcoholism is progressive, it is permanent, and if not
treated, it is fatal. I feel confident any further
information on the topic a person may need is as close
as a telephone. Whether a person is a problem
drinker, an alcohol abuser, or an alcoholic makes
little difference. If he has any kind of a problem
because of his drinking, then he has a problem. It is
that simple. As we argue among ourselves over who is
and who is not an alcoholic, the problem of alcoholism
is mushrooming. We do not have time to indulge in
arguments of this nature. We only have time for
constructive action regardless of how small our
contribution may be.

As the probing for more knowledge on alcoholism
continues, astonishing facts keep coming to the
surface. Just one example should be sufficient to
excite our curiosity. During the past fifteen years,
because of intensive work with alcoholics, a new light
has been turned onto the behavior of the non-alcoholic
persons involved in the human drama. These people who
are closest to the alcoholic are called, "The
Significant Others". They are sometimes given other
titles as well. For example there is "The Enabler"
and "The Rescuer". It is believed now the disease of
alcoholism involves a complete circle of people all
playing a specific role in order for the illness to
stay alive and active. There is sound proof to
substantiate this belief.

If you know an alcoholic, direct him to Alcoholics Anonymous or a rehabilitation center for help. If you are married to an alcoholic, you owe it to yourself to look into Al-Anon. Children of alcoholics should be given the opportunity to avail themselves of the help Alateen offers. For anyone enmeshed in the madness of alcoholism, enough is known to help him turn any destructive reaction into constructive action. Yes, an alcoholic is a sick person who needs help. He/she is worth helping, and the proper help is available. But whether the alcoholic responds to help or not, the people close to him/her need help in coping with circumstances in their lives. They are no longer forgotten victims. The proper help is available for them also. It is no longer a shame to have alcoholism in a family. It is only a shame if the family insists on covering it up and living with it.

During my drinking days my thinking
was just as abnormal as my behavior.
It was not my drinking that got me
stinking --- it was my stinking
thinking that kept me drinking.

INTRODUCTION

I am told that people are always interested in other people. For this reason I would not feel I have been just to my readers if I omitted at least a thumbnail sketch of my childhood. Then too, I am inclined to think if a reader happens to be a professional, he may be disappointed if it is not included. Some professionals may even feel the work would be incomplete without it.

I hesitated to write even a partial history at first, lest anyone think I was trying to place the responsibility for my alcoholism elsewhere. A good part of my reluctance probably came from a guilty conscience because for years I would have loved to have done just that. I do not know whether my early environment had anything to do with my alcoholism or not. Some experts say yes, some say maybe, and still others argue that it is mostly in the genes. I do not care. I will leave that discussion with the psychiatrists and psychologists where it belongs. How or why I became an alcoholic is unimportant. If I was to live, I had to take responsibility for reshaping my life facing the fact that I was an alcoholic.

In keeping with the anonymity theme in this book, and to protect the living members of my family, I have assigned fictitious names to everyone. Even our surname, Carpenter, is an alias. It was taken from my father's occupation.

FOR YOUR CONSIDERATION

This story was written to provide an historical account of how one alcoholic survived his dysfunctional childhood, his alcoholism and his eventual recovery from that dreaded disease. The author does not claim that his decisions and his actions, in any given situation, would produce the same successful results in any reader's particular case. In fact, the opposite results may be experienced.

Every individual has different strengths and weaknesses; every situation is uniquely different.

This story is not meant to be a therapeutic guide. The author knows only too well how addicts insist on working out their problems all by themselves. Some of them can't ask for help, others won't ask for it and still others hate to.

Many an addict, knowing the practice of keeping to themselves with their problems is dangerous, still continue to indulge themselves much to their own chagrin.

Remember, for many of us, the diseases of alcoholism and/or drug addiction are only symptoms of a grave mental, emotional and spiritual disorder. The more confused, angry and unhappy a person is in the beginning of his/her recovery the more help they need to keep on track.

For Your Consideration Continued

Every alcoholic and drug addict needs a sponsor or two. Many of us need a counselor as well. Still others need a therapist and a sponsor. And a very few of us need psychiatric help along the way.

Please let this story be a compliment to whatever method you are using in your efforts to get well, not a substitute.

If you can feel comfortable in accepting the limitations of this book, please read on and may God bless you in your efforts.

I am in the program as long as I
have been because people told me
to keep coming back until I got it
right --- I think I've almost got it.

PART ONE

INSIDE A DYSFUNCTIONAL FAMILY

A PERSONAL INTRODUCTION

THE CARPENTERS

I was born in Halifax, Nova Scotia, Canada, March 12, 1920. World War I had ended over a year before but everyone was still excited about peace being restored. Peggy, my mother, had given birth to two girls and a boy before I came along. However, Albert, her second child, was born with serious stomach problems and died before he was six months old. Because of mother's loss, I was told I was a most welcome son. Eleven months after my birth, another son was born and we became a family of six.

When I was a little over three years old, my parents decided to come to America to seek their fortune. What an adventure that was for me! A huge steamship delivered us to Boston Harbor, Massachusetts, in late May of 1923. I vaguely remember bits and pieces of that journey but not much.

Three months after we moved into our new home, mother gave birth to her first American-born child, a girl. She named her Eileen and I had another sister. We were then a family of seven.

CHANGING TIMES

The first few years in America were good years as I remember them. But when I was about six years old things began to change. For one thing, Bruce, my father, was around the house during the day and that was strange to us; later we learned he was not working. At first we liked having him home because he played with us and we had a lot of fun. However, at night, after we children had gone to bed, mother and dad would begin to argue. At times their arguments would become violent and we would be terrified they would hit each other. I began to hate my parents then. I hated my mother the most because I blamed her for everything.

I BEGIN MY SCHOOLING

When I was seven years old, I started my schooling. Mother enrolled me in a Catholic school nearby, a school where my two older sisters were already attending. For some strange reason I was terrified of everything, including school, and it showed. It did not take the other children long to learn I could not or would not defend myself no matter what they did to me. Every class had a bully or two, even in a Catholic school, and we had ours. Almost daily I would come home with a black eye or a bloody nose until they tired of the sport and left me alone most of the time.

In spite of all the confusion I experienced during my school years, I am grateful to the nuns for many things. There were some warm and loving nuns whom I got to know. I liked being close to them and would stay after school to erase blackboards and clean desks just to be near them for a while longer before I had to go home to my cold house. Then there was the quality of my elementary education. The nuns were excellent teachers and disciplinarians. They taught, and we learned. Because of circumstances beyond my control, that education was to be all I had for a long time. I was able to go a good distance with it. Then, later on, when I had the opportunity to further my schooling, my instructors were pleased with my basic knowledge.

THE FAMILY MEMBERS

As my story unfolds, the characters of my mother and father would take on a certain hue. The same would be true of my brother and four sisters. And so, in order to make their individual personalities better understood, I will introduce the members of the Carpenter family one by one.

PEGGY MY MOTHER

My mother, Peggy, was born in a small mining town somewhere in Canada. Her father was a coal miner and she was one of six children. I never knew my maternal grandparents and can remember meeting only one aunt. There were two uncles, but I never saw them that I can recall. Just after we moved to the United States, my grandfather was killed in a mine explosion. Mother was heartbroken and as far as I know never went back home after that.

Mother was a pretty woman but she was dictatorial, no one could communicate with her about anything. She made a statement about something and we kept our mouths shut, or we would be sorry we hadn't. If we tried to develop a conversation, she would quickly tell us, "Children should be seen and not heard, and they should not be seen too often". I had the feeling that if God Himself wanted to speak to her, she would force Him to make an appointment!

Mother was also cruel. For instance, once when my sister Erma was about twelve, mother sent her to the corner store for a few groceries. Mother had given her just enough money to pay for everything, about fifty cents as I remember. On the way to the store Erma lost the money. Like the rest of us, Erma was too terrified of mother to tell her, so she bought the groceries and charged them to a neighbor's bill. That particular neighbor was a person who watched her

27

spending closely. At the end of the week when our neighbor went to pay the grocer, she learned what Erma had done and told mother. It was only then, while mother was slapping her face, that Erma admitted she had lost the money. I remember Erma was cowering on a chair near the kitchen stove where I had firewood piled high in the corner. Mother became so enraged she grabbed a large piece of wood and came down on Erma's head. Later, at the hospital, mother told the doctor Erma had fallen and we dared not say differently. It took six stitches to close the gash.

Mother would not let us show her any affection and she gave none. It seemed that she felt once she got us through infancy, we were too big to hug or hold. Anytime we went to kiss her, she turned a cold cheek to us and did not kiss us in return.

Although mother had only a third-grade education she loved to read, and over the years she had taught herself to read well. One of her favorite pleasures was to read aloud to us children and we spent hours at a time listening to her. I was fascinated with her books and loved to sit on the floor at her feet while she read to us about far-away places and courageous people. Mother passed on to me a love for books which I shall always be grateful for. However, as things kept getting worse between her and dad, even those precious moments faded.

MY FATHER BRUCE

No one ever told us where our father, Bruce, was born. Dad never talked about himself and so mother became our only source of information. According to mother, dad was raised by his mother and an aunt. As mother did not have a kind word for either of them, we children were told very little about their lives. My father's childhood, as far as I was concerned, was as if it never happened.

However, he was a first-class carpenter and

cabinetmaker. Because of his education and his skills, it was difficult for me to understand why he was out of work so often. The answer to my dad's periodic unemployment began to dawn on me as I grew older. With all the talents my father possessed, which should have guaranteed him a comfortable income, he had a serious problem in getting along with people.

ERICKA MY OLDEST SISTER

Ericka was the first born in our family and was five years my senior. My first lasting impressions of her began when I was about five years old. She was a tall, thin girl who was rather sickly all during her early years. Because of astigmatism in both eyes, she was forced to wear thick glasses from the time she was about seven. Her eyesight was so poor she had to put her glasses in one of her shoes each night in order to find them as soon as she woke up; she could not see a thing without them. However, as she grew older, her health steadily improved and by the time she was in her late teens, except for her eyes, she was as healthy as the rest of us.

In school Ericka told me she was not a star pupil. Although she received good grades in all subjects, she said she had to work hard for them, and if she neglected her studies even for a short time, her grades would suffer. However, she continued to apply herself and graduated from both elementary and high school in the allotted time.

Being the oldest in the family, Ericka was given the responsibility of taking care of the rest of us much of the time. A short time after her twelfth birthday mother began leaving Ericka in charge of the house in the evenings so she and dad could take in a movie or visit friends.

In fact Ericka became our surrogate mother, as the responsibility for our behavior and our welfare fell more and more on her shoulders as we grew up together. Ericka seemed to be more concerned about us than our own mother was. It was she who came to school to see our teachers when anything went wrong. Whenever I was kept after school, she never went home without checking on me first. If I was being beaten by a bully, again it was Ericka who would wade in and pull the villain off me by the scruff of his neck. Many a lie she told to protect us from our parent's wrath. I know now that Ericka had no life of her own; she actually lived for us. And I also realize now that without her, we may not have survived our childhood.

ALBERT MY OLDER BROTHER

Albert, mother's second child, was born a year after Ericka, but as recorded earlier, he died in his infancy. According to our aunt, mother was completely crushed by Albert's death and suffered a nervous breakdown. She was placed under a doctor's care and for a long time showed no desire to get back on her feet. However, mother was a healthy young woman and soon found herself pregnant again; she was ecstatic and began to improve rapidly. She told everyone she wanted a boy to take the place of her lost son.

MY OLDER SISTER ERMA

Our aunt told Ericka that when mother found out she had given birth to a daughter she went into hysterics and refused to accept the child. The story goes she even told father to give the baby away, to get her out of the house. I don't know just how they were able to resolve that problem, but the relationship between mother and Erma was never a good one.

What made matters worse, Erma wet the bed every night and as she got older she became obese.

I was the next child to be born in our family after Erma. There were twenty-eight months between us. Because of the unique circumstances surrounding our family at the time, I was greeted with open arms by everyone. Ericka told me that mother wanted a boy badly to replace her lost son Albert. Ericka said that for the first five years of my life I was the "star of the show" and loved every minute of it. Dimly I remember some of those years; I was a happy child then. However, because I was loved and pampered those first few years, it was most confusing and difficult to adjust when that love was suddenly withdrawn. I began to feel, at a very early age, that there was something wrong with me, that I had become unlovable. The idea was not a clear, concrete thought at the time; but rather an uncomfortable feeling in the pit of my stomach that I could not define. Later on, when I entered school, I found out why I was so unlovable. In that Catholic school I learned that I was a sinner, a bad person. My self-esteem, what was left of it, fell to a lower level and stayed there for years. From that day on I had the feeling I was worthless and was destined to remain that way.

MY BROTHER JAKE

Jake made his grand entrance into the world just eleven months after I did. But he was different. Most babies lose their so-called baby fat as they grow and become active; not so with Jake. He not only retained his original weight, he added to it each year. Before he was five years old he was fat enough to have earned several nick-names: "Tub-Of-Lard", "Bowl-Of-Jelly" and "Jelly-Fish" were a few of the most popular. Eventually, "Tub-Of-Lard" was shortened to "Tubby", and that nick-name stuck with him throughout his life.

31

Like Erma, he too wet the bed every night and was always an embarrassment to us.

EILEEN MY YOUNGER SISTER

Then there was Eileen, mother's first American-born child. What a beautiful baby she was! With her white complexion, her red hair, and a nose dotted with freckles, she was a miniature of mother. As she grew, she even developed an identical superior attitude and a haughty air about her. Mother and Eileen became inseparable. It was Eileen who always got new clothes while the rest of us had to be content with Salvation Army seconds.

Eileen was three and a half years younger than I, and I noticed that after her arrival I was no longer the "star of the show". I resented her very much.

LISA THE BABY

Lisa was born in September of 1929. I was nine years old at the time and becoming aware of all that was going on around me. By then I was conscious of the fact that mother hated children. At the very least, we knew she thought her children were a burden she had to endure. We knew because she told us so --- often. The night Lisa was born mother let each of us hold her for a few minutes before we went to bed.

Looking down at her in my arms, my heart swelled with pride. Even before she had a name I knew I loved her. She was "my" baby sister. An overpowering urge to protect and take care of her flooded through me. I had something worthwhile in my drab life at last. I had someone to love. They named her Lisa, and she proved to be the last addition to the Carpenter family.

THINGS GOT BETTER

All during 1926 and 1927 my father had been forced to take one temporary job after another. For months he had been bringing home just enough money for us to exist on. It was during that time I first came to know what hunger was. Many nights we were put to bed without dinner. The hunger was terrible and I cried myself to sleep often. However, like everything else, that too changed. It was a day of excitement for us when dad came home to announce he had been hired by a large contracting firm. The work would be permanent and the pay excellent. Dad jubilantly declared that things were going to be good for us from then on. There was plenty of food and fuel once more; everyone was happy again.

Only a short time after he started his new job, dad bought his first automobile. It was a two-year-old Reo, but it shined like a new one. Our family held a prestigious position in the neighborhood then, because not many working men could afford an automobile in the 20's. Then too, we could go for a ride or a picnic on Sundays instead of staying in our back yard all the time.

WE MOVED TO THE COUNTRY

The next big surprise came about two months after dad had bought the car. One evening just after dinner, he told us we would be moving. He said he had bought a house in the country about twenty miles from Boston and he expected to move us within a month. We were really excited, and when I learned I would be taken out of the Catholic school I was jubilant.

After waiting for what seemed like forever, moving day was on us. When dad came home from work that evening we had a quick dinner and piled into the car.   It was uncomfortable with all the bags and boxes, but we were glad to be on our way at last.

It was only twenty miles to our new home, but it seemed like a hundred to us kids. We knew we were far away from the city because even after we left the macadam highway, we traveled several miles on dirt roads and there was not a street light to be seen anywhere. With each passing mile our excitement mounted. We arrived at our country home about nine-thirty; the night was pitch-black. The stars were so big and looked so close I felt I could reach up and pluck them right out of the sky. It was magnificent!

The summer of 1928 was one of the best times of my life. We kids were so engrossed in our country adventure nothing could tarnish our pleasure. There were large fields all around us to play in, big ponds and lakes to fish in, and most exciting, there were miles of woods to explore. Even the insects and mosquitos trying to eat us alive could not dim our spirits. That was a time when mother was busy getting settled in her new home and left us in Ericka's care much of the time. I couldn't get out of bed fast enough in the morning to see what new adventure the day would bring.

WE ENTERED PUBLIC SCHOOL

The summer was over all too soon, and it was time to think of school again. All of us, except Eileen, were going to school at the time, so mother enrolled us in a public school, the only school for miles around. Public school proved to be a wonderful experience for me. The boys and girls were in the same classroom, and the teachers were dressed like real people. The children seemed to be different than the kids in the Catholic school too. They were less mischievous when the teacher had to leave the room, for one thing. And, on the way to and from school, there was much more playfulness and less fighting. In fact, during that whole school year I personally was not involved in one fight. But most enjoyable of all, there was no catechism to memorize and little talk, if any, about sinners going to Hell. What a relief!

WE FACED REALITY

As the summer faded into winter that first year, and as the days became shorter and colder, the charm disappeared from our adventure. We began to see our "Country Home" from a more realistic perspective. What we saw did not make us happy at all.

Our house was not a house but a four-room unfinished cottage. The outside walls were intact, the roof was on, and the windows and doors were in place but that was about all. There was not one inside wall finished. The partitions between the rooms had not been installed. The floors were rough lumber and we could put our hands in the spaces between the boards. Spiders and bugs of all kinds had free access through those cracks. There were no ceilings and the place became an oven in the summer months. During the winter we could not get the house really warm, either. Electricity had been run into the house, but we had only one light bulb hanging from a rafter, the rest of the wiring had not been put in. Our water came from an old rusty pump in the front yard, and there was always a fight to get it primed.

Then there was the land. It was more like a rock pile. Down in one corner of the yard, where the privy was, a few small trees had taken root and were struggling for growth. But nothing else could grow anywhere in the yard because of the stones. The cottage was built on a huge, almost-flat rock, the top of which was just above ground. Even the privy had been in disrepair when we first moved in.

To make matters worse, all the other houses in our neighborhood were finished homes. Most of them had running water and inside bathrooms. Our privy was one of the last four still being used "On The Hill".

The old feeling of being different soon returned; I felt degraded because of our living conditions. It seemed we were living like a family on a permanent camping trip and I began to hate the place.

OUR GOOD FORTUNE ENDED

We settled into a routine of living as people will and things were pretty quiet and normal for a while. But just before Christmas of 1928, something happened that was to signal the beginning of the end of our good fortune. One evening dad did not come home for dinner at the usual time. As the hours dragged on, mother started pacing the floor and wringing her hands. The worried look on her face and her nervous actions conveyed very clearly her fears and we children picked them up easily. About three hours later than usual, my father came walking up the country road. Evidently something dreadful had happened because his head was all bandaged and his right arm was in a cast. He said he had been in his first automobile accident. After the initial shock wore off and we found he was not seriously hurt, mother started to browbeat him.

He explained he had been forced off the road by a driver coming from the opposite direction. "It had almost been a head-on collision," he said. Mother appeared not to hear a word. According to her he was careless, reckless and stupid. She said,

"I'll bet you fell asleep behind the wheel; you would have fallen asleep many times except I was with you to keep you awake." I was dumbfounded by her callousness. As I saw it, dad had nearly been killed. I could not understand how she could be so insensitive.

Naturally, dad could not go back to work for a long time. There was no unemployment compensation in those days; in fact there was no money coming in at all for a while. Soon we were hungry again and mother was verbally attacking dad as before.

Several times during that period we found boxes of food at our door early in the morning. Some wonderful person had delivered them during the night. I knew that mother's pride would not let her accept them if she knew who our benefactor was. Maybe the donor knew that also. There were canned fruits and vegetables of all kinds, meat, bread, frankforts, everything. We were so hungry that the boxes seemed like gifts from Heaven. But I still remember feeling shame because people "out there" knew that we were poor and felt sorry for us.

When dad went back to work, about three months later, he had to use public transportation for a long time before he got another car. That meant a walk of over a mile every morning to catch a bus and the same long walk home after a hard day's work, but I can't remember ever hearing him complain.

Christmas of that year was a bleak one indeed. We could not exchange gifts with each other for the first time. Santa Claus came all right, but he could only leave one small present for each of us. Our tree was a scrawny pine stolen from the woods across the road. We even had to make all the decorations for it ourselves out of paper and string. The cold and hunger seemed to be the worst I have ever known.

MY DOG JIMMY

On my ninth birthday dad gave me a puppy. He was only ten weeks old. He was full of life and I loved him immediately. He was all white except for a brown spot that covered most of the left side of his head. There was another brown spot, the size of my hand, at the base of his spine. His body was chunky and his legs were short but he was strong. He was just a mutt but to me he was a beauty. I named him Jimmy and we became inseparable. He slept on the foot of my bed at

37

night, greeted me when I came home from school every day, and even when there was little food in the house, I gave him part of mine.

Jimmy was a consolation to me in every situation. When I was punished for anything I could go off in a corner with Jimmy and it would be all right. When I was angry at Jake or anyone, I could tell Jimmy all about it. He would listen intently at my ravings and it helped. Jimmy was the only thing in the world I could call my own. Even my clothes had to be shared with Jake, but Jimmy was mine and mine alone.

A short time after Jimmy came into our home dad bought his second car. It was a five-year-old Chevrolet sedan, but it looked like a new car and we loved it. Dad could drive to work again, and he brought a carload of scrap wood home with him each night for the fire. That saved me a lot of work scrounging for dead wood all the time. Things were looking good.

FATE TURNED ON US AGAIN

In November of 1929, just two months after the birth of Lisa, the construction company my dad worked for went bankrupt. They owed my father two weeks wages, but he told mother there was no money for anyone and he did not expect to get his. Mother ranted and raved as usual and our house sounded like old times again. The Stock Market Crash of 1929 that spelled doom for so many families, had very little effect on us. We were in serious trouble long before that. The crash may have been responsible for my dad not finding work with a large construction company again. I don't know. But on the surface we saw nothing different in our house. The Christmas of 1929 was not as bad as the year before, but it was not a real good one either.

I LOST JIMMY

Late in 1930 I experienced the first personal
tragedy of my life. I lost Jimmy. The trauma was
much greater than it might have been because of the
way in which I lost him. It so happened our car had
been put in the garage for a minor repair one day.
The mechanic had told dad the car would be ready by 11
A.M. the next day. As we were getting ready for
school the next morning, I heard dad tell mother he
would not be going to work until after he picked up
the car. When we left home that morning, dad was
chopping wood and Jimmy was staying close to him. At
11 A.M. the lunch bell rang and we were out the door
before the echo of the bell had completely faded. As
we raced to the end of the school driveway we saw a
large crowd of people in the front yard of a house
directly across the street from school. They all
seemed to be looking at someone on the ground. We
kids were very curious. I thought someone had been
hurt. I was surprised when, still a good distance
away, I recognized my father in the crowd. On getting
closer I saw it was not a person on the ground
everyone was looking at, it was my dog Jimmy! He had
been hit by a car. The driver had not stopped. Jimmy
was not dead but he was badly injured. Although there
was no sign of broken bones and he was not bleeding
anywhere, he could not move his hind legs; they were
paralyzed. He tried to crawl to me but could not and
I could see the pain reflected in his eyes. My heart
went out to him and I was devastated. I learned he
had followed my dad as he walked to the garage for the
car. Jimmy had been hit right in front of the school.
Another two hundred yards and he would have been at
the garage and safe. For the first time in my life I
was so moved that I screamed at my father for letting
Jimmy come with him. Dad was taken by surprise by my
outburst, but seeing I was nearly hysterical he did
not reprimand me for my disrespect. Instead, he told
me, in as gentle a voice as I ever heard from him,
that he tried to chase Jimmy home and said he had
thought he had succeeded. But I could not believe

Jimmy could follow anyone for a whole mile without that person being aware of it.

However, Jimmy was still alive and I thought sure I could nurse him back to health. Someone had handed me a blanket and suggested we slide Jimmy onto it; they said it would be easier to handle him that way. I was crying so hard I could not see to do anything. A man next to me took the blanket and spread it out alongside of Jimmy. When they eased him onto it, he was in so much pain he yelped loudly and snapped at one of the men. Meantime, dad had gone to the garage and gotten his car. Gently they lifted Jimmy on the blanket and placed him on the floor of the car and we took him home.

There would be no afternoon school for me that day; no one could get me away from my dog. Once home, I made a thick pad of blankets in back of the kitchen stove where it was warm and settled Jimmy on them. I was determined to see he would get well again, but it was not to be. At first I could not get him to eat or drink, but by using an eye-dropper I was able to force feed him a little. He would not let anyone but me go near him. He would snap at anyone else if they tried. Jimmy had lost control of his bladder and his bowels, and mother was angry if I was five minutes late in cleaning up after him. I could see he was getting weaker and I was heartsick. I would wake in the night two or three times to go into the kitchen to see how he was. This went on for two days and three nights. Early on the third morning, when I went to see how he was, Jimmy was gone. I asked everyone if they had moved him. No one had. I knew he could crawl a little but I did not think he could go far. I had visions of him hiding under the house with no one to take care of him. He could not have opened the backdoor and gotten out by himself, but a ten year old boy would not be able to reason that out for himself, especially if he were blinded by grief. All that next week, every spare moment I could get, I crawled under the house daily with a flashlight looking for Jimmy. As the house was built on a large boulder, there were many places too narrow for me to get into, but I knew Jimmy could have wriggled into one of them if he had wanted to. My concern drove me to force myself into areas that were so close to the floor nails bit into my back and once I almost got jammed in so tight I thought I would not get out. I would have nightmares, and in them I could see Jimmy dying in a back corner under the house just below my bedroom. In my dreams I tore up the entire floor of the house without finding him. I looked for him for several days. I can't remember just how many. I cried myself to sleep every night for a long time over losing him.

Many years later, when I was married and had children of my own, Ericka told me dad had taken Jimmy out into the woods that night and had put him out of his misery. I guess he just did not know how to tell me because of my erratic behavior.

I WENT TO WORK WITH DAD

With the coming of spring my father started to get a trickle of carpentry work. As the temperature began to rise so did our hopes that things would get better for us. My spirits rose to new heights as dad began to take me to work with him. On the job I took a keen interest in the work and learned fast. Dad taught me how to frame doors and windows, how to build a dividing partition between rooms and how to lay a hardwood floor. A new feeling of importance flooded through me. I thought, "Gee, here I am, only eleven years old, helping dad with work he is being paid for. I am being a help instead of a burden. Surely I will now enjoy a position of importance in the family."

Because of the work we were doing together I began to see another side of my father, a side I would not have known otherwise. I watched in awe as he turned a bare room into a modern kitchen with built-in cabinets that he created right on the walls as he went along. I felt privileged to watch a house being built from the ground up. My respect for my father grew

41

immensely as I watched him putting his skills to work. I thought there was a closeness developing between us but it was evidently one-sided. Nevertheless, I became bold enough a few times, to say a word or two on my father's behalf when mother would make derogatory remarks about him. Those efforts got me a cuff on the ear or some other form of mild punishment, but I felt it was worth it.

MOTHER AND DAD CONTINUED THEIR FIGHTING

Sometime near midnight one night when I was in a deep sleep I felt a hand on my shoulder shaking me; someone was whispering in my ear. It was Ericka and she seemed frightened.

"Freeman, Freeman," she whispered, "wake up."

I was instantly awake. I could sense her anxiety and became apprehensive myself.

"What's the matter?" I whispered back to her.

"Mom and dad are fighting again," she said; "they are going at it hot and heavy and I am afraid dad will hit her."

"I wish to hell he would," I said, "but he doesn't have the guts."

I listened in the dark for some time but I heard nothing. I thought maybe they had ended their argument and I started to drift off to sleep again. I was almost asleep when mother's voice jarred me into consciousness. She hollered at dad so loudly I was sure one could have heard her way out on the street.

"Goddam you, Bruce, don't you pretend to be asleep when I am trying to talk to you. School starts soon and I don't have money for school clothes," she said. Dad mumbled something I could not make out, but whatever it was it made mother furious.

"You spineless bastard!" she screamed, "Mr. Jones from the bank was here today. He said you haven't paid the mortgage in four months. You told me all along you were paying it regularly. What the hell is the matter with you?" She was so distraught her voice was a high-pitched scream by the time she finished her tirade.

All of us children were awake by that time, listening and whispering back and forth. We were terribly frightened when mom and dad fought like that and the fear stayed with us for days afterward.

NEIGHBORS BEFRIENDED US ONCE MORE

Early one morning, when Jake went outside with the chamberpots, he found four large boxes of groceries on our doorstep. I had never seen so much food at one time. Mother said it was probably from a local church. There was almost everything a person could think of in those boxes. A large ham, a seven pound roast beef, frankfurters, hamburger, sausages, flour, fresh vegetables of all kinds, canned goods, bread, cookies, and even some candies. All the time that mother was unpacking the food she was berating dad for not being able to provide for his family. She was angry because neighbors knew of our plight and were forcing charity on her. She said if she knew who put the boxes on our doorstep, she would make them take their groceries back. I was afraid she would. I had seen her do other things just as crazy many times before. I was thankful she never did find out who those generous people were. Hunger had quickly helped me to overcome the humiliation I felt because of some kind person's charity. Whenever boxes of food were left at our door, except for the first time, I found myself being very thankful that there were concerned and generous people in the world.

Even though mother said she wished people would stop embarrassing her with gifts of groceries, she was like a kid with a Christmas present. She tried to

43

hide her pleasure but it shone through her eyes in spite of her efforts. All that day she spent in the kitchen with her pots and pans. The house was so warm from her cooking stove it was uncomfortable. The aroma of baked goods coming from her oven made the whole neighborhood aware of her talents. That evening, at dinner, what a treat we had! Mother had baked bread again. She had made a large pot of ham and cabbage with boiled potatoes, carrots and parsnips. It had been a long time since we had that much food on the table. We could hardly constrain ourselves until mother called us to eat. Once seated it was difficult to watch our manners, but we knew we must or mother might send us away from the table with our stomachs still empty. I was cramming food into my mouth as fast as I could while keeping an eye on mother, when suddenly another serious problem was thrust upon me.

MY TEETH BEGAN TO BREAK

As I was chewing furiously on a large piece of ham, a tooth broke off even with the gum. When the hot food hit that open nerve I thought the top of my head was coming off. I was too hungry to stop eating, but that shock slowed me down a lot. After the first stab of pain subsided I cautiously put small bits of food into my mouth on the right side away from the broken tooth. I found if I chewed slowly and eased the food down my throat, I could keep the tooth from acting up on me. In that manner I was able to put away quite a bit of food in spite of a bad tooth.

But that night, as I lay in bed, the tooth started to throb again. I had no idea there was pain so intense and so persistent! Until that night I had thought all pain was alike. For example, when I hurt an arm or a leg the pain slowly subsided and sooner or later it would be completely gone. It took a toothache to teach me differently. I found that when a bad tooth started to ache the pain went on and on. It left when it was ready to go and not before.

Over the next three years I had several more teeth break as the first one had. I became very familiar with the torture of aching teeth from then on. The cure for one toothache never seemed to work for the next one. It came to the point that when I had a toothache, mother would give me anything she happened to have in the medicine cabinet at the time and hoped that it would do the trick. Once she gave me a jar of red, jelly-like salve and told me to rub it on my face next to the bad tooth. The salve was so hot that my face was badly burned! All the side of my face became fiery-red and very hot to the touch. I soon forgot about the aching tooth and began to concentrate on my burning cheek. It took a lot of cold water before all the redness was gone from the skin.

Many times the medication was of no use at all and I would continue to cry with the pain. If that went on for long mother or dad would accuse me of being a crybaby and threaten to give me something to cry about if I did not shut up. I learned to cry silently into my pillow whenever my parents were in one of their nasty moods. Often when the tooth would finally stop aching, I could not be sure just what I had used that brought about the relief.

Finally, in the fall of 1934, the school sponsored a dental program and I saw a dentist for the first time. By then several teeth were beyond saving. Those that had broken off had to have the roots dug out to insure against infection. Even with the help of good dentists my teeth continued, year after year, to rot and break. One by one I lost them until in my early thirties I had a full set of dentures. But I am getting ahead of myself so let us return to late summer of 1931.

DAD FOUND EMPLOYMENT AGAIN

My father did find work one day shortly after mother threatened to put him out if he didn't. For the time being there was a truce between them. But still, at night, there was a lot of muffled talk coming from their bedroom. However, they were not at each other's throats and I was grateful for that.

Going to school that year was the first time we were not newly dressed from head to foot. Each of us had at least one or two pieces of new clothing but not much more. Jake and I had no underwear at all by then and I felt that most keenly. Our clothes, or lack of them, became one more reason for me to feel different than the other children. I felt more awkward than any previous year. I was skinny, weighing only sixty-two pounds. I was four-foot five inches tall and a bundle of nervous energy. I could not sit still for five minutes, I was constantly biting my finger nails, and I was afraid of my own shadow. The other boys in school still terrified me, but Ericka said she would take care of me and she did. Once when a bully was pushing me around, Ericka came on the scene and gave him a good thrashing. From then on I was ridiculed for being a sissy who needed a girl to fight his battles for him. I don't know which was worse, to be called a coward or a sissy. I felt the embarrassment all during my school years, the more because I felt I deserved the titles.

WE MOVED BACK TO THE CITY

Only six weeks after school started we were to be jolted again by a drastic change in our lives. One Friday when we came in from school we found mother packing all her dishes, pots and pans, and knickknacks. She told us we were going to move that weekend and sternly warned us not to tell anyone. The very next evening, after dark, a big truck pulled up to our door with three men ready for a night's work. Within three hours, with mother, dad and all of us kids helping, everything we owned was in the truck and we were on our way back to the city. I could sense the urgency and the need for secrecy even if I could

46

not understand why. I interpreted the move to mean that we had to escape from some dreadful enemy only mother and dad knew about.

We moved into a large apartment that time. It was on the first floor of a huge three-story house. There were two apartments on each floor, all rented except the one we were moving into. That was the first house we lived in that had a bathroom. We kids were excited because it had not only a toilet but a washbasin and a bathtub. We thought we were in paradise. Finally, after a lot of work, we flopped into bed. It was then past midnight and we were exhausted. Although we slept soundly the rest of the night the newness of the whole thing would not let us sleep late the next morning. We were up at 6:30 A.M. and out the door to see where we were. After just a bit of exploring in the neighborhood, we realized we were then living only a half mile from where we had lived just over three years before.

The following day we learned, to my horror, that Erma and I would be going back to the same Catholic school we had attended before. Jake and Eileen would be going there also but it would be their first experience in a Parochial school. Ericka was more fortunate; she would be going to a public high school since she was in the tenth grade and the Catholic school only went to the eighth.

OUR FIRST ENCOUNTER WITH THE LAW

We were in our new apartment less than a month when I was catapulted into my first brush with the law. It began on a rainy Saturday; late in the afternoon I was reading a book in my room when Erma came running in.

"Freeman," she said, "do you want to take a walk uptown with me?"

47

Uptown was only ten blocks away and I was bored with reading anyway. The rain had turned to a fine mist by then and so I said,

"Sure, let's go."

I hadn't noticed until we stepped outside, that Erma had two paper shopping bags under her arm.

"What are you going to do with the bags, Erma?" I asked her.

"We are going to fill them with toys and things," she answered.

"How are we going to do that?" was my next question. She frightened me with her answer but I would not let her know I was afraid.

"You and I are going on a shoplifting spree," she said.

I was deeply concerned but said nothing. I didn't want Erma to tell the others I was a coward.

The first store we went into that day almost turned into a disaster for us. It was a large, famous-named department store. The toys were in their basement and so we headed straight down the stairs. The first half hour Erma spent teaching me how to shoplift. She showed me how she could sneak an article off the counter right under the nose of the store clerk. Dresses would disappear off a rack as she walked by. She was fast and slick; I had a good teacher. When she thought I had been taught enough she told me we would have to separate so we wouldn't attract too much attention.

"You stay in the toy department," she said "I will come back here as soon as my bag is full."

I was really scared but I wanted Erma to think I was as courageous as she was. Using the techniques she had taught me, I went to work. I stole several small items off the first counter I came to, boldly dropping them into my bag as though I had paid for them.   In a short time I had stolen a couple of brightly-colored balls, four decks of playing cards, a few boxes of crayons, a handful of lead soldiers, and a couple of tin racing cars.   Still I had used only a small portion of the shopping bag.   "I will never fill my bag at that rate," I thought.   I was amazed at how easy it had been, and began thinking of stealing something bigger to speed up the process.   Just then Erma came up to me and said,

"I'm ready. My bag is full."

I saw a couple of stuffed animals and a doll in her bag and I thought, "No wonder she filled hers so quickly. All the things she stole are big."   Erma was very excited.   Her big eyes seemed larger than I had ever seen them and they were sparkling.   Her whole face was lit up and glowing.   I could sense she was really enjoying this as a sport of some sort.   She became cross when she saw how little I had in my bag, but her excitement would not let her stay cross for long.   I pointed out to her that it was my first attempt at being a thief.

"OK" she said, "I'll tell you what we'll do. When we first came in I saw a big display of chocolates at the bottom of the stairs. We will get a box of them on the way out and your bag will be full."

"All right," I said.

I wished desperately to be out of that store and home safely in my room with my book. Seeing how much Erma had in her bag had scared me all over again. As good as my intentions were, when we got to the display of chocolates I found I could not reach the top boxes and I dared not pull one from the middle. Again Erma solved the problem.

"You stand close to the counter with your bag open between your feet," she said, "and I will pop one of those five-pound boxes into it when the coast is clear."

I had to wait about five minutes but she did it.

"Now just walk naturally up the stairs and out the door," she said, "I will be right behind you."

Suddenly I felt as if every pair of eyes in the store were on us. My hands were trembling and sweating profusely, my knees were knocking and I was slightly sick to my stomach. I prayed the ordeal would be over soon. The box of chocolates was sticking so far out of the top of my bag I could just barely stretch my fingers across the box and get a grip on both handles. But I finally managed it and started up the stairs. It was then that I noticed a small tear in the bottom of the bag. I had known all along the bag had become damp from the rain but I hadn't given it another thought. However, with sharp toys on the bottom and a heavy box of chocolates on top of them, the bag was in danger of splitting; I had to walk gingerly to avoid an accident. Just then, from the bottom of the stairs, a man's voice boomed out,

"Hey you, the boy in the green and white jacket."

I turned my head and saw two huge store detectives coming up the stairs. One of them was pointing at me, the other at Erma. When he saw me looking at him he hollered,

"Stay right where you are, boy --- don't you take one more step."

I was paralyzed with fear. But at that moment Erma's voice shot through me like a bolt of electricity,

"Run, Freeman, run!" she screamed in my ear as she streaked past me headed for the door.

Instantly I shot into action and bolted for the top of the stairs. The two detectives were shouting to anyone and everyone,

"Stop those two little thieves, stop them!" they cried.

Luckily everyone around us seemed to be stunned by all the fast action and no one made a move toward us. However, as I shot up the stairs, the bottom of my bag split wide open and my entire loot went cascading down the steps, amid the feet of several customers. I turned my head again in time to see the box of chocolates bouncing, end over end, down the stairs headed directly at one of the detectives. In fact he had one arm outstretched to stop it. I took advantage of the confusion by dropping my bag, then empty and tattered, and I streaked out the door.

Erma was a good three yards or so in front of me but I was determined to follow her wherever she went. She seemed to know every backalley and side street. About ten minutes of running and Erma stopped to catch her breath. I was right beside her by then and we sat down on the curbstone to rest. When Erma was finally able to talk again, she turned to me and said,

"We'll be safe now; those two detectives are too fat to chase us this far."

I knew she was right and began to relax. Through all the excitement Erma had managed to hang onto her bag and she was quite pleased with herself. I was so unnerved by the experience I became as angry as I had ever been at her. In no uncertain terms I told her to never ask me on one of her crazy junkets again. She ignored my anger, laughed heartily at my fears, and seemed to enjoy the whole thing. Her attitude enraged me. I sensed she was actually glad we had almost gotten caught. The danger had a strange exciting effect on her and she seemed to love it. I found myself thinking once again that there was something really strange about my sister Erma and I did not want to be with her. She promised not to ask me to go with her again if I would promise not to tell our parents on her. I quickly agreed. After that, every once in a while, I would see Jake and Erma sneaking off together. I knew where they were headed and I was glad to be out of it.

MY TWELFTH BIRTHDAY

March twelfth arrived and I was a year older. We had a party that day. Mother baked a big chocolate cake and the twelve candles on it were impressive. "I am growing up fast," I thought, "one more year and I will be a teenager." We had a grand time that day. I felt good and I believed all our troubles were behind us.

ERMA AND JAKE WERE ARRESTED

Meanwhile, Erma and Jake were going out at least once a week on their adventures. They brought back clothes, shoes, jig-saw puzzles, games, toys, all kinds of things. Remembering the close call we had when I was with Erma, I wondered how they were getting away with it. Then, too, I wondered why mother hadn't noticed all the toys and things that began showing up in our rooms. They must have been very conspicuous because we had almost nothing of our own until then. Ericka said she believed mother did know what was going on but pretended not to.

About the end of March the inevitable happened. Jake and Erma were caught. One evening, just before dinner, a police car pulled up in front of our house. Out of curiosity I ran out the door to see what was going on. The policeman asked me where the Carpenters lived and I pointed to our front door. After showing the officer where we lived I ran up the stairs leading to the apartments over us and sat on one of the landings close to the wall. Although I could not see our door from there, I knew I would be able to hear everything. When mother answered his knock, the officer asked,

"Are you Mrs. Carpenter?"

"Yes I am," mother answered. "What's wrong?"

Instead of answering her question, the officer asked, "Do you have a daughter named Erma and a son named Jake?"

"Yes I do," mother answered. "My God! What's wrong? Did they get hurt? Where are they?"

"No, they are not hurt," the officer said, "but they have been arrested for shoplifting. They are in the juvenile detention home and will be kept there overnight. At ten o'clock tomorrow morning they will be brought to court and the judge wants you to be there."

"I don't have any way to get in town," mother snapped at him. "My husband takes the car to work every day and I have no money for the bus."

"I could send a police car for you if you have no other way," the officer said.

"No you won't," mother shot back at him, "I will get there by myself; I'll be damned if I'll let anyone see me getting into a police car like a common criminal."

The officer, seeing he could do nothing more, turned to leave. As he did he said,

"Good day Mrs. Carpenter, I expect to see you in court in the morning." Then he was gone.

Mother raved all that evening about her wayward children. She was in a terrible state by the time dad came in from work. She was crying hysterically and ranting about how her children had betrayed her. She reminded dad, and all of us, how hard she works for us and how unappreciated she was. She went on and on, and I wondered how dad was able to keep his sanity. I was afraid that her voice would drive me nuts and I was not even in the same room with her.

Mother kept Ericka home from school the next day so she would not be alone when she went to court. Early that morning they took the bus into town. They were gone all day, but when they came home, about four o'clock, they had Erma and Jake with them.

Later that evening Ericka told me what had happened in court. She told me that when the judge asked mother if she knew what her children had been doing, she went into one of her familiar acts. With big tears flowing down her cheeks she painted a picture of a loving, overworked, doting mother --- a mother with a houseful of children and a spineless husband who could not keep a job. She convinced the judge she could take care of her children and that their stealing days were over. With a stern warning not to show up in his courtroom again, he released Erma and Jake to mother. However, the punishment they received at home was worse than anything the court would have meted out.

As soon as they got in the house mother began to scream at them.

"You goddam little thieves; I'll teach you!" she hollered. "Disgrace me in front of everyone will you? I'll put a stop to that damn quick."

Without stopping her verbal barrage she had grabbed one of dad's leather belts and began beating them. She had both of them cowering in a corner of the kitchen as she swung the strap freely letting the blows fall where they would. Even out on the front steps where I was sitting I heard her scream,

"Bring shame on the Carpenter name will you? I'll see you dead first, you little bastards."

I was terrified for them and felt the beating more than if it were laid on my own back.

Suddenly I heard Erma let out an ungodly shriek.

I thought mother had really hurt her and I rushed in to put a stop to the massacre in any way I could. What I saw froze me in my tracks. Erma had become so enraged she had turned on mother and had grabbed the strap. Her eyes were wide-open and wild-looking. Her face was beet-red and as I watched her struggle with mother over the belt I saw every cord in her neck stand out as if to burst. I was sure mother would kill her, and the courage with which I had rushed to the rescue of her and Jake evaporated right on the spot. I found I could not move even if I had wanted to. As I continued to look on, the redness in Erma's face spread quickly down her neck and even her ears turned the same color. Mother's face was just as red as Erma's as she fought for control of the belt. As Erma struggled in vain to wrest the strap from mother's grasp, she screamed at the top of her voice,

"You bastard you, why didn't you leave us in jail? You don't want us anyway!"

I was shocked. Nobody talked to our mother that way; it was forbidden. Erma had done more than talk back, she had sworn at her, had called her a "bastard" and I thought she was done for. But mother had turned white at Erma's outburst and I was afraid she was going to faint by the looks of her. Then, when Erma found she could not get the strap from mother, she let go of it, spun on her heels, and fled into her room, slamming the door behind her. Erma had released the strap so unexpectedly mother bounced off the wall and almost fell to the floor. Mother surprised me by not going after Erma as she ordinarily would have. In fact, Erma's attack seemed to sober mother somewhat and she stopped beating Jake. However, she sent him to his room with the warning there would be no dinner for either of them that night.

After that frightful episode, everything settled down again for a while. Erma and Jake seemed to be extra careful around mother. Jake even helped me to take the ashes from the kitchen stove and cleaned up his room without being asked. One could not ask for children to be better behaved than those two were for the next few months. But things were not completely quiet and calm in the Carpenter household even then -- - they never were.

DAD LEFT HOME

The first week in May of 1932 my father disappeared. That day had started like any other. Before we children were awake dad had left for work as usual. We were up at our regular time and off to school. Home again, we took care of our different chores and then did our homework. Mother cooked dinner, set the table and waited for dad to come home. Dinner was always served between 6:00 and 6:30 P.M. in our house, but it wasn't that night. Six o'clock became six-thirty and then seven. Dad still hadn't come home. Mother began pacing the floor and wringing her hands. Aloud she speculated he had wrecked the car again, or he had been injured on his job. She was such a nervous wreck within a short time she had us all scared.

Finally, at eight o'clock, mother let us sit at the table to a cold dinner. But even as hungry as we were, we could not eat; our apprehension had spoiled our appetites. Right after dinner we were put to bed, but as nervous as we were it took a long time for us to fall asleep.

We had no telephone so mother walked the ten blocks to the police station and reported dad missing. The police checked all the local hospitals and anywhere else they could think of without locating him. Late that night they sent mother home with the promise they would let her know if they learned anything. The whole night passed without a word about him.

In the morning we had to get ready for school regardless of what was going on. Mother was like a wild animal by that time. Her long red hair was disheveled, her eyes were glassy and red as if she

56

hadn't slept a wink. Her appearance and her actions scared us very much, but we got ourselves off to school. Mother was so preoccupied I don't think she knew when we left. Ericka stayed home with her that day. She told me later she was afraid to leave mother alone.

When we came home from school, Ericka filled us in on the day's happenings; her account only helped to deepen the mystery. As soon as we had left for school, Ericka told us, mother had called a taxi and they went to the housing development where dad worked. On talking to his foreman, mother found out dad had been in an altercation with a co-worker and had quit his job. The foreman said it had been a week since he had seen dad and he did not know where he was.

My emotions were all mixed up about that experience. I was afraid for dad's safety but secretly I was glad to be rid of him. I was also afraid for our future without him because mother seemed to be afraid; at the same time though, I was delighted mother seemed to be stumped. For the first time in my life I saw that mother was unsure of herself. She did not know what to do next. Then I felt guilty about my feelings and angry at myself for being scared.

I don't know how mother found out where dad was living but she did. One afternoon, right after school, mother took Ericka and me to a rooming house on the other side of town. The landlady told us dad was living there but he was out looking for work. Mother said,

"That's all right. We will wait for him to come in." Saying that, mother pushed herself past the stunned woman, almost knocking her over, and sat herself down on a sofa in the small reception room. Pointing to two big stuffed chairs, mother made us sit next to her. When my father came in that evening he found us waiting. He did not seem as surprised as I thought he would be and that puzzled me.

As soon as dad walked through the door, mother pounced on him.

"Well, you're a smart one you are," she said. "What the hell do you think you're doing?"

Dad ignored both her question and the sarcasm in her voice as he smiled at the three of us. He looked at mother with tenderness in his eyes and said,

"Hello, Peggy. Gee! I'm glad to see you."

As he spoke, he walked up to mother and tried to kiss her but she pushed him away.

"What the hell is the big idea, Bruce?" she asked, "Why are you living here when you have a home to come to?"

"I was laid off from work a few weeks ago and could not find another job," dad said. "I thought you would not want me home if I was not working."

"You're a goddam liar," mother screamed. "Your boss told me you quit your job, you did not get laid off. What the hell kind of a fool do you take me for anyway? You know it took you a long time to find that job. How are we supposed to pay our rent and buy the groceries now?" she ranted.

Dad stood stunned as he seemed to be trying to collect his thoughts. He did not answer right away and mother became impatient.

"Come on you damn fool, I expect some answers, you owe me that much at least," she snapped.

Another minute went by before dad spoke. In a trembling voice he said,

"Peggy, I quit my job because I had a fight with Frank, another employee. It was not the first one either. In fact, he had been a problem for me since the day I went to work there. He was always running to the foreman criticizing my work. He would use my tools without asking for them and then leave them all over the place. The day I had my last fight with him, he had knocked my lunch-pail over onto the muddy ground and I had no lunch. He said it was an accident but I don't believe it was. That was the straw that broke the camel's back and I could not take it one more day."

The echo of dad's last word had not faded before mother snapped back,

"A likely story. Do you really expect me to swallow that one? You never could stand up for yourself, Bruce, and you never will."

Without waiting for him to answer she continued,

"Why the hell did you rent a room here? Do you realize you scared us half to death not knowing where you went or what happened to you?" mother asked.

"Peggy, when I could not find another job right away," dad said, "I was afraid you would not want me home, especially if you found out I had quit my job."

As he spoke he began to cry and I was shocked; I had never seen him cry before.

"I love you so much Peggy," dad continued, "I could not take it if you put me out. I just did not know what to do, I am so sorry. I want to be home with you and the kids again. If you forgive me I will never do anything foolish like that again."

The room we were in had become hot and stuffy and I wished the whole thing was over. I hated to see dad beg and I was embarrassed by their emotional display in front of dad's landlady.

"Pack your goddam bag," mother said, "and come home where you belong, you poor excuse for a man you."

Meanwhile the landlady had been standing in the

background not saying a word. She was watching mother and dad in open-mouthed disbelief. I was not surprised; mother affected many people that way.

Dad had only a few things to get out of his room, and after he had a quiet conversation with his landlady, we all piled into the car and headed home. The little respect I had left for dad disappeared that evening, never to return. From that time on I answered him back whenever he reprimanded me for anything. Usually dad would ignore my retorts and that alone was something new. As I got away with my belligerency, I became bolder and it was not long before I began to challenge his right to be the head of our family. But now I am getting ahead of myself again.

With dad back home, mother turned into her old self again. She walked around like a haughty queen, in full charge of everything and everybody once more. Dad, on the other hand, was as meek as a beaten pup and practically licked the back of her hand. Through that whole charade I was consumed with a deep hatred for both of them. That hatred was shared by all of us children. In fact it was the one thing we had in common. It was so deep that it almost ruined my life. In the next three years the experience was to be repeated at least two more times. Dad would disappear, mother would go looking for him, drag him back home, etc.

MOTHER WENT TO WORK

In desperation, mother began to work two days a week as a domestic. As more time passed and dad did not find work, mother's nagging became more constant. She was downright nasty because she was earning money herself for the first time, and she wanted everyone to know it. Again and again she threw in dad's face the fact he had quit a good job for no apparent reason. One particular evening I heard her say to dad, among other cutting things,

"You had better find work, Bruce, because I am not going to feed the children and you too." I cringed inwardly and felt his shame acutely.

Naturally, dad was around the house more when he was not working. He was most difficult to live with during those times. The slightest thing would send him into a rage and he did not hesitate to use his belt on us. This gave us another good reason to justify our hatred for him and that relieved my conscience somewhat.

However, our circumstances changed again. Just before school started that year, 1932, dad found a job. Actually, he did not find it, it found him. A contractor, who had known dad for some time, came to our house one day and offered dad a job! Just like that he was working again. It took a while for us to get used to dad working regularly, he had been out of work for such a long time. But because he was earning a salary each week the atmosphere in our house gradually got better. We began to depend on, and look forward to, seeing dad come home each Saturday with his pay envelope; they paid in cash back then.

WE MOVED ONCE MORE

For a time there was food and fuel aplenty and peace reigned in the Carpenter household once more. My anger and resentment began to fade; it was a good time --- a peaceful time. And good fortune continued to smile on us for a while longer. Early in November dad found a house for rent not far from where we were living. It was a double house with tenants already living in one side; not the single home mother would have liked, but it would get her out of the apartment house that she hated and pacify her for the time being. I had hoped to get away from the Catholic school again by moving but our new address was in the same parish and so we did not have to change schools. I was disappointed to say the least, but I was excited about moving just the same.

61

The house was located on a very busy thoroughfare with traffic constantly whizzing by at forty miles an hour. If we forgot for a moment and put one foot off the curb without looking, we would have lost it to the first truck that came along. Then too, there was a fire station directly across the street. They had two regular fire-engines and a hook and ladder that seemed about a hundred-feet long. The noise of the siren and the clanging bells scared the daylights out of us and woke us up many nights. However, after living there a few months we found that we could sleep through any fire.

Because of mother's unusual fear for our safety, regardless of how nice the weather was, we children were made to spend much of our time indoors all the while that we lived there. When she did let us out to play, which was seldom, we were told to play on the side steps. Mother would warn us not to leave those steps for any reason. And if we strayed a bit, as kids are wont to do, mother would pounce on us from out of nowhere and bring us back into the house. Often we got a sore bottom for our mini-adventure, and we would lose our outdoor privileges for the rest of the week as well.

I RECEIVED MY FIRST HOLY COMMUNION

Of all the things that happened to me up until I was twelve, the most traumatic was my First Holy Communion. In the Catholic faith a child is considered to have reached the age of reason by the time he is seven. It is assumed that everyone knows the difference between right and wrong by then. Therefore, when a child reaches his seventh birthday he is obligated to receive his First Holy Communion at the earliest opportunity. The Catholic school I attended set a particular Sunday aside each year for that important event. That day is a milestone in a Catholic's life and is looked forward to with joyous anticipation by most of the children. But before a child could take part in the ceremony, he or she had to know a lot about Catholic doctrine. That doctrine was taught through the Catechism, and instructions in that good book began the day one entered the first grade. It was as much a Catholic's education as any other subject.

My teacher was strict and I learned my Catechism well. We had to know our lessons by the first Sunday in November, the day set-aside for us by the Monsignor. Anyone who failed his test would have to wait until the end of the school year before he could try again. November was the month chosen in order for the entire school to receive Holy Communion together on Christmas Day. I passed my test easily and was ready for the big day ahead of time. However, I did not receive my First Holy Communion that year. In fact it was to take five more years before I made it to the altar. I knew all about the Holy Trinity and everything else in my Catechism, but I learned there was more needed than knowledge of the Holy Eucharist in order to take part in the ceremonies on that Holy Day.

For instance, our clothes had to be considered. Everything had to be just so. That meant we all dressed alike. The boys had to wear a dark blue suit consisting of short pants and jacket. They also needed a white shirt, blue tie, and black shoes and stockings to complete their wardrobe. The girls were to be just as nicely dressed. They were to wear a pleated blue skirt, the same color and material as the boy's suits. To complement the skirts they needed white ruffled blouses, white shoes and stockings and blue neckerchiefs that matched their skirts. All the pomp and ceremony was designed to make us pleasing in the eyes of God and therefore our Communion more meaningful I guess. However, the special clothing that was required kept me away from the altar that year.

As a matter of fact, my clothing had always been a source of embarrassment to me. Mother bought much of our clothing from the Salvation Army and many of my shirts had frayed collars and cuffs. My pants hardly ever fit; they were either too big or too small, and everyone could see that they were threadbare. Then too, in those days, boy's pants had buttons to keep them closed in front. I usually had a button or two missing from mine. Because of that I had to be very careful whenever I moved or sat down.

However, it was my shoes that caused me most of my discomfort. Mother bought shoes for us only when it was absolutely necessary. As a result, my shoes had holes in the soles of them much of the time. But if I said anything about needing another pair I would get a lecture for not taking better care of the ones I had. She would usually end her reprimand by saying something like, "I saw you deliberately jumping in that mud puddle yesterday. What do you think shoes are made of anyway, iron?" Rather than listen to her ravings, when I needed shoes, I would keep quiet and wait for her to broach the subject. Of course, while I was waiting I would leave my worn shoes in strategic places all around the house where she could not help but see them. However, even with that maneuver, there would be times when the entire sole would be gone from both shoes before mother bought another pair.

Meanwhile, in school, we had to kneel on our seats to say our prayers as soon as we arrived each morning, and again in the afternoon before we left for home. During those times I could feel the eyes of all the children, who happened to be kneeling behind me, staring at the bottoms of my tattered shoes, and my neck and ears would turn red and begin to burn from shame. All my thoughts would be centered on those damn shoes, not on the prayers that I was supposed to be offering to God. It was even more humiliating when I had to kneel at the altar every Saturday afternoon as we practiced receiving Communion. It seemed that I could never find a place at the altar where I could keep the bottoms of my shoes hidden.

With the home situation being what it was, I found myself being on guard all the time. I did not want to rock the boat and get something started. My motto was simply, "Let sleeping dogs lie". And because I knew that mother ranted hysterically every time one of us needed something, I was not about to tell her that I would need a whole new wardrobe for school. As it turned out though, I didn't have to. Our priest solved that problem by sending everyone in the parish a notice in the mail.

When mother received her's, she really went wild. She made it clear to everyone within hearing distance that she was not made of money, and that she was not going to spend money that she didn't have on clothes that were only going to be worn once. I knew better than to pursue the matter further. Her reaction had been exactly what I had expected it would be, and so I was not surprised nor disappointed. I had a feeling all along that I would not be allowed to be a part of the big event. The priest had made it clear that no one could receive Holy Communion unless they were dressed properly. I felt that it was just one more time that I had to step aside while all the other kids went on and did their thing "together".

However, when there was just three short weeks left before we were to march to the altar, something happened that kindled a spark of renewed hope in me. It began to look as though I had a chance to be with my classmates after all.

Early on a Monday morning, even before we had said our prayers, the priest came into the classroom to give us some final instructions. He spent the first twenty minutes expounding on the importance of our First Holy Communion, and what it should mean to us. The more he talked the more excited he seemed to get. All of a sudden he slammed his clenched fist on the sister's desk, making it jump an inch off the floor, as he thundered, "Boys! I want every one of you to receive Holy Communion next month. It is your birthright as a Catholic, and it is your duty to God as a Christian!" He had everyone's attention at that moment. I remember he scared the hell out of me! "Now," he continued, "if there are any of you whose parents can't afford to buy the necessary clothing for the occasion tell them I will buy them for you. Tell

65

them to come to the rectory and see me any day next week and we will make arrangements to get what you'll need." Then, before the echo of his last words had completely faded, he turned on his heel and walked briskly across the room and out the door. As unexpectedly as he had appeared, he was gone. However, the aura of authority he left behind lingered for sometime, and it was almost a half an hour before the class had settled back to normal.

I could hardly wait for school to let out that day. I raced all the way home to tell mother that the church would buy everything. I had expected that mother would be as excited about the news as I was. Instead of being pleased though, she acted as if she was angry. She said she didn't want to take charity from anyone and she would not beg for anything. Under these circumstances I usually kept my mouth shut and accepted defeat. That time though, I really pleaded with her. I wanted all those new clothes so badly, especially the shoes. It took a lot of effort and a long time to win her over, but finally mother agreed to go and see the priest.

Early the next morning mother set off for the rectory and I thought everything would be all right. I don't know what happened between those two, but she was boiling mad when she came home. She did not tell us what took place, but she raved for hours about sanctimonious people, and she even threatened to take all three of us out of Catholic school. Whatever it was, she did not get the clothes for me, and so I could not receive Holy Communion with my classmates.

My reaction to all that was to pretend I really did not mind very much one way or the other. I thought that I could just stay home that Sunday and forget about the whole thing. However, I was not even allowed to use that escape either. Missing Mass on Sundays was forbidden in our school; the sister said it would be a sin. And so there I sat on that fateful day, in our assigned pew, way in against the wall so I would not interfere with the other boys going and coming. My clothes were clean and presentable but I certainly felt out of place, not only with my classmates but with the whole church. If ever I was aware of being different it was on that particular Sunday.

Nevertheless, the ceremony was beautiful just the same. It was an impressive sight to see all those children, dressed alike, slowly and solemnly moving down the center aisle of the church toward the altar. Especially impressive was the priest. He was dressed in sacramental robes and was carrying a huge silver cross as he led the procession. Then, just behind the priest, four abreast, came twelve altar boys. They wore their regular black and white habits and each one was carrying a lighted candle in a tall silver candleholder. Then, behind the altar boys came the children. The boys were first, four abreast, with the tallest in front. Next came the girls in the same order. Two assistant priests in beautiful robes stood just inside the altar rail facing the procession. Both of the priests held a gold chalice in their left hand and in their right between thumb and forefinger, a Host ready to serve Holy Communion. The choir added a beautiful aura as the organ played and they sang, very softly, the hymn, "Come Holy Ghost, Creator Blest".

I was humbled by it all, and the feeling of not being a part of the world around me was very acute at that moment. Then, after my friends had received Communion for the first time, I thought that they had been magically touched by God in some way and were then different than before they went up to the altar. The chasm between us, although wide enough already, was then so great I felt I could never bridge it. And so I did what I had done thousands of times before --- made believe I did not care anyway. But God I did care; I cared very much.

There was not much time to be concerned about all of that though, because soon after, I withdrew from the Catholic school when we moved into the country. All during our years in the country there were no churches in my life, no talk of God, and certainly no prayers were said in our house. However, although it was not visible, whenever I had some quiet time, I was aware of an uneasy feeling in the pit of my stomach about this God business. The fact that no member of the Carpenter family had a chance of entering Heaven bothered me constantly, but I could tell no one.

Coming back to that same Catholic school after more than three years absence was an ordeal for me also. First because the monsignor would not accept me into the fifth grade, the grade I was in at the public school. He claimed that the public school education was inferior to theirs and he said I would not be able to keep up. So into the fourth grade I went whether I liked it or not. And secondly, although the children were getting ready for their First Holy Communion again that year, the monsignor would not let me join them. He said that because I had not kept up my religious obligations while living in the country I would need special training to catch up with my classmates.

However, it turned out better than I thought it would because I was not alone that year. There were four other boys in my class who had just moved into our parish. Only one of those boys had received Holy Communion before, and he scoffed at the whole thing and said it was all a bunch of foolishness.

I was attracted to that scoffer and all five of us became friends. Together we brought our sister a lot of trouble. We drew funny pictures of the nuns and priests on the blackboard whenever we had the chance. Many times we would sneak in before class and write funny bits of poetry on the blackboard and sneak out again. The kids always had a good laugh when they came in the room later and saw our handiwork. Whenever the sister left the classroom one of us would start throwing spit-balls or erasers across the room. If the sister was away for more than a minute or two the whole class would be throwing things by the time she came back.

One day I really thought we had done it. Our

fourth grade sister was rather a large woman in her
late thirties. She could grab two of us at a time,
one in each hand, and bang our heads together with
ease. She liked doing that I guess because she did it
often. That particular day she had left us alone for
a long time, a dangerous thing to do. When she
returned, the whole class was having a grand time,
throwing everything they could get their hands on. As
the sister walked through the door, she was plastered
right in the kisser with an eraser from the
blackboard. The blow knocked her big hood sideways
and the white powder from the eraser covered her face.
With a stunned, surprised look, and her peculiar
stance, she was a funny sight standing in the doorway.
There was not a sound from anyone. The classroom had
become as silent as if no one were there. The scene
looked like a picture in a book because no one moved
for a long time. Luckily for us there were so many
kids involved that the class was punished rather than
a few individuals. The whole class was made to stay
after school for a half hour every day for a week to
pay for their few moments of fun.

One of my new friends had a lot of spending money
and we gathered around him. He became our leader and
we were known as the school punks. I got a certain
amount of pride from the title but did very little to
earn it. I was still afraid of everything and
everybody, but I was learning how to hide it so no one
knew. It was with that group of boys that I learned
how to smoke before I was twelve. We spent a lot of
time in back of the stores near our school, smoking,
telling dirty jokes and laughing at the kids who took
their school work seriously.

Time passed and the big day for Holy Communion
was on us. That day there were about twelve kids from
all over the school who could not receive Communion
for one reason or another. We were allowed to sit
together in the back of the church during the
ceremony. I did not feel as odd as the first time and
we got a couple of new recruits for our gang. But I
still felt different than the rest of the world around
me. I had found a few friends who were in the same

boat as me, that was the only difference.

During the school year one of the gang got himself expelled for rowdyism. Two others moved away and one turned chicken and began to avoid us. That left just three of the old gang, myself and two others. After several beatings with a big long pointer, we three finally got the message and settled down. Besides, I got tired of the sister twisting my ear and making me sit next to her every Sunday at Mass. I buckled down, worked hard and my grades went up again. And as a result I was able to receive my First Holy Communion in November of 1932 when I was almost thirteen.

However, it was not a joyous experience for me as it was for many others. Because of my inability to tell the truth even in the confessional, my First Holy Communion only added to my feelings of guilt. Then, too, there was another burden to carry I brought on myself that day. We were told right from the beginning that we were not to eat or drink anything after twelve o'clock midnight on the day we were to receive --- ever. If we ate or drank anything even by accident we could not receive Christ; it would have been considered a sacrilege if we did and God would punish us severely.

It so happened, the night before I was to receive Communion, I had to get up during the night to go to the bathroom. As I walked near the kitchen door I smelled molasses cookies. Mother must have baked them during the evening after I had gone to bed. I sneaked silently into the kitchen and there they were. About twenty-five big, soft molasses cookies with plenty of raisins in them were sitting on the table to cool. I did not think to look at a clock, all I could think of was the taste of those cookies. Without a moment's hesitation I crammed one of them into my mouth, went to the bathroom, and back to bed. But the next morning, as I was putting on my blue suit and white shirt, a flash of fear shot through me as I remembered the cookie. "Was it after midnight when I ate it?" All kinds of thoughts were running through my head, thoughts like, "What am I going to do now? Should I tell mother?" One look at her solemn face and I knew I had better not. I was in one hell of a fix. I continued to think, "If I ate that cookie after midnight and receive Holy Communion, God might strike me dead or worse. If I did not receive with the rest of the class, after all the rehearsing, the sister would kill me anyway." I did not know which way to turn. However, when I got to church that Sunday morning and took one look at our sister in full regalia, I had no trouble making a decision. She was standing there with her feet planted firmly on the floor, with her hands on her hips and a stern look on her face that said, "I dare anyone to spoil this show for us in any way." I knew then that God would have to wait. My sister was a real force that I had to deal with then and there. So I kept my mouth shut and received my First Holy Communion at last.

In the solemn procession I was the oldest and the tallest that day. Even the three boys alongside of me did not come up to my shoulder. My suit was a half-size too small, it made me look like a scarecrow. I felt very conspicuous and awkward throughout the whole affair. But mostly my mind was on my problem with God. I knew that my confession had not been completely honest. Even if I had eaten the cookie before midnight my Communion was shadowed in deceit and I was sure I would be punished. But the uncertainty of what God's punishment would be and when it would come down on me was difficult to handle. I felt like a Judas and was positive I was not worthy of God's love and grace, whatever those mysterious things might be. From then on, every time I went to confession, I felt guilty, remorseful and full of fear. And we were forced to go to confession every Saturday afternoon as long as I went to that Catholic school. I swore then that as soon as I could get away from the school I would never go to church again. I thought that even if I could not do anything about being a sinner, at least I could do something about being a hypocrite and so I stopped attending church when I left school at sixteen. But the spiritual turmoil continued just the same.

ERMA AND JAKE WERE ARRESTED AGAIN

All of us, except mother and dad, knew Erma and Jake were still shoplifting. They had not stopped their forages into department stores just because they had a cruel, self-righteous mother at home. For several weeks they had been bringing home a lot of expensive toys and things for all of us. There was so much in our rooms I was afraid we would all be punished if they ever got caught. And I was sure they would be; it was just a matter of time. But even Eileen, the family stool-pigeon, would not squeal on them because she too was sharing in the loot. And besides all the toys and games we were getting, things we would not have gotten otherwise, Erma and Jake were bringing adventure and excitement into our lives. Although I would not admit it to anyone, I admired their courage. I used to love to listen to Erma as she told of their narrow escapes and of how they were able to elude the store detectives every now and then.

However, just before Labor Day of 1933 they were caught with over one hundred dollars worth of toys and clothes in their possession. They had three shopping bags full and were filling a fourth when they were nabbed. The store detectives were furious and called the police. Erma and Jake found themselves in jail once more, but they were not going to make it easy for anyone. They would not tell the police who they were nor where they lived. Even when they were separated and questioned they remained mute.

Jake told me later they had made a pact between them. They had reasoned that if the police could not find out who they were they would not be able to send them back home. "Any place would be better than home," Jake said.

I wanted to get away from mother as badly as they did, but I did not want to jump out of the frying-pan into the fire to do so. Still I sometimes wished I had a bit of their craziness. As a result of their silence, mother did not learn of their arrest until the next day. And she only found out then because she had reported them missing. When they did not come home by eight o'clock that evening, and we could not find them in the neighborhood, mother became frantic and called the police. As I listened to her telling one of the officers how terrified she was that something may have happened to them, I felt a strong revulsion toward her. She spoke as though she were a loving mother afraid for her children's safety. We all knew how she really felt toward us and I hated her for trying to deceive everyone. My frustration was made worse because so many people seemed to believe her.

It was through the efforts of the local police that their whereabouts finally became known. However, it had taken until three o'clock in the morning to make the connection. Several more hours were to pass before mother was informed. Although she needed to be told, the way she learned was rather cruel and insensitive, at least I thought it was.

About ten-thirty the next morning, a big impressive-looking limousine pulled up in front of our house. It was all white with a big, round, black and gold Sheriff's Office insignia painted on each front door. The officer who got out of that car was a huge man, over six feet tall. He stood as straight as a soldier, and his uniform, by its very strangeness, was intimidating. He even walked with an air of authority about him that seemed to demand respect. I moved out of his way when I saw him heading toward our house. But as curious as I was, I could not stay away. Silently I crept up behind him just as he knocked on our door.

Almost immediately the door was thrown open and Ericka was face to face with that strange apparition. I could tell by the expression on her face that she was as impressed as I was. Her eyes reflected surprise and fear at the same time. The moment Ericka appeared in the doorway, the officer spoke:

"Is this where Mr. and Mrs. Carpenter live?" he asked.

His deep voice was in keeping with his overall appearance. Ericka did not answer him but called over her shoulder into the dark house,

"Mom, somebody wants you at the front door. You better come quick."

The tremor in her voice indicated how nervous she was. In less than a minute mother appeared behind Ericka wiping her hands on her apron. When she saw the sheriff standing on the steps, a look of deep concern crossed her face.

The officer took off his hat as he asked,

"Are you Mrs. Carpenter?"

"Yes," mother said, "I am."

As she spoke she pushed Ericka aside forcefully and I was afraid she would drive me away also. However, she seemed not to notice me as her eyes focused on the sheriff.

"Are these your children?" he asked, as he held out two small pictures for her to look at.

"Oh my God," mother cried, "what has happened to my children? Where are they? How did you get their pictures?"

"They have not been harmed," the officer said. "They have been arrested for shoplifting, and we are holding them in jail for a court hearing."

The officer told mother that he was from the sheriff's office in Boston and explained to her how Erma and Jake had been apprehended the day before. He said they were being held for a hearing which was going to take place the next day. He told mother she would have to be in court when their case was called

74

before the judge.

As soon as mother heard that they had been arrested she changed from a concerned mother to an angry parent.

"Those goddam kids," she said, "they are at it again!"

The sheriff became interested at once.

"What do you mean, they are at it again?" he asked. "Have they done this kind of thing before?"

The tears began to roll freely down mother's face as she told the officer about Erma and Jake being arrested the year before. She was convincing as she told him how hard it was for her with six children to care for. She blamed Erma for always causing her trouble both inside and outside the home.

"You can tell the judge all about that Mrs. Carpenter," the sheriff said. "You can ask him to declare her an incorrigible and he would take her off your hands."

"Can I really do that?" mother asked.

"Yes, you can," the officer said, "it is being done often these days when someone has a child who has become unmanageable."

He told mother again that she must be in court the next morning and said dad should be there also if it was at all possible. Then, handing her an official looking paper, he said,

"Please bring this order with you tomorrow; you will need to present it to a bailiff to get into the courtroom."

As he finished speaking, he put his hat back on, turned on his heels and came down the steps almost knocking me over as he brushed by.

I stayed out of the house as much as I could all the rest of that day. I did not want to hear mother's constant ravings about her ungrateful children and of how hard we all made life for her. Besides that, whenever she was in one of her nasty moods, anyone of us could get a beating for the slightest wrong move.

By the time dad got home that evening, mother had worked herself into a frenzy. All during dinner she kept up a constant barrage about her no-good children, her weak and spineless husband, her ill-furnished home and her unhappy life. When dad finally got a chance to speak, he said,

"Peggy, I will take tomorrow off and drive you into town. I would like to be in the courtroom with you this time."

But mother's mood changed abruptly. From a whining, distraught parent she jumped into the role of a coolheaded, competent person. A person in charge of everything.

"No, Bruce," she said, "there is no reason for you to lose a day's wages over those two little bastards. We are having enough trouble trying to pay bills and buy food as it is."

"But Peggy," dad said, "I was not able to be with you the first time this happened. I feel terrible letting you go alone."

"You go to work tomorrow," mother said, "I will take the bus into town, and I think that I'll take the kids with me." Again dad tried to protest but mother said,

"Bruce, that is the end of the conversation, I don't want to hear another word."

Dad clamped his jaw tight, and that was the end of that. Mother had the final word as usual. I was always amazed at how quickly she could change her mood to meet different situations. For that very reason I felt she was not genuine, that she was acting most of the time.

I was excited over the prospect of an adventure into town, but I was afraid mother would change her mind before it was time to go. Many times she had promised to take us to one place or another and called it off at the last minute. However, at seven o'clock the next morning we were called from our beds to get ready; we were really going.

Once in the courthouse, among a group of policemen who were huddled in a corner, we saw the sheriff who had been to our house. He spotted us at the same time and came over to speak with mother. They spoke in very low tones for a couple of minutes and then he told us to follow him. He led us across the lobby to another officer who was standing behind a narrow counter outside one of the courtrooms. The sheriff told mother to give the officer the paper he had given her the day before. Seeing that done the sheriff left us.

After the officer read the paper he told mother to wait until her name was called. He pointed to a long bench along the wall and said we could sit there until needed. Ten minutes later the courtroom opened and we were allowed in.

The prisoners were in a cage-like section of the courtroom in full view of everyone. Erma and Jake were among those prisoners.

I saw them, but I said nothing to mother about seeing them because my emotions were still all mixed up. I was afraid for Erma and Jake and really sorry they had been caught. However, at the same time, I was relieved that everything was in the open. I had been worried about all of this to long not to feel relief. Then of course I felt guilty about being relieved. I felt like a secret traitor even though I had not told a soul about them.

After we were seated, the other courtroom doors were opened and the public was let in. They filled the rest of the seats quickly. Only a few minutes after the last seat was filled, and all the doors closed, I heard a strong voice boom out, "Hear ye, hear ye," he went on in a singsong voice for a few more minutes, but the people made so much noise I could not make out his words. The noise came from everyone standing up at the same time as a large man in black robes came through a door in front of us. Majestically he took his seat behind the bench. The court was now in session.

The first cases were the derelicts. Evidently they were a morning ritual. The judge even knew some of them by name. Three months for Harry, thirty days to Joe and only ten days to Mike.

Then a man by the name of Gene came up before the judge. "Gene," the judge said, "you have been in front of me six times in the last five months. You are killing yourself with booze and I want to see if I can help you save yourself before it is too late. I'm going to hold you in the county jail for ten days while I get a psychiatric report on you. I would like to place you in the State Hospital for six months or a year if I can." Gene was a man about fifty I guessed. He was a small man, weighing about one hundred fifty pounds but he looked sick. As he walked back to his seat, I could sense that he felt tired and beaten. My heart went out to him. As I was watching him intently mother grabbed me by the arm so hard I winced. I looked up at her to see what she wanted, but she was staring straight ahead at the judge. She was like an animal poised for a kill.

It was then I realized the bailiff had called Erma and Jake to the front of the room. As they stood in front of the judge the officer read the charges. All the things they had stolen were on a table near the judge's bench. I could not believe they had crammed all that stuff into three shopping bags; I wondered how they had carried it all. I could tell that even the judge was impressed because he took one

78

look at the table, turned to Erma and Jake and said, "My, you two have been busy ones, haven't you?" They did not respond to that comment at all. I'm sure they were not expected to.

The store detectives testified against them and told the judge they had been in the store many times before. They said they had suspected them for a long time, but they could not catch them with anything until now. The judge was rather stern as he asked why they had let the children steal so much before they decided to move in on them.

"If you look at the store labels, Your Honor," one detective said, "you will find that there is something there from almost every store in the immediate area. Those stores have been notified. Those two kids came into our store with most of the stuff already in their bags."

"What do you have to say for yourselves?" the judge asked Erma and Jake.

They both continued to look at the floor and shuffle their feet, but would not say a word. The judge then looked in our direction and asked,

"Are the parents of these two children in the courtroom?" Mother jumped to her feet and said,

"Yes, Your Honor, I am their mother."

"Where is Mr. Carpenter?" the judge asked.

"He is working, Your Honor," mother answered. "He had been out of work so long that I would not let him take the day off; we need the money so badly."

"All right," the judge said, "will you please step up and take a seat alongside of your daughter."

Erma shocked the courtroom by jumping out of her seat and screaming,

"Don't let that bastard near me, she is a witch and only wants to kill me. If she comes near me I'll scratch her eyes out, so help me I will."

Erma's face was distorted with rage and fear. Her eyes were bulging and she was backing away from the table as mother started to approach. Mother froze in her tracks at the outburst and seemed not to know what to do next. Even the judge was startled. He had jumped to his feet as he called for the bailiff to grab Erma and put her back in her seat. Erma was kicking the bailiff in the legs and screaming as he dragged her back. Mother wisely backed away from her and stood bewildered in the aisle. She sat down only when the judge indicated another seat a good distance away from her two children.

"What do you say, young Jake?" the judge asked, "do you think your mother wants to kill you?"

Jake did not answer. He sat slouched in his seat with a sullen look on his face. He seemed to be unmoved by all the commotion. I had a strong impulse to jump up and shout at the judge, "Yes she does want to kill Erma and maybe the rest of us as well," but I dared not. I knew I would be going home with her later, and I did not want to end up being a victim of her wrath. However, I felt as though I had let Erma down by not speaking up and I was ashamed of my cowardice.

Meantime, the judge had turned to mother and said,

"Mrs. Carpenter, what do you think about your daughter's outburst?"

It seemed that mother had been waiting for a chance to speak for she sprang to her feet the moment the judge addressed her.

"Your Honor," she said, "Erma has been a thief since she was old enough to walk. She has stolen from neighbors, from the corner grocery store and even from me a few times."

At that moment Erma jumped up again and with tears flowing down her cheeks she screamed,

"You're a goddam liar."

The judge pounded his gavel loudly and said,

"Bailiff, if there is another interruption of that kind I will ask you to remove Miss Carpenter from the courtroom. Is that clear to you young lady?" the judge asked.

"Yes," was all Erma would say, but she kept quiet after that. When order had been restored, mother continued to tell the judge all the problems Erma had caused her, especially about her being arrested the year before. She ended by saying,

"Your Honor, I can't handle her any more. She is corrupting her brother. Jake is a good boy but he is easily led. He would not do anything like this if it were not for Erma. I just don't know what to do with her."

"Would you be willing to have Jake placed on probation under your supervision Mrs. Carpenter?" the judge asked.

"Yes, but I can't handle Erma; I don't want that little thief in my house again," mother said.

"There is no question there is bad blood between you two," the judge said.

Then he turned to Erma and said,

"As this is the second time you have been apprehended for shoplifting, I believe you did not benefit from the last experience. I can also see there are intense bad feelings between you and your mother just now. For everybody's sake, the merchant's, your mother's and yourself, I am going to sentence you to three years in a girl's reform school."

Erma said nothing and did not even look up as the judge spoke.

Next the judge looked at Jake and said,

"I am going to place you on probation indefinitely and send you home under the supervision of your mother. If there is any complaint from her to this court at any time about your behavior, this court will send you to a reform school also. Is that clear to you, Jake Carpenter?" the judge asked.

When Jake did not answer, the judge said,

"Young man, I am talking to you; I will not tolerate insolence. If you do not answer me now I will hold you in contempt of court and it will be a long time before you see your family again. I will ask you just once more if you understand the conditions under which you are being allowed to go home with your mother and how you are to behave?"

"Yes, I do," Jake answered. The judge turned to the bailiff and said,

"Bailiff, please release Jake to his mother and turn Erma over to Policewoman Watson to be transported to the reform school."

Without waiting to see his orders carried out I heard the judge call,

"Next case, please."

It took mother about an hour after we left the courtroom before she had all the necessary papers signed and we were headed home with Jake. I hated sitting next to him on the bus because he smelled so strongly of urine. I was sure everybody else could smell him also. Jake was exceptionally quiet all during the trip. Mother sent him to his room with the warning he would get it from his father when he came home from work. I sympathized with him because I knew from experience that the waiting was far worse than the actual punishment. Of course there would be no dinner for Jake that night either. Mother did not even bother to ask Jake if he had been given any food at all that day. When dad got in that evening his first duty was to administer the strap to Jake's back. Jake never went shoplifting again, but he stole everything he could from anyone. He just could not be trusted.

I did not find out how dad felt about Erma's incarceration, in fact I hardly ever knew how dad felt about anything as we were growing up. Nevertheless, we had lost a member of our family even if it was for only three years, I was going to miss her. However, the events of the next few weeks helped to take our minds off of Erma, because dad had found another house for us and we moved again.

OUR LAST MOVE AS A FAMILY

Prodded by mother's constant complaining, dad finally found a safer place for us to live. Interestingly it was back in the neighborhood we had moved away from just ten months before. In fact, it was only a block away from our old address; it was on a side street away from traffic and that alone made it attractive.

None of us, except mother and dad, had seen the house before the day we moved in. Early in the morning of that day, dad drove all of us to the house with brooms, pails, and scrubbing brushes. We were to get the place clean and ready for our furniture while he went to borrow a truck from his employer. As soon as we got there, and dad had gone, I began to explore the place. I immediately found the house was similar to the one we were moving from. The one big difference though was a much bigger yard to play in.

During the next few weeks I took every chance I could get to explore our new neighborhood. It was exciting, not only because of what I found but also because I was taking a risk just getting away from mother even for a short period of time. The more I explored, the more I knew that I was going to enjoy our new surroundings. The street we had moved onto was only about one quarter of a mile long. The first two-thirds of the street had an even mixture of apartment houses and private homes; all the buildings were wood. However, the last third of the street had been zoned commercial and as a result it was always bustling with activity. On one side of the street a huge automobile repair garage and gasoline station took up several hundred feet. Directly across the street, another garage specialized in repairing trucks and tractors. All of these buildings were made of bricks and steel. About fifty or sixty men worked in the shops and one can imagine the noise and the language that emanated from that end of the street constantly. Mother declared that section "off-limits" to us and made it clear what would happen if we disobeyed her. Naturally, that meant I had to sneak down there every chance I could get. It was fascinating to watch all the exciting things going on, and I could not understand why I was told not to go near the place. Needless to say, I was beaten often because I could not seem to resist the attraction the area held for me. Over a period of time I made several acquaintances and a few friends in the garages, and it proved to be a good thing I did. It was not long after we moved onto that street that I needed help desperately and a couple of my new friends came to my aid.

In just a few short weeks we found ourselves settled, and aside from missing Erma every once in a while, our life continued as it had been. However, one could always count on Jake to break any routine before it became too dull. About six or seven weeks after we moved in, Jake was responsible for the Carpenter family being in trouble again. Sadly, his misbehavior involved our new landlord, who lived only two houses away, and this episode almost caused our eviction.

JAKE MAKES NEW ENEMIES FOR US

Once Erma was gone, Jake found himself without a buddy. He was isolated from the rest of the family by mutual consent. Now that he no longer could go shoplifting, he began to look elsewhere for excitement. Of the many possibilities he had to choose from as ways to amuse himself, he had to pick on our landlord's beautiful angora cat. As usual, we found out about it after the mischief had been done.

One Saturday, late in the afternoon, someone came banging on our back door. The pounding was so loud and insistent that it frightened both mother and me. When mother opened the door, our landlord was standing there with his cat cradled in his arms. The cat was all roughed up as though it had gone through a windmill. Its nose was torn and bleeding and its eyes clearly showed its fear. The landlord had all he could do to hold it, it was so unnerved. We could see that the landlord was in a terrible rage. In fact, he was so angry his voice trembled and cracked as he spoke.

"Mrs. Carpenter, what the hell is the matter with that son of yours?" he shouted as soon as mother had opened the door. Then, without waiting for an answer, he went on.

"That crazy son of yours almost killed our cat this afternoon. He and another kid took a piece of rope and tied our cat and another cat together by their tails. Then they threw the cats over a clothesline and they came together with a thud, upside down. The boys were standing back laughing hysterically while the fur flew in all directions as the cats tore into each other."

Mother cut in on him,

"Are you sure that it was Jake?" she asked.

"I know it was," Mr. Jones said, "because I saw the whole thing from an upstairs window, but I was too far away to stop them. As I came running around the corner of the house to rescue the cats, the rope slipped off and the cats fell to the ground. Instantly the animals took off in opposite directions as if the devil were after them. It took us over an hour to find our Tabby. He was hiding behind some trash cans three blocks away. He was so terrified that when my son went to pick him up, he was badly bitten on the hand. I had to put these heavy gloves on and go get him. I am on my way to the veterinarian to have him treated, but I wanted you to see what your son did to him first. I expect you to pay for Tabby's treatment and you better hope that he is not seriously hurt."

With his anger somewhat spent, the landlord paused and glared at mother, expecting a response. The experience had taken us by surprise and it took mother a few minutes to regain her composure. Just as I was beginning to be uncomfortable with her silence, she spoke.

"Mr. Jones, I am sorry about your cat," she said, "I really hope that it is not badly hurt. I don't know what's got into Jake lately, he has me at my wit's end. For some time now he has been causing me trouble one way or another. He seems to be into everything. But he will be punished for this and he won't bother you again."

"Mrs. Carpenter," the landlord said, "this is the second time we have had trouble with Jake since you moved here. Just last week he cut my son's football with a knife and ruined it. I am fed up with his tricks. I was going to ask you to move by the end of the month but my wife interceded on your behalf. For her sake I won't ask you to go, but I want you to keep your son away from my house, my children, and my pets. In fact, if we have any trouble from anyone in your family, you will have to move. Is that clear?"

When mother answered meekly with a "Yes" the
landlord stalked off, still angry, leaving us standing
there with the door open.

Mother took just a minute to come to life after
Mr. Jones had gone. She practically tore the kitchen
apart looking for the dog leash. By the time she had
found it she had worked herself into a frenzy. She
always frightened me when she went through that kind
of transformation; she became like a mad-woman. Out
the front door she flew, looking for Jake, with her
favorite strap in hand.

About ten minutes later she came up the middle of
the street with Jake running in front of her. She was
lashing him across the back and screaming at him with
every step. Her face was red and distorted with rage.
I felt sorry for Jake even though I had wanted to kill
him just moments before. I was also embarrassed for
my mother because I felt that she was making a
spectacle of herself in front of the whole
neighborhood. When they got close enough to the
house, Jake made a dash for the front door to escape
her wrath. When that happened mother just stopped
dead, still in the street, and screamed at the top of
her voice for Jake to come back to her. Jake was too
terrified of her not to obey her command, so he slunk
back. Mother continued to beat him the rest of the
way into the house. Of course she sent him to his
room and told him there would be no dinner for him
that night. Even that didn't satisfy mother because
she demanded that dad give him another strapping when
he came home, and, as always, dad followed
instructions.

It was over an hour after dad finished beating
Jake that I went up to bed. Jake was still curled up
in a ball, in the middle of his wet bed, sobbing
quietly. I didn't say a word to him but I felt an
intense rage toward our parents because of our
helplessness under their care. I slipped into my bed,
turned my back to Jake, blocked his sobbing from my
ears with a pillow and tried to escape from it all
through sleep.

Evidently the cat had not been seriously hurt because mother had to pay just the one bill from the veterinarian and the landlord said no more about it.

I began to think that Jake was really crazy, and I was uncomfortable sleeping in the same room with him from then on. As our lives unfolded he became more bizarre and continued to confirm my ideas about his sanity. It was at that time in his life that he started staying indoors more than usual. His hours of sleeping increased noticeably as well, so much that I was sure there was something wrong. However, the Carpenter family had things much more serious to be concerned with than Jake's sleeping habits.

ADJUSTING TO OUR NEW ENVIRONMENT

Just before we moved, mother had begun preparing us for school once again. Even in the confusion of moving, we managed to be ready on time and we looked like store-front mannequins in our new outfits. That year mother had enough money for all our needs and we felt special with so many new clothes. We were better-off than many of the families around us as several of the men in our neighborhood were out of work and had been for some time. Although it was not pleasant to see other people hungry, it was nice to be on the other side of the situation for a change.

A month after I started school that year an overgrown bully entered our classroom. Within two weeks he had beaten up a few of the boys, including me, in order to establish his kingdom. Then he demanded tribute as insurance that he would not beat us up again. I hated him with a passion, but I was also afraid of him so I gave him whatever he asked for. However, the end of his tyranny came one day when he wanted an expensive deck of playing cards I had brought to school. The cards belonged to my father and if I did not return them, dad would have given me a severe beating. I told the bully I would give him anything he asked for but I could not give him the cards. Without saying another word, he punched me right in the face with all his strength. My nose gushed blood and my eyes filled with water so that I couldn't see. But even in that condition, when the bully tried to pull the cards out of my hands, I went into a blind rage and jumped on him bodily.

All the fear and hatred that had been bottled up for weeks erupted like a volcano and I almost killed that kid. My attack had caught him by surprise and he went down on his back with me straddling his chest. With both hands on his throat I was choking him and banging his head on the hard ground at the same time. We were both bleeding by then and there was blood everywhere, but I was not conscious of what I was doing. It took two sisters and a priest to pry us apart, but I was not aware of that either. However, I did keep my dad's cards and the bully left me alone after that. He told everyone that I was crazy and warned them to stay away from me. I enjoyed my classmate's respect the rest of that school year because I had beaten the bully and they were still paying him tribute.

Up to that time I had been afraid to fight because I did not want to get hurt. I still had that fear, but now I had another one as well. I realized that there was an intense rage in me that made me want to kill at times. I became afraid of that rage because I did not want to hurt anyone --- it was not my nature. I was terrified I would lose control someday and hurt someone badly. Because of my fears, I usually took a lot of abuse from my peers and did not fight often. If I were pushed far enough though, I would explode and someone would get a severe beating. The priest threatened to expel me a couple of times because of attacks on classmates, but I managed to avoid that somehow.

DAD WAS OUT OF WORK AGAIN

From the latter part of 1929 when the stock market crashed, businesses had been closing their doors at an alarming rate. Companies were filing for bankruptcy by the hundreds of thousands annually nation-wide. Daily, thousands of banks were closing without returning a nickel to their depositors. Panic swept over the nation like a raging fire that was being fed by gasoline. Every day the newspapers were reporting names of prominent people jumping from high buildings or shooting themselves because overnight they had lost everything. Security for anyone in any venture was precarious at best.

We had been very fortunate during the past year because of dad's steady employment. In fact, he had found his job at a time when most of the men who were out of work had become so discouraged they had stopped looking. Dad had been working so steadily we felt safe, and we took our good fortune for granted. All that came to an end one day in late October 1933. Without a word of warning, two of the four partners in the corporation dad worked for disappeared, taking the funds of the company with them. On the day that it became known, one of the two partners who had been left to face the consequences, shot himself to death. The one man remaining had to face the forty-two men who were still working on the six half-constructed buildings.

Dad had gone to work that morning at the usual time and everything seemed normal. However, he was back home again before we got out of school. He never got home before six o'clock and so we wondered what was wrong. Mother and dad were both in the kitchen when we entered the house, and although they were not speaking to each other at the moment, the atmosphere was electric. We knew something bad must have happened just by looking at dad. His face was white as though he had seen a ghost. We did not dare ask what the trouble was, but when dad went to the car and took his toolbox out of the trunk, I knew that he was out of work again.

Early the next morning dad enthusiastically started looking for another job. Every evening there was a nasty scene because he had not been successful. As the days mounted into weeks and then into months, dad's spirits began to fade. Two weeks before Christmas, the finance company came and took our car. Business men had become like vultures. If a person missed one payment on anything, regardless how much of the principle had been paid, the person lost whatever it was. Dad was never able to buy another car and therefore became limited in his efforts to find work. It was almost impossible to carry his big tool chest with him when he was using public transportation to get around. Yet, if he found a job he would be expected to go right to work, and so he had to have his tools with him. My heart went out to him as I saw him hoist that box on his shoulder every morning and head up the street to the bus stop. It was worse watching him come home, tired and dejected every evening. Mother became terribly cruel to him verbally and I wondered why he came home to her each night. Finally, the day came when he too stopped looking for work. One look at him and anyone could see that he was a beaten man.

Meanwhile, mother had found another job as a domestic, one that gave her six days work each week instead of three. A general housekeeper was paid two dollars a day, twenty cents for car-fare, and was given one meal a day. Although the pay was small, it was in keeping with the times. For example, a large loaf of bread was only seven cents, a dozen eggs were fifteen cents and a twenty-five ounce can of vegetable soup was only a dime. Our rent was eight dollars a month and a ton of coal was nine dollars and fifty cents.

In her new position, mother was doing the cooking as well as housecleaning. After serving dinner she was allowed to bring the leftovers home. Many

91

evenings our dinner was the scraps from her employer's table and that was all. I hated eating other people's leavings, but it was food and I knew better than to say a word about my feelings.

ERICKA IS OFFERED A JOB ON STAGE

Christmas of 1933 was a bleak one indeed. Ericka and I stole a Christmas tree from a corner store or we would have had none. The few toys we had were from the secondhand store and they were either broken, soiled, or had some pieces missing. We were cold, hungry, scared, and angry all through that winter, and although we fought with each other, we were drawn closer because of our misery. In that gloomy atmosphere any good news would have been appreciated. For that reason, if for no other, we were excited when Ericka came home from school one day and told us she had been offered a chance to work onstage as a comedienne. It seemed that she had been in a school play and there had been a talent scout in the audience. Ericka told us that the scout had watched her in several performances before approaching her with his offer. She had an opportunity to earn money and do what she loved to do, make people laugh. We could hardly wait until mother came home that evening to share the news with her and ask for her consent. We should have known better. Mother practically screamed her "No!" at Ericka. All that evening she had to listen to mother rave about the evils of the theater, "Only tramps work onstage!" mother said. Ericka said nothing, but began working in a theater only a mile away from our house. Mother was away working during the days and dad was sleeping on the sofa much of the time, so no one paid too much attention to Ericka as long as she was home when mother came in around eight o'clock each evening.

Ericka kept me abreast of what she was doing and how she was getting along. She loved being onstage. By her own account she was doing well. With her ability to twist her long arms and legs into grotesque positions, she put on a good show. She developed a stand-up comedy routine that was hysterical, and as a result she began to attract a small following. Ericka told me that the manager wanted her to put on an evening performance as well as the matinees but because of mother she did not dare. "But you just wait," she told me, "mother can't hold me back much longer, you'll see."

ERICKA AND MOTHER CLASH

One evening Ericka was invited to a movie by one of the men she had met in the theater where she worked. Passing him off as a local suitor Ericka asked for mother's permission to go.

"Yes you may go," mother said, "but you must be home by ten-thirty."

"But mother," Ericka protested, "the movie doesn't get out until eleven; I could be home by eleven-thirty."

"No you won't!" mother said. "I can't go to bed with you out roaming the streets and I have to go to work in the morning. I need my sleep. The dead line is ten-thirty. Take it or leave it!"

Ericka went to the movie with her new friend and did not come home until eleven-thirty. Mother was waiting up for her and she was furious. As soon as Ericka stepped through the door, mother began to scream at her. She called her a dirty tramp and a few other choice names. When Ericka did not say a word, mother hauled off and slapped her across the face so hard that she knocked her glasses clear across the room and broke them. In a flash Ericka tore off one of her shoes, and holding it in her hand by the toe she screamed at mother,

"You bastard, you will never hit me again! If you don't believe me just try one more time! Come on,

93

you son of a bitch, hit me!"

Ericka was standing with her feet spread wide apart, eyes wild, face red on one side from mother's hand print and white with rage on the other. She was waving her shoe menacingly just begging mother to come close enough. It was mother's turn to be afraid. She ran to the foot of the stairs and called dad who was in bed sleeping as usual. When dad came downstairs, mother demanded that he take care of Ericka and teach her a lesson. Dad took his leather belt and beat Ericka across the back and legs until she ran up to her room to save her skin. As she was still running up the stairs mother hollered after her, "No goddam tramp is going to live in the same house with me, and you had better remember that." And another nasty scene was over for the moment.

Ericka could hardly see without her glasses and she was bitter. That night, while mother and dad were still downstairs talking about her, she came into my room and told me she wanted to kill both of them. She said the only thing that kept her from trying was the fact that she might fail and they would kill her instead. From the strong emotion I heard in her voice and the hatred on her face, I believed her. Secretly, I wished that she would kill them, and I was horrified that I could even think such a terrible thing. However, Ericka, like the rest of us, swallowed her anger and her hatred and kept up the pretense that everything was fine.

Mother never hit Ericka again, but the tension between them was so high from that time on I knew anything could set off another explosion. School for Ericka, and mother at work, kept them apart much of the time, and that was a blessing for everyone concerned. Ericka was without glasses for five weeks, and then it was the school, not our parents, who finally bought her another pair. Of course Ericka could not perform onstage without her glasses, so her only pleasure in life was lost for those five weeks. Because of that her resentment toward mother became full-blown.

MOTHER LOSES HER JOB

Because my father refused to apply for public assistance, the only income our family had was mother's meager earnings. It was not enough for everything we needed, but we were surviving. However, mother's fiery temper and her sharp tongue were forever getting her in trouble. About the middle of February 1934 her big mouth got her fired. She had overstepped her bounds one day when she decided to give her employer a piece of her mind. Not only was she fired, but the lady made sure that she would not get another decent job as a domestic in the area. Of course mother did not know that, and no agency could tell her outright she had been blackballed; but none of them would send her on a job. We were destitute again in a very short time.

When mother refused all suggestions of applying for welfare aid, the school officials contacted someone and informed them of our plight. As a result, a representative from the welfare department came to see mother and he asked her a lot of questions. When mother still insisted she did not need, nor would she accept, charity, I heard the representative tell her that if she did not apply to the welfare office by the end of the week, he would start court proceedings to take her children away from her. I remember the fear that stabbed my heart at the thought of being taken away from my parents and yet I had wanted to get away from them for years; it did not make sense to me. After he left, mother was raving mad, and as usual she called him every dirty name she could think of for interfering with her personal life. I was thrilled that someone had some power over her at last. By the end of the week, mother had gotten her temper under control again, and she was able to swallow her pride and report to the welfare office. Immediately good things began to happen. We were given a large box of food, two boxes of clothing, and a ton of coal. We began to eat regularly again and much of our fear vanished, but that was not all they were able to do for us.

DAD WAS PUT TO WORK

When President Roosevelt took office in March of 1933, one-third of the work force in America was idle. The president immediately began to create organizations to get the unemployed back to work and thousands of young men off the streets. Two of the organizations were: the Works Progress Administration, the W.P.A., and the C.C.C., or the Civilian Conservation Corps.

Just six weeks after Roosevelt's inauguration, young men began to leave the cities to enter C.C.C. camps in the forests. The conservation project was under way. In the next nine years over two million young men served in that ambitious program, in which they planted millions of trees, saving our forests from fire and floods; restocked streams, and protected wildlife. In return for their labors they were given room and board and a monthly salary. However, the money was sent to their parents in order to relieve the situation at home. The morale of the young men was high because they felt as if they were a part of the solution rather than a part of the problem. It seemed that everybody benefited through the activities of the C.C.C.'s. I was too young to join their ranks when it first began and later, when my age qualified me, other events intervened.

Although the Carpenter family had no boys to send to the C.C.C. camps, dad was eligible for the W.P.A. In fact, he had little choice after he had signed onto the welfare rolls. Once on the W.P.A., dad was guaranteed three days work each week repairing roads or building new ones. The W.P.A. was responsible for many projects that were beneficial to the country besides their road work, but the men working on the streets were visible to everyone. Standing around old metal drums in which they were burning scrap wood to ward off the morning chill, groups of about forty men could be seen at intervals along every highway and main thoroughfare.

A few of the men publicly expressed their gratitude for the opportunity to help their community and themselves through the W.P.A. projects. However, many more of them said they felt humiliated by the experience. Because of their attitude their hearts were not in the effort even though the projects warded off starvation for thousands of families. Unfortunately dad was one of those men who seemed to feel degraded and embarrassed rather than grateful for the work. I thought that it sure beat loafing, and it paid a lot more too. However, dad hated the whole experience and many days when he should have been out on the road working, he would be in bed sick. How I wanted to tell him what I thought about him and his passivity but I couldn't.

I think I was old enough then to realize, more clearly than ever before, that there was no significant communication between dad and me. In fact, dad did not seem to have a relationship with anyone. Even his contacts with mother were all negative. I can't remember ever seeing them being mutually tender and loving with each other. It seemed as if dad paid attention to us only when we had to be corrected.

We began to ignore him much of the time. Once in a while Ericka or I would challenge his authority in subtle ways. As I grew older I became reckless in showing my defiance and disrespect. For example, one day when I was almost fifteen, dad called to me from the kitchen, I came running in from the backyard to see what he wanted. When I entered the kitchen I saw dad standing in the middle of the floor, belt in hand and his feet planted wide apart. Jake was standing in front of him completely naked. As I came through the door dad said,

"I am going to teach this bastard a lesson he

will never forget for wetting his bed. I want you to hold his hands flat against the wall so he can't run away on me."

I was horrified, scared and angry all at the same time. I don't know where the courage came from, but I looked dad right in the eyes and said,

"You're a savage bastard. I can't stop you from beating Jake, but I'll be a son of a bitch if I am going to help you."

I spun on my heels and ran out of the house. I could not bear to hear Jake's screams; I would rather have taken the beating myself. I was shaking like a leaf and sick to my stomach. I was sure dad would come after me when he was finished with Jake but he did not. The fact that he didn't only added to my confusion, but it also seemed to give me a new license to express my contempt for him openly from then on. In spite of all the confusion, I found ways to keep myself busy and therefore could avoid a lot of the turmoil that was constantly going on.

ERICKA AND I VISIT ERMA

Because mother was no longer out working, Ericka became afraid she would find out about her performing onstage so she quit. However, Ericka had made many friends in the theater and she had no intentions of giving them up. In fact she was "going steady" with a fellow named John whom she had met through the theater manager. John was a pleasant young man and I liked him. We got along together very well. He owned an automobile too, one that had a rumble seat, and he often took me for a ride.

About the middle of April 1934, Ericka had talked John into driving her to the reform school to see Erma, and she asked me if I wanted to go with them. Early on a Saturday morning we started out. It was a beautiful spring day with plenty of sunshine. The ride in the rumble seat was quite chilly but it was also an exciting experience riding in the midst of so much fast traffic. The reform school was only twenty-five miles away, but because of the heavy traffic it took us over an hour to get there.

I was awed by the beauty of the place. It looked like a millionaire's estate rather than a house of correction. A tall wrought iron fence surrounded the entire area. The huge iron gate was ornate. A uniformed guard opened the gate and checked us through. Once inside, I saw five large two-story, redbrick buildings spaced evenly over a few acres of land. The doors and windows of all the buildings looked as if they had just been painted. Everything was so neat and clean it looked as if the whole place was new. There was a thick carpet of green grass everywhere and many early spring flowers were poking their heads out of the ground. The area was so quiet and peaceful no one would have guessed it was a girl's reform school, where over a hundred and fifty girls were living and working. We learned the place was a small farm with about fifty acres of crops that the girls planted, cared for and harvested. We were told they had some cows, a few pigs, and about five-hundred chickens to care for as well.

Ericka and I were ushered into a huge reception room that looked big enough to accommodate a hundred people. With thick rugs on the floor and overstuffed furniture everywhere, the room, had a quiet elegance about it. The atmosphere was such that it invited silence. When I felt compelled to talk to Ericka at all, I automatically spoke in a whisper and she answered the same way. There were a few other visitors scattered throughout the room and they too were talking to each other in subdued tones.

We had only been sitting for about five minutes when a door in a far corner of the room was thrown open and the inmates came flooding in. There were about twenty excited girls in that group, and they set up a terrible din with their chatter. Erma was one of the last girls through the door, and when I saw her I was stunned. I hardly recognized her --- she had changed so much. In a little over six months she had become a beautiful young woman. She had slimmed down, her hair was combed and shiny, and her clothes fit her perfectly. She even had shoes and stockings on. However, it was the happiness I saw on her face that impressed me the most --- her face actually glowed.

As soon as Erma spotted us, she raced across the room and grabbed Ericka in a bear-hug. She began to cry and she pulled me to her without releasing her hold on Ericka. All three of us were crying and I was thankful the room was so large, none of the other people were paying attention to us.

When Erma finally got herself under control, she told us we were the only visitors she had. She began to tell us everything that had happened to her since she arrived. She said she was assigned to work in the barn where they had several cows. Twelve of those cows became her responsibility and she loved working with them.

"Ericka, I am truly happy for the first time in my life," Erma said, "and I have only wet the bed a few times since I have been here."

There had been so much news to share the visiting hours were over before we realized it. With a promise to come again as soon as we could, we left. Ericka and I managed to get to see Erma three more times in the next eighteen months before she was released.

ERICKA RUNS AWAY FROM HOME

Ericka had graduated from high school in June of 1934. Two months later she had turned nineteen and John, her boy friend, wanted her to go back to work in the theater with him. Because money was so scarce in our house at the time, Ericka thought mother would be more receptive to the idea than she had been. So one evening she asked her. All the rest of that week

100

mother nagged Ericka about becoming a tramp. However, Ericka was determined to have her way, and although she didn't tell mother about it, she went to work onstage just the same. She told mother she had taken a job as a waitress in a nearby Chinese restaurant in order to keep peace in the house. Sadly, she only got away with that deception for a short time before mother found out what she was really doing. There was a heated argument that evening, but mother ended it by saying,

"Ericka, if you go up on that stage one more time I will pull you off of it in front of everybody. See how you'll like that, you damn tramp."

"You dare do something like that, mother, and so help me you'll live to regret it," Ericka threw back at her.

"I'll teach you to talk back to me," mother said, as she jumped out of her chair to strike Ericka.

But Ericka had dashed out the backdoor and ran to a neighbor's house. Later that evening when Ericka came quietly back there wasn't a word spoken between them, but the tension was electric.

Sometime after midnight I felt a hand on my shoulder shaking me gently awake. The room was so dark I couldn't make out who it was and I became frightened.

"Sh-sh," a voice whispered in my ear, "it's me -- - Ericka."

"What's the matter?" I whispered back, more afraid than before.

"Nothing's wrong," Ericka responded, "I am running away from that goddamed woman, and I wanted to say goodbye to you. I am going to miss you and Lisa the most," she said.

I could feel the tears on her cheek as she put

her face to mine and I started to cry too. As she hugged me I could feel her trembling and I knew she must be afraid. I did not want to lose her, but I knew she had to get away from mother and I didn't want to say anything that might discourage her. She whispered in my ear again,

"John is going to pick me up at the corner and take me into Boston where mother will never find me."

We held each other silently for a long time and then she really scared me when she said,

"God I hate to leave you, I am terrified to think of what is going to happen to you kids once I am gone." With tears flowing down my face I whispered,

"We'll be OK. You must go while you have the chance, but please come and visit us some time when mom and dad are not home."

She whispered, "Oh, I will, I will!"

My ears followed her as she sneaked down the stairs and I heard a faint "click" as she quietly closed the backdoor behind her. I held my breath for a long time and prayed mother would not wake up and stop her.

Of course Eileen had to dash into mother's room early the next morning to let her know Ericka had not slept in her bed that night. Mother made a big fuss about it all day, but she did not call the police as I thought she would. After a couple of days mother stopped even mentioning Ericka, and I got the feeling she was glad Ericka was gone. It was a sad time for me because I still missed Erma and now I felt I had lost Ericka as well. It was a scary time also, because the Carpenter family seemed to be falling apart. Even Eileen had begun staying away more by sleeping at her friend's house. It was not unusual for her to be gone three and four days at a time. The puzzling thing about that situation was mother's reaction to it. She would not let any of us out of her sight, I had been refused every time I asked to be away just for an afternoon. Why she never said anything to Eileen or why she let her stay overnight in someone else's house was a mystery to us. However, we were glad to have her out of our hair so we didn't ask any questions.

At that time, with Eileen spending so many hours with her friends, Lisa, Jake and I seemed to be the only children in our family. That put me in the position of being the oldest, and I tried to become more responsible because of that. But because we were fewer in numbers did not mean that our family became more peaceful and serene. On the contrary --- the deterioration seemed to accelerate. In fact, the very next situation I became involved in proved to be the most frightening of my life up to that time.

DAD ATTEMPTED SUICIDE

It was a cold, dark Saturday in late October of 1934 when dad scared me more than I had ever been frightened in my life. That day mother had decided to clean and wax the linoleum in the living room. She had sent Lisa and Jake out to play to get them out from under her feet, but she kept me with her to help with the heavy work. Dad was upstairs in his room directly over the living room. He had said he was not feeling well and wanted to lie down for a while. An hour or so later mother and I were right in the middle of stripping the old wax off the linoleum when I thought I heard dad say something to us. As we were making so much noise, I could not make out what he had said; so I went to the foot of the stairs and called up to him,

"Did you say something to us, dad?", I asked.

His answer was muffled and seemed so far away I could not understand a word. I ran lightly up the stairs then, and as I got to the bedroom door I said,

"What did you say dad?"

Dad was lying on his bed, fully clothed, except for his shoes, and he had a white rag over his face. At the same time I saw him, I was hit full in the face with a sweet sickening aroma that was so thick I couldn't catch my breath. Dad moved the rag away from his face just then and said,

"I just told your mother goodbye. I took chloroform --- I'm killing myself."

First my heart fell into my stomach like a hunk of lead; next it leaped up into my throat. There was a flash of diarrhea and I felt sick. I was afraid I was going to vomit right there. My knees had turned to water and my legs became wobbly. However, I knew there was no time to think of anything, I had to act, and fast. There were sixteen steps down to the living room where mother was, and I covered all of them in less than a second. In fact I only hit about three of them on the way down. I burst into the room and screamed to mother,

"The son of a bitch is killing himself with chloroform!"

I was crying hysterically by then, and for once I was glad to have mother to run to. As soon as mother saw me, she was in action before I had finished my sentence. She dropped her mop on the floor and headed for the stairs as she said,

"Oh yeah! We'll see about that."

I knew it would be all right then. Dad would not dare commit suicide because mother would kill him if he did! Moments later mother came flying downstairs and out the front door as she hollered to me over her shoulder,

"I'm going to call the police."

I was really frightened then because I thought,

"It must be bad if mother has to go for help." We had no telephone so mother had to run a block to the nearest store where there was a pay phone.

Ten minutes later an ambulance arrived, just as mother got back, and they took dad to a nearby hospital. The police came as the ambulance pulled away, and they asked mother a lot of questions. Mother kept saying dad was faking, that he didn't have guts enough to kill himself. I was furious at her for her callousness. Later on though, I began to believe she may have been right.

The next day one of our neighbors drove dad home from the hospital as no damage seemed to have been done. I was consumed with anger because he had scared me half to death, and it looked as if mother had been right. He had probably not been serious at all. Then too, I began to wonder what the "jerk" would try next. From then on I could not believe anything he said, and the only reason I didn't defy him openly was because he was bigger and stronger than me.

Christmas of 1934 was a terrible one for us. The W.P.A. checks that should have been paid two days before Christmas, for some unknown reason, did not show up until eleven o'clock Christmas eve night. All the stores were closed; we could buy nothing. We had food in the house, but not one toy for any of the children, and for the first time we had no Christmas tree. Mother tried to make up for our disappointment by buying some toys and games the day after Christmas but it wasn't the same. However, we survived that ordeal only to be confronted by another problem.

MY FIFTEENTH BIRTHDAY

March 12, 1935 came and went without fanfare. Mother had baked a chocolate cake and with it we had homemade ice cream, but she said I was too big to expect a party. She promised to take me in town to a movie as my birthday present, but she never got around

105

to it. However, I noticed a significant change in her
attitude toward me. She began telling me I was old
enough to start looking for work. Whenever she became
cross at me for any reason she would say,

"You're too goddam big for me to support. You
have to get a job and help me to feed this family, I
can't do it all by myself."

She said that one day when I was feeling a bit more
courageous than usual, and so I said to her,

"What kind of a job could I apply for, mother?"

"Don't you get smart with me, you little
bastard," she answered, "you know damn well you could
sell papers or run errands, there are plenty of things
out there a big kid like you could do."

I found it useless to tell her there were twenty
boys after every job available. I knew she would not
believe me if I told her about the street bullies.
They roamed the streets in groups of threes and fours,
and when the boys who were working got paid they would
strong-arm their thirty or forty cents away from them.
I sold newspapers whenever I got the chance and I
learned how to duck the tough guys in order to get
home with my few pennies. However, it was Jake, not
mother who finally got me mad enough to take the risk
and run away. I'm glad I didn't know what was in
store for me or I probably would not have been so
brave as I started on a journey that took me over one
thousand five hundred miles.

I RAN AWAY FROM HOME

Of the few boys who could be called my friends,
there was one in particular whom I liked very much.
His name was Roger, and he was the same age as me.
His father had been killed in an industrial accident
when he was only eight years old. His mother had to
go to work and as he was an only child he was lonesome

106

much of the time. He enjoyed being with me and even helped me to cut wood a few times. I think we were drawn to each other because we were both very sensitive children and easily disposed to periods of melancholy.

We were sitting on the steps of his house one evening bemoaning our lot. Feeling angry, sad and depressed, we made a pact to run away together the next morning. We had no plans, no idea where we would go or how we would get along. We both knew one thing only --- we were unappreciated, unwanted and unhappy.

Early the next morning, after a sleepless night, I called at his house. We made three sandwiches, all the food that was in his house, and we started out toward Boston. Roger had fifteen cents his mother had given him, but I had nothing. On the outskirts of Cambridge, we came to a big freight yard with trains shuttling in and out. We watched the men shifting cars around for a long time, fascinated. Roger turned to me and said,

"Let's hop a freight."

"But we won't know where we will be going then," I said.

"What's the difference," Roger said, "we don't know where we are going anyway, do we?"

I had to admit he had me there. And so, watching out for the railroad police, we found a train all made up with several empty boxcars in a row. We hid in the bushes alongside the tracks for about an hour, but the train finally started to move and we jumped into an empty car. We were off to --- only God knew where!

Within the hour I was to have my first brush with death. The train had slowly gathered speed and we soon left the freight yard behind. I was on my hands and knees looking over the landscape and trying to guess where we were headed. For some unknown reason the engineer applied his brakes hard and then released them. When he did, the big door that had been wide-open, came sliding closed on its track and jammed my head against the frame of the car. I was almost knocked unconscious. My head had a big gash on one side that was bleeding profusely and I saw stars for a good ten minutes. I know if there had been just a bit more force behind that door, the top of my head would have been taken off and Roger would have found himself alone. However, I was all right after a while and we continued to think of our adventure and where we were going.

Several hours later we found ourselves in another freight yard. When we tried to see where we were, we were spotted by some railroad police and had to flee the yard to keep from being arrested. We learned we were in Bangor, Maine. We had been traveling north. Where do we go from here, I wondered.

"Hey Freeman, I have grandparents in Prince Edward Island, Canada; what do you say we head for there?" Roger asked.

"That suits me fine," I said, "but how the hell do we get there? I don't have the foggiest idea where Canada is, let alone Prince Edward Island."

"Don't worry," Roger said, "all we have to do is keep heading north. Just stick with me and we'll get there."

We tried a couple of times to catch another freight car heading north, but each time the railroad police drove us out of the yard and we became afraid to push our luck, so we took to the highway to continue our journey.

Long miles of roadway were still unpaved, and when a car went by the dust was intolerable. Our clothes were covered with it before we had traveled ten miles. Add to that the uncomfortable fact one could not see a thing for fifteen minutes after a car had zoomed by. However, automobiles were rare in 1935, especially in the state of Maine, and trucks were almost as scarce. There were times when an hour would pass without us seeing a vehicle of any kind, and once we were stuck on a lonely road for seven hours before we were given a lift.

Soon after we left Boston our sandwiches were gone and we were hungry again. As our hunger increased we began to feel we had made a serious mistake by running away. Nevertheless, I was too afraid of mother to go back and too proud to admit defeat; we had no choice but to press on. I had read stories about boys on adventures such as ours and of how they had worked for their food as they went along. Bearing that in mind I went up to a farmhouse and knocked on the door. When a big farmer answered my knock, I said,

"Pardon me, sir. My buddy and I are hitchhiking from Boston, Massachusetts, to Canada. We are hungry and we were wondering if we could cut some wood or do some other work for you in return for a bite to eat."

That appeal had taken all the courage I could muster. I was trembling inside and my knees were knocking when I had finished. We stood there holding our breath waiting for the man's answer. We didn't have to wait long.

"You goddam bums get off of my property," he shouted at us. "Don't come to me with your damned problems, I have enough of my own. Go on, get out of here or I will call the police on you."
The police were the last people we wanted to see, so we took off in a hurry. I had been humiliated and I was angry. I promised myself I would never ask another person for a handout again regardless of how hungry I was, and I never did.

To relate all the adventures we had on the way to and from Prince Edward Island would require a book in itself. However, there were a few highlights that must be mentioned. For one thing, there were the people we met. Most of them were nice folks who were impressed with our courage and wanted to help us in some way. Some of them gave us a ride of only a few miles while others took us over a hundred. More than one person took us farther north than they were going just to get us near a better place to hike from. Many more gave us a little money as we got out of their car. A quarter, a half-dollar, and one older man even gave us a dollar. Twice we were taken into a restaurant and invited to eat with the people who had given us a lift. However, even with the help of those good people, there were many times we bought a loaf of day-old bread for five cents and washed it down with spring water we found in the woods. We were hungry more than we were not throughout the whole trip.

Sleeping was another problem. We were too terrified to sleep at night wherever we found ourselves, so we took turns sleeping during the day when we had the chance. A few times we both fell asleep in someone's car as they were giving us a ride and they were good enough to let us sleep until they had to let us out. One night we were allowed to sleep in a hayloft of a big barn. It was an interesting place in that it was not a regular barn but a taxicab company. Their taxicabs were horses and buggies rather than motor vehicles. The company had ten of those rigs, and six drivers on hand to meet the trains at the station which was only a hundred yards down the road.

Slowly, one dusty mile after another, we continued northward. Five days after we left Boston we found ourselves at the Canadian border. That presented another problem --- we could not go through customs because we had no papers. Besides, we were kids and big people always asked kids too many questions. So into the deep woods we plunged and began to circle around the back of the customs house. We were just outside of Holton, Maine, when we slipped into the woods. We walked more than five miles into Canada before we felt safe enough to come out onto the road again. The Canadian border had been crossed; we were in Canada. A strange, scared feeling came over me, "Now you've really done it," I said to myself, as I realized we had left the United States behind us.

110

It was a feeling of finality, as though I had locked a door on my past life, and I was afraid. I could not let Roger know I was scared, though. He had always looked up to me because of my strength. Besides, Roger was not emotionally very strong and I was afraid he would fold up on me if he saw me fearful.

On and on we went. Five more days passed and we had not reached Prince Edward Island. I was weary and discouraged, but still kept up a good front. I began to experience my first taste of homesickness. As bad as it had been to live with my family, I began to wish I was back with them. I especially missed my little sister, Lisa, and much to my embarrassment I found myself crying silently in my arms at night. What a terrible lonesome feeling that was! I was on the verge of turning back regardless of how Roger felt when something happened to give us new hope.

The next automobile that came along that day was a big black Buick and the driver was a middle-aged business man. He was going all the way to Prince Edward Island! It was only then we learned that one could not get to Prince Edward Island by land. It was an island and it took an hour or more on a ferry to get there. Seeing how crestfallen we were when we heard there would be a fare to pay and we had only a dollar between us, the business man said he would pay our way across, and he did. And so, twelve days after we left Boston, we set foot on Prince Edward Island, Canada!

The only automobiles we saw on the island were the two that came over on the ferry with us. All the islanders appeared to be farmers and they traveled in horse and buggy. They seemed to be everywhere. Everybody knew everybody else on the island and when we asked for Roger's grandparent's place, one farmer offered to drive us there even though it would take him out of his way. Six miles on a dirt road in an open buggy was a strange way to end such a long and exciting journey, but we were so glad to finally reach our destination we didn't much care how uneventful or unglamorous the last few miles were.

Roger's relatives were overjoyed and dumbfounded to see us; they had no idea we had run away from home much less that we were on our way to see them. That made it so much more fun for us. They were completely stunned by the fact that two fifteen year-old boys would dare to set out on an adventure of that magnitude, and succeed in their attempt. Even though it was way past dinnertime, they sat us down to a marvelous home-cooked meal. And as would be expected, we ate too much. Then we were tucked into a real bed again for the first time in almost two weeks. We were dead to the world for the next twenty-four hours.

Although Roger's relatives welcomed us with open arms they had serious problems of their own they were dealing with. They were still in a state of shock because of the death of Roger's grandfather the month before. He had died with a sudden heart attack and although he was in his late sixties, he had always been healthy. The atmosphere we had stepped into was sad and gloomy. His loss was felt keenly by everyone, especially so because he was the only man on the one hundred sixty acre farm. Helen, Roger's grandmother, Sadie and Winnifred his two aunts, and two small girls belonging to Sadie made up the entire household. There would be no man to till the soil that year. Roger had not known his grandfather very well, having seen him only twice, and so he did not feel the loss. He was content to lounge around the farm and eat home-cooked meals, but not me. I had been taught one must earn every bit of food one eats. I just could not feel comfortable taking so much from strangers without giving something in return. To satisfy my need to feel productive I went to work on a neighboring farm.

While I was looking for work I learned the whole island was aware that two boys had hitchhiked all the way from Boston, Massachusetts. We were celebrities! Because of that I had no trouble finding a job. I think I was hired only because I was one of those boys, not because the farmer needed help. I was paid one dollar a day and two meals for a twelve-hour day, and I gave him his money's worth. The Canadian dollar was much larger than the American dollar back then and

I felt very rich with a few of them in my pocket.

Roger and I stayed in Canada for ten weeks, but my homesickness had become unbearable by then and we had to leave. Because I had worked most of that time, I had been able to save thirty-six dollars for the return trip, but Roger didn't have a dime. The day we left though, his grandmother gave him ten dollars --- not a great amount of money for a trip of over a thousand miles, but it was every cent she could spare.

When we left Prince Edward Island we were not as afraid as we had been when we left Boston. We knew we had enough money to guarantee we would not go hungry on our way back. Then too, since we had learned quite a bit about hitchhiking on our way north, we felt confident about our abilities as we started for home. Our only real concern was getting across the Canadian-United States border. However, when we finally did get back to it, we had no difficulty traveling the same general path through the woods that we had forged on our way north.

There seemed to be more people traveling south than there had been going north. Whereas it had taken us twelve days to travel from Boston to Prince Edward Island, it took us only nine days to make the return journey. We headed straight for Roger's house because I didn't know if I would be welcomed in mine. As we anticipated, Estelle, Roger's mother, was overjoyed to see us back unharmed. They had such an emotional reunion I felt awkward in their presence, and so I slipped out onto the front stairs and sat there feeling alone and lost. Roger must have told his mother about me being afraid to go home because she came out to me and said,

"Come on Freeman, I'm taking you home. Don't you worry one bit though," she said, "if your mother doesn't want you, you can come back here and live with us."

With an offer like that I felt somewhat comforted, but still I was apprehensive going to face mother.

Much to my surprise mother was as glad to see me
as Estelle had been to see Roger. Or at least she
acted as though she was and that was good enough for
me. My return home was cause for everyone to make a
fuss over me and tell me how much I was missed ---
everyone except dad. When he came in that evening, he
acted as though I had never been away, or as if I was
still not there, I couldn't tell which. However, I
was so glad to be home I ignored his slight.
Surprisingly, within a few weeks things seemed back to
normal, and our trip to Canada began to seem like a
dream, as though it never had happened. But of course
some things had changed while we were gone.

For one thing, Erma had come home from the reform
school. She had been given time off of her original
sentence because of her good behavior. I was
delighted by the way she had changed. She had gone
away an overweight, bed-wetting, fourteen year-old
girl. She came home a very good-looking seventeen
year-old young lady. There was even a steady
boyfriend in her life and she seemed happy. However,
her boyfriend, Pete, was ten years older than she and
he was a blustering blowhard. Erma had met him in a
carnival that had passed through our neighborhood a
few weeks before. He was operating the Ferris wheel,
but to hear him talk one would think he owned the
whole carnival. I disliked him immediately but Erma
seemed to be in love with him. Pete had promised to
marry Erma as soon as she turned eighteen which was
not far off and so she was in a world of her own. It
was so good to see Erma happy for a change I didn't
want to say or do anything that might spoil things for
her, so I kept my dislike for Pete to myself. At the
same time, things were not going well between mother
and dad. In fact the animosity seemed to be too deep
by then to ever be resolved.

DAD LEFT HOME AGAIN FOR THE LAST TIME

The first week in December of 1935, the final argument erupted between mother and dad, and dad left home again. At that time, mother was working three days a week and dad was still on the W.P.A. There was some money coming in and we were better off than we had been for some time. However, mother had become cynical and bitter, especially toward dad. She nagged him constantly over everything, and every day she found new ways to belittle him.

The day dad left home had started off no differently than many other days. In fact, it had been rather peaceful all morning. It was just after lunch when the trouble began, and as usual it was mother who started it. She was rocking gently by the window in her favorite rocking chair. Dad was sitting on the sofa reading the newspaper, and I was lying on the floor with some comic books. No one else was home at the time and everything was quiet. But, I could tell mother was itching to start something by the way she was acting. She was darting angry glances at dad, and as she did, her rocking became more animated. After a while I heard her speak to dad in a very low voice.

"You call yourself a man, for Christ's sake; you can't even feed your family. What the hell kind of a man are you anyway? If it wasn't for me working, this family would starve."

Her voice kept rising as she spoke and I could see her anger was mounting as well. I cringed the moment she started to speak because I knew she was going to create a scene. I watched dad as he sank lower into the sofa, and I saw him bring the newspaper closer to his face as if to shut her out. Mother didn't miss his maneuver either, and she became furious.

"Bruce, you put that goddam paper down while I'm

115

trying to talk to you," she screamed at him.

Dad lowered the paper onto his lap and turned to face mother with a resigned sigh. She continued her tirade.

"You call yourself a man," she repeated. "If you were really a man you would get the hell out of here and stop eating the food I bring home for the kids. I'm tired of going to work while you stay home doing nothing. You don't even do the housework to help me," she said. "The least you could do, if you can't find a job, would be to leave us alone. We can get along much better without you."

Mother had started to cry then and she turned her face toward the window.

Dad folded his newspaper very carefully and laid it on the sofa. There was a deep sadness in his eyes. He stood up and faced mother then, and said to her,

"Peggy, do you really want me to leave?"

"Yes --- for God's sake, yes," she answered, "I want you out of my life. I never want to set eyes on you again."

Without waiting for another word, and without answering her, dad went upstairs, packed a small suitcase, and walked out the front door. I watched him as he walked up the street toward the bus stop and out of our lives.

I was almost sixteen when that happened, and I never saw my father again. My feelings over his departure were mixed. For one thing, I didn't know whether to take him seriously or not. There was the possibility he was grandstanding, that he would come slinking home again in a couple of weeks as he had done before. Yet at the same time, I sensed there was something different about the way in which he left that time and I felt he was really gone for good. Then, too, I was thrilled to think that he had finally found enough guts to walk away from mother. However, I resented him for turning his back on his family. I think I was afraid we could not survive without him. Daily, all the rest of that winter, mother nagged me about finding a job. I went out looking for one a couple of times, but my heart was not in it. I wanted to graduate from grammar school as I was in my eighth and final year. I was able to stall until my birthday, but after that there was no more schooling for me for a long time.

MY SIXTEENTH BIRTHDAY

March 12, 1936 was not the magical day I had expected it would be --- I didn't feel any different being sixteen. For some strange reason I had thought I would. We had cake and ice-cream, but we older children had stopped having parties on our birthdays a few years before. Mother gave me two pairs of pants for a birthday present, but she handed me a shock with them. As she passed the package to me she said,

"Freeman, this is the last present you are getting from me. You are sixteen now and I can no longer support you. I expect you to get a job as soon as you can find one or you will have to leave my house."

"Mother, can't I finish school first?" I pleaded --- "I will be graduating in three months."

"We can't wait that long," she answered. "Since your father left, we don't get a check from the W.P.A. as we used to and I need help with this family. You must get a job now."

"I'll find a job," I said, slowly but angrily. "Don't worry, you won't have to support me any more, I'll take care of myself from now on."

I was so frustrated and angry I went into the cellar and cut firewood all evening. I was throwing the wood all over the place and crying most of the time I was working. I cursed my father for dumping his responsibilities on me; then I felt guilty for not wanting to shoulder my part of the load with mother.

Nevertheless, I had to quit school two months before graduation and join the army of men and boys who were looking for employment. I made a firm resolution to do a better job of being the man of the house than my father had. I was going to solve all of our problems. That even included forcing Jake to become a responsible person. The family was getting smaller and so I thought the job could not be that awesome. Lisa had just started her schooling and was taking care of herself much of the time. Eileen was spending so much time with her friends she was hardly a part of the family any longer. Erma had gotten a job as a waitress in a local restaurant, and most of her spare time was spent with Pete, so she was no problem. That left Jake as my sole concern. I didn't think I would have very much trouble getting him in line. However, I did not believe I had the right to order anyone around unless I was holding down a steady job. Finding work became my immediate goal.

MY FIRST EMPLOYMENT

The day after my birthday I went to the garage at the end of our street and let everyone know I needed a job. A couple of the men who knew me, introduced me to several street peddlers and as a result I was working for one of them in less than two weeks. I had been hired as a helper on an ice truck, and I was to be paid seventy-five cents a day. Those were the days before refrigeration was available to the general public, and in hot weather ice was an important commodity. All during the summer months it was not unusual for us to be on the streets from seven A.M. until eight or nine o'clock in the evening. On Saturdays, when all our customers needed ice for the weekend we would not finish our route until two o'clock in the morning. When the ice season was over,

118

we sold wood and coal to keep busy. Later on, range oil was discovered and I became proficient converting wood-burning stoves into oil burners.

At the peak of the season there would be three, sometimes four, helpers on the truck. Work, eat and sleep became a way of life for me for a long time. It was with that group of hardworking young men I had my first drink of alcohol, and a whole new world opened up to me.

For many years I refused to become a team player until Alcoholics Anonymous showed me the value of compromise.

PART TWO

MY INTRODUCTION TO ALCOHOL

THE BIRTH OF THE MONSTER

MY FIRST DRINK

I had been working less than three months when an early hot spell hit our area. The first four days of the week had been extremely hot and we had record-breaking sales each day. We were at least three hours later finishing our route every evening. When Friday turned out to be a chilly day, with a fine, misty rain falling, we welcomed the break. By noontime, it was obvious our customers had bought all the ice they needed --- at least for a while.

Our boss decided to quit work early and take all of us into Boston for a spaghetti dinner. He said the dinner would be our reward for the extra work we had done. As it turned out, we got much more than dinner that evening.

Prohibition had been repealed just three years before; taverns and barrooms were opening all around. People no longer had to sneak into a speakeasy to buy a drink. They no longer had to look over their shoulder for the law as they shared a bottle of moonshine with a friend. There was a holiday excitement in the air as people once more could sit at a bar and legally drink whatever they chose. Even the bartenders did not look too closely at one's identification, they were so elated over the new freedom.

As we pulled up to the curb in front of an

Italian restaurant in downtown Boston, our boss said,

"Before we have dinner, let's go in that tavern over there and get a glass of beer."

The four of us went in together, and piled noisily into a booth. Immediately a pretty waitress appeared with her order pad in hand.

"How much is your beer?" our boss asked.

"Five cents a glass," the waitress said, "but you can buy six glasses for a quarter."

"Then how much is that big pitcher of beer on that table over there?" he asked.

"That's thirty-five cents," she said, "but it's worth it because you get ten glasses of beer out of it."

"Good," he said, "bring us a pitcher of beer and four glasses."

When the waitress placed the beer and the glasses on the table, a feeling of terror came over me. All of my teachings in the Catholic school had been that alcohol was the devil's brew. It was to be avoided at all cost. Then mother, through her hysterical outbursts over the evils of drink, whenever she saw someone drunk, taught us the same. Nevertheless, I wanted to be accepted by my friends so badly I would have done most anything. Just the same, as our boss filled our glasses from the pitcher, I became almost frozen with fear. I sat there, eyes fixed on my glass, seeing nothing else and not knowing what to do next. Finally, Charlie, one of my friends said,

"What's the matter Freeman, are you afraid of a little beer?"

Before I could think of an answer, Amos, my boss said,

"Here, for God's sake, it won't hurt you. It will do you the world of good."

Saying that, he pushed the glass closer to me, and to avoid anymore teasing I put the glass to my lips and took a sip. It tasted bitter and I did not like it. After a while though, Charlie was after me again.

"Come on, Freeman, for crying out loud, drink up will you!"

With that prodding I angrily grabbed the glass and emptied it in two big gulps. The moment the beer reached my stomach a warm sensation spread throughout my whole body. It started in my stomach, crept down my legs, warmed my feet, and traveled back up to my head. My face became flushed and my ears started to burn. And then the miracle happened. I experienced a feeling of freedom such as I had never known before. Until that exciting moment, I had been an awkward, shy, fearful individual who could talk to no one. I had always felt out of place, inferior to everybody. I felt as though everyone was talking about me. My emotions were so sensitive I would cry or fight with the least provocation. When a girl would come near, although I might be attracted to her, I would not know what to say or how to act.

All my life I had a feeling as though I had a knot in the pit of my stomach; it felt as big as my fist and seemed to be growing with each passing year --- I had become so familiar with that feeling I never considered there would be any way to get rid of it. The knot eased somewhat as I got involved in my work, but it always came back again as soon as the workday was over.

Sometimes it came back stronger than it
had been. With the first glass of beer
I felt that knot dissolve all by itself.
I began to talk to everyone with ease.
I felt bold and confident for a change.
I even made a date with the waitress, a
date I didn't have the courage to keep
when the time came. For the first time
in my life I felt a part of the gang, and
I loved the feeling. At that moment I
believed I had found the elixir of life
--- alcohol.

        I didn't wait for my boss to pour
the next round, I did that for him. When
the pitcher was empty I began to sneak
drinks out of the other glasses when my
friends weren't looking. I offered to buy
the next pitcher of beer because it wasn't
coming fast enough for me. My thirst for
alcohol was insatiable from the very beginning.

The only way our boss was able to get us away
from the tavern so we could have dinner, was to
promise us we would come back later. Dinner turned
out to be the most joyous time I had ever had. I ate
until I couldn't eat another bite. We carried on and
laughed until our sides were aching. Then, with
dinner over, we went back down the street to the
tavern for more beer. Needless to say I got mildly
drunk that night and felt very grown up.

        When the boys let me out in front of my house
about midnight, they hollered loud enough to wake the
whole neighborhood, "Freeman's drunk as a skunk.
Freeman can't take his booze, Freeman's a rummy. Ha
ha ha."

        I was so afraid mother would hear them I
wouldn't knock on the door until they had driven
around the corner. When mother did let me in I told
her that we had a busy day and I was tired. In that
way I was able to get past her and I went right up to
bed.

I woke up the next morning with a terrible hangover, but I was not concerned about that. My very first thoughts were centered around how soon I could experience that marvelous feeling again. I thought I would have to wait until we had finished work that day. But it didn't work out that way. Circumstances worked in my favor and I was drinking before nine o'clock that morning. My behavior that Saturday should have served as a warning that my drinking was different than that of my friends, but it didn't.

Our first delivery that morning was in a liquor store. In the state of Massachusetts, the liquor stores were privately-owned. That particular store bought three hundred pounds of ice, and, as I was the last man to leave the store, I had to collect the money. As I was being paid I got a sudden impulse and asked the clerk for a quart of port wine. Much to my surprise, and to my delight, he sold me a bottle of wine for sixty-nine cents with no questions asked.

I dashed out to the truck thinking I would be hailed as a hero. Because I had wanted more of the good feelings I had experienced the evening before, I thought my friends would also. To my chagrin they wanted nothing to do with me or my wine. They told me bluntly they only wanted to get on with their work. They made me feel ashamed and guilty about my desire to drink and I became angry at them. They even called me a "dammed rummy" and asked me to get away from them with my booze.

For a few moments I felt embarrassed, but after I took a good swig from the bottle, I did not care what they thought of me. I did not need their approval anyway. I had the only real friend that mattered --- Alcohol.

And when I realized I would not
have to share my wine with them I was
pleased. That meant all the more for me.
I thought I would have enough for the
weekend. How wrong I was! I drank that
whole quart of wine in about three hours.
Before it was half gone though, I went
into my first blackout. Imagine my
horror when I drifted back out of that
fog and found myself behind bars. I had
no idea what I had done to cause my
arrest nor how long I had been in jail.
The last thing I could recall was arguing
with my friends. I remember telling them
I was not too drunk to do my work and I
would not go home as they told me to.
That had been sometime Saturday morning.
After that, my mind was a complete blank
until I woke up in jail.

About an hour after I reentered the world of
reality, I heard keys rattling, and a guard came into
the cell-block. He came right to my cell and unlocked
it. As he did, he said to me,

"Well! I see you're awake; that's good. Now
come with me because someone wants to talk to you."

Walking behind him I asked why I had been
arrested.

"You were drunk and raising hell," he said,
"they brought you in about six o'clock last night
according to the report on my desk."

A clock on the wall told me it was ten-thirty
Sunday morning. I quickly calculated I had lost about
twenty-four hours somehow.

I wanted to ask several more questions but we
had stopped in front of a door marked "Interrogation
Room". The officer unlocked the door and threw it
wide open.

"Go in and take a seat," he said, "someone will be in to talk to you in a few minutes."

I stepped through the door and found myself in a room not much bigger than the cell I had just come from. The heavy mesh grating bolted on the outside of the only window was a grim reminder I was a prisoner. A large, heavy mahogany table, with three chairs on each side of it, almost filled the room. As I heard the guard lock the door behind me, leaving me alone with my thoughts, a feeling of despair and helplessness enveloped me and icy fingers of fear gripped my heart. I did not know what to expect next.

The room was as quiet as the inside of a church as I sat there shivering from the cold and wondering what was going to happen to me. Faint sounds of traffic drifted to my ears --- a dog barked some distance away, now and then a door would slam somewhere in the building. Footsteps in the corridor a couple of times gave me a start, but they passed on by and I relaxed again. I could hear the ticking of a clock in the next room. Twenty minutes passed very slowly, and then I heard a number of men's voices just outside the door. With a noisy flourish the officer unlocked and opened the door all in one motion, and the room seemed to fill with people. Actually it was only the guard and three other men. The men were all big, very tall and burly. They were well-dressed and carried an air of authority about them. In contrast I felt like a drowned gutter rat. Towering over me, they told me they were detectives and they demanded to know the name of the person who had sold me the wine. I knew if I told them where I had purchased the bottle, our customer would be in serious trouble and might even lose his liquor license. Even though I was terrified of the detectives, I could not become an informer. I insisted I had found the wine on the backstairs of an apartment building when I had gone in to see a customer. I suspected they knew I was lying, but they could not shake me from my story.

Finally, after what seemed an eternity, one of the men became enraged and grabbed me by the front of my overalls lifting me right out of my chair. Holding me at arms length in one hand he raced down the corridor. I was paralyzed with fear; the look of anger on his face suggested I was going to be thrown into some dark dungeon to be left forever! The next thing I knew, he had opened a door behind me with his free hand and pushed me through it. To my utter amazement I found myself on the sidewalk outside the building.

"Go home you goddamed stupid jerk," the detective shouted just before he slammed the door.

I had been freed so suddenly it took a few minutes for it to register in my whirling brain. It was then just after noontime on a beautiful Sunday. I felt so ashamed I started slinking towards home by staying as close to the buildings as possible. It seemed that everybody I passed on the street was dressed in their Sunday best making me look the worst in my dirty work clothes. I guessed they were all going to or coming from church, while I was on my way home from jail. I had an odd feeling that "Jailbird" was written all over me. I was sure anyone who looked in my direction could tell where I had spent the night. Still shivering from the cold, sick to my stomach from the wine, and very apprehensive about facing an angry mother, I slowly continued my trek homeward. As I trudged along I began to rack my brain, trying to remember what I had done the day before. The guard had told me I had been locked up about six o'clock Saturday evening. That meant seven or eight hours had to be accounted for. "What had I done during those hours? Where had I gone? How and why had I been arrested?" After a while though, I had to give it up; I just could not recall anything.

THE MYSTERY WAS UNRAVELED

Halfway home I met my brother, Jake, and my boss, Amos. They were driving to the police station in my boss' car to see if they could get me out of jail. As I climbed in the back seat and slouched in the corner, I was grateful to have a place to hide. My boss said he felt responsible for me because he had started me drinking.

When I told them I could not remember what had happened, they did not believe me at first, but after a while they at least seemed to accept the idea and began to tell me about the trouble I had caused. First Amos told me that as I drank the wine that morning, I kept getting more boisterous and I would not let the other fellows do their work. They finally had to call him from a pay phone and ask him to do something with me. He said he had driven me home three different times and then had to threaten to beat me up before I would stay there.

"I just heard this morning that you had been arrested and I came down to bail you out if I could," he said.

Then Jake spoke up and told me that when I came home, about three o'clock, I started to beat him up and a neighbor had called the police.

"You even tried to fight with the cops when they showed up," he said, "and so they put handcuffs on you and took you away in the police car."

My boss let me and Jake out in front of our house and drove away. I had to go in and face the music.

After an hour of lecturing mother had spent her anger and left me alone. I got away from her as fast as I could and stayed away from her the rest of the day.

ERMA GETS MARRIED

While I was struggling with my own changing role Erma was having her own problems.

Very soon the beautiful young lady who had come home from the reform school vanished, and an over-weight, unkempt woman took her place. The transformation was so rapid it was frightening and we left her alone most of the time. Erma had a different boyfriend practically every month and there was not one of them that didn't have serious personal problems. For instance, there was George --- he was only twenty-five, but he had been married and divorced twice. Then there was Larry --- he could not keep a job of any kind and he did not seem to be bothered about being out of work and broke all the time. Next Tom came into the picture --- he was in jail for minor offenses more than he was out. So it came as no surprise to me when Erma announced she had decided to marry Ed. Ed was a down-and-out local drunk. He was twelve years older than Erma and he had not been able to keep a job since the day he began to work. Erma was only twenty at the time and it certainly seemed as though she really had jumped from the frying pan into the fire. That marriage was horrible from the day it took place. More about them later. For now let's return to me and my problem in trying to drink like a man. My first experience scared me so much that it was two weeks before I dared try again.

I GOT DRUNK A SECOND TIME

One Friday evening, when we had again finished work early, my friends coaxed me to go out with them for a few beers. Evidently they had forgotten how crazy I had become the last time. I was very confident by then that I had learned the dangers of "drinking too much" and I was sure I would be careful. Nevertheless, as soon as I drank the first glass of beer, the same warm glow began in the pit of my stomach and all my inner tensions slowly relaxed --- I felt wonderful. The warm sensation spread rapidly throughout my entire body and I felt free again. All of my fine resolutions flew out the window. By the third glass of beer I was beyond caring about anything. Alcohol had given me the feeling of belonging once more and nothing else was of any importance. Although I got good and drunk that night, I did not have a blackout, and I was able to get into my own bed without mother realizing I had been drinking again. The next morning, though, I had to go to work with a terrible hangover and not enough sleep.

I ATTEMPTED TO CONTROL MY DRINKING

During the next nine months I made a serious effort to control my drinking. My fear of alcohol had increased immensely because of my unpleasant experiences with it; and yet I wanted desperately to enjoy the feeling of freedom that only alcohol provided. From June 1936, when I had my first taste of beer, until Christmas of that year, I drank five or six times. However, each time I had gotten drunk in spite of my good intentions not to. Through all of those drunks I honestly believed my difficulty was just a matter of learning how to .... drink like a gentleman. Nevertheless, every attempt at control failed, and I began to believe I was a weak-willed person. If that were so, all I needed to do would be to strengthen my will power. "In other words", I thought, "I would have to grow up and become a man". For a long time I was confident I would learn how to do that. At no time did I ever consider giving up alcohol completely; I liked what it did for me too much to let it go. Besides, I had no idea I was up against something too big for me to handle. My definition of a man, at that period in my life, excluded a quitter, so I was obliged to stay with the struggle and solve the dilemma. When the Christmas season approached I promised myself I would not drink even though I wanted to. Although there was plenty of alcohol around me throughout the Christmas and New Year holidays, I was able to abstain. In fact, it was after my birthday before I took another drink. My first real effort to not drink had lasted over four months.

My seventeenth birthday arrived on a Friday that

year, but there was no celebration. Mother, and I were busy working long hours; there was no time left for pleasantries. Besides, at that manly age, I didn't want a party anyway; parties were for kids. However, I would have liked to have had mother bake a chocolate cake like she used to, but I pretended it didn't matter. Needless to say, it did matter, and I stewed inwardly for over a week about it. Then, feeling sorry for myself one day, and angry at mother, I bought myself a present. It was ten cans of my favorite brew, Ballantine Ale, ice-cold and ready to drink. I kept the cans of ale buried in our load of ice all day as we covered our route. It was all I could do not to touch a can of it until our day's work was finished, but I succeeded. Finally, about six o'clock that evening, I stood behind the parked truck and downed two cans before I even left the garage. Two more cans disappeared while I was eating my dinner and by that time I was as high as a kite. A few friends I had met on the street corner were glad to help me drink the rest. The ale was all gone by eight o'clock, but someone in the gang bought more so the party could continue. Sometime during the evening I went into another blackout and knew nothing until I woke up, hours later, in jail for the second time in less than a year.

That time, I found myself in a small community on the opposite side of Cambridge from where I lived. I had never heard of the place before and didn't know where it was in relation to my own neighborhood. The police station was in the basement of a large building but had very little space of its own. There were three cells in the jail, each one big enough to accommodate one prisoner. It had been a Wednesday morning, about six A.M. when I woke up there, and I found myself alone. There were no other prisoners and not even a police officer at the desk.

I prayed silently, "Dear God, please get me out of this mess without being sent to jail and I will never take another drink again as long as I live." No prayer had ever been more sincere.

Another half hour passed, and then I heard a car drive up near the building and park. A minute later a young police officer came into the station and went straight to the desk. The scowl on his face and his businesslike manner discouraged me from hollering out to him as I had started to. About forty-five silent minutes later he got up from his chair and came right to my cell. As he unlocked the door he said,

"I guess you're sober enough now to turn you loose, but someone ought to kick you right in the ass before it's too late, you damn jerk."

The look of contempt on his face forced me to keep my mouth shut and slide past him to get to the outside door. However, out on the street a few minutes later I forgot all about him and even the promise I had made to God. I had other problems to worry about just then. I had to find my way home with no money in my pocket and I had to cook up a good story for both my mother and my boss about where I had been all night.

When I finally found my way home by hitchhiking, some two hours later, mother was wild. Someone had told her I had been arrested again and she had stayed home from work to find out what I was up to. The lecture I had to endure for the next two hours was worse than if she had given me a beating.

"Let me tell you something, Freeman," she screamed at me, "now that your father is gone, you are the man of the house. I will not put up with your foolishness; I need your help with the other three kids and by God you are going to give it to me. You had better straighten yourself up damn quick or you can get the hell out of my house. I work too damn hard for you kids to have a snot nose kid like you bring me all this trouble."

She had started to cry then and I felt worse than if she had used the dog leash on me. I felt ashamed for not doing more to help her. I made a silent vow to become more responsible and to be more

133

involved with the family.

Later that afternoon, when mother had finally
exhausted herself lecturing me, I went to see my boss
to square things with him for not going to work that
day. I was all set to lie to him, but I didn't get
the chance. He too had heard about my escapade and he
wasn't happy. He did not seem to mind that I had lost
the day's work, he just said he would dock my pay.
Nevertheless, I had to listen to a Dutch uncle lecture
for an hour before he told me I could come to work the
next morning.

I CONTINUED TO DRINK

Just a month after my second arrest for being
drunk and disorderly, I went out drinking again. As
before, I had convinced myself it would be different
because I was going to be careful. Although I got
drunk that night, I had been amazed at how much beer I
had to drink to get that way. It seemed almost
overnight my tolerance for alcohol had increased
threefold. I took that as a sign I was learning how
to drink properly. Even though I had gotten drunk
against my wishes, I felt I was on the right track and
it would not be long before I had even that under
control.

As my tolerance for alcohol increased, it began
to cost me a lot more money to drink. In order to
keep up with my additional expenses and not let mother
know how much I was spending, I began to steal from my
employer. That was not hard to do because I was
handling a lot of his cash. Some of the methods I
developed were foolproof and if I could have used only
them I probably would never have gotten caught.
However, when those methods were not available, I
began to alter my account book. It was only a matter
of time before that kind of juggling would catch up
with me. Several times I avoided the inevitable with
lies and clever maneuvers, but discovery had to happen
sometime.

I GOT FIRED

One day in June, just before the ice business was due to start in earnest, Amos kept the books off the truck. He said he had to work on them, but I had a strong intuition he was looking for discrepancies, and I was apprehensive all day because of what he might uncover. We were near the end of our route, about four o'clock in the afternoon, when he drove up to the truck and got out of his car. He fumbled with some papers on the front seat for a while, then he straightened up and looked in our direction.

"Freeman, come here will you?" he hollered.
As I approached I saw he had my account book in his hand and I knew I was in trouble. He began to ask me questions about many of the entries, questions I had a hard time answering. Finally, he snapped the book closed and said,

"Freeman, you goddamed little thief, get the hell off of my truck while you can still walk. If I ever see you near my truck again I will personally knock your head off!"

I can still remember the anger on his face and his efforts to control himself. He had frightened me with his rage, but my fear was not as acute as my guilt and shame. I was angry, too, because he had humiliated me in front of the other men. I dared not look in their direction, but I could feel their eyes on my back. I knew they were watching the whole thing. Jamming both fists deep into my pockets, with my jaw clamped tight and my head down, I stormed away from the job I had worked on for more than a year. Everything had happened so fast my head was spinning.

Without a job I felt lost; feeling sorry for myself, I walked two miles to the nearest barroom and proceeded to get drunk. I got so drunk that night I didn't make it home. Instead, I woke up at five o'clock the next morning behind a local factory. I had slept on their loading dock all night. My head was killing me, my tongue was so thick and dry I could hardly swallow, and I was sick to my stomach. I had no idea how I had gotten there or anything else about the previous evening except that I had been drinking. Immediately I thought of mother, and wondered what I would tell her about being out all night. I was terrified of what she would do if she found I had been fired. I reasoned, however, that if I could find another job before I went home it would be to my advantage. With that in mind I went back to the garage where all the peddlers hung out, the garage where I had been hired by Amos in the first place. Needless to say, it was difficult for me to show my face around there because I believed everyone would know why I was looking for work.

I FOUND ANOTHER JOB

No one seemed to know I had been fired by Amos, and I was thankful for that. Then, to my pleasant surprise, I learned that all the peddlers who knew me considered me a good worker and, since one of the men did need a helper, he hired me to start work the next day.

My new job promised to be more exciting because the company had horses and wagons, no trucks. The company had twelve different routes throughout the city and were talking about putting two more teams out that year. If things went well, I was told, I had a chance for advancement.

That evening I was home when mother came in from work. I was shaking in my shoes, but I figured being home first would be the easiest way to face her wrath, I had to get it over with.

I was able to satisfy her with a lot of fast talk but I got through the ordeal rather easily.

I MADE AN EFFORT TO CHANGE

The next morning I was up at five o'clock, eager to start on my new job. I had been told to be there by seven, and I wanted to be on time. The barn was two miles from my house, but I found I could walk that distance in about forty minutes. Being fired as a thief had shaken me deeply; I didn't want that to happen a second time, nor did I want to face mother again because of something stupid I had done.

The fact I would be working in a completely different environment, with strangers, led me to believe I had a chance to turn over a new leaf and start all over again. I wanted desperately to get ahead with the company, and earn everyone's respect, so I had done a lot of serious thinking during the night. As a result, I had made a firm resolution not to steal again and to stop my drinking. So it was with a new spirit I presented myself to the men in the barnyard that morning. I felt sure there would be no more foolishness from me because I had decided to direct my life into more constructive channels. My future looked promising and I felt great.

Mr. Day, my new employer, welcomed me into the company, gave me a few important facts about my job, and then introduced me to the man whose "helper" I was to be. His name was Jim O'Brien.

Jim was thirty-seven years old, one of the three oldest men working for the company. He had been with Mr. Day less than a year, but already he had a route of his own. He was working on a commission basis rather than a weekly salary. That fact alone reinforced the notion that I too could get ahead fast if I worked hard enough.

Instantly I was awed by that tall, skinny, almost toothless, bald man. Not only was he to be my boss, but he was more than twice my age, therefore I thought, much wiser. Besides, I learned he carried a

137

pint of whiskey in his back pocket, and he drank right out of the bottle. Often I watched him drink a half pint of whiskey even before we had breakfast. One of his favorite comments was, "You got to get fortified for a hard day's work if you expect to do a good job." Then, as we worked together, I was amazed at how he nipped from his bottle all day, every day, and yet he never seemed to run out of booze.

Jim and I liked each other from the beginning. He said I was too young to know much about anything, but he would correct that very quickly; he was going to teach me "plenty". I was thrilled anyone would take an interest in me, and I was anxious to learn as much as I could.

I TOOK MY FIRST DRINK OF WHISKEY

The second day we worked together, Jim offered me a drink from his bottle. I became frightened and refused. I thought of the problems drinking had already caused me and of the promise to myself not to drink again. With much prodding, Jim was able to get me to tell him a little of my past experiences and about some of my fears.

"No wonder you got in trouble," Jim said, "there are so many bacteria in wine and beer they effect the brain and cause a person to do all kinds of crazy things. I would never drink that stuff even if you gave it to me. Now you take whiskey," he continued, "it is pure alcohol. Bacteria can not live in it. In fact it is so strong nothing can live in it. You just stick with me, kid, and I will teach you how to drink a man's drink like a man."

I wanted so much to have Jim think highly of me I would have done anything he suggested. Besides, I had secretly wanted all along to find a safe way to drink alcohol again if I could. All the rest of that day

138

Jim kept talking about the virtues of whiskey. He was saying everything I wanted to hear. We were the last ones in the barn that evening, everyone else had gone home. As I was unhitching the horse Jim took a drink from his pint and then turned to me and said,

"Look, Freeman, there's only a little left, why don't you kill it? I have another pint under the seat of the wagon."

Very gingerly I tipped the bottle and let a little whiskey run into my mouth. It burned my tongue fiercely, and when I tried to swallow, my throat contracted in a spasm. My eyes filled with tears; my nose was running profusely, and I could not catch my breath. I began to cough so violently I thought I was going to choke. I even threw up. Meanwhile, Jim started pounding me on the back and he was laughing so hard he had tears in his eyes. I was embarrassed and angry at myself for being a weakling. Finally, when I could breath again, Jim put his arm across my shoulder and said,

"Hey, it's OK buddy, I did the same thing when I had my first drink of booze. Here, let me put a little in this coca-cola and you will be able to drink it that way."

I wanted to refuse but for some strange reason I could not. Slowly, a sip at a time, I drank about half of the bottle of coke. Again there was that warm feeling in the pit of my stomach, only that time it was much warmer, almost hot. Then it seemed to radiate, very rapidly, to all parts of my body. Within minutes I experienced that wonderful feeling of euphoria I had come to regard as precious. I learned that whiskey was marvelous, just as Jim had predicted it would be.

However, getting to sleep that night proved to be difficult. My mind was racing from one subject to another with lightning-like speed. If there had been a speedometer attached to my brain it probably would have clocked eighty. Every nerve in my body seemed to be on edge, and as tired as I was, it took hours for me to unwind and drift off to sleep. Back at work the next morning I felt as though I had been run over by a truck. But, even though every muscle was sore, I was excited because I thought that Jim was going to teach me how to drink like a gentleman, and all my drinking difficulties were going to be left behind. Slowly, and with several disastrous episodes, I learned how to drink, but not like a gentleman.

Whenever I drank, I always ended up drunk. Blackouts became common! Because I did not want to lose my job, I quit drinking during working hours, but I made up for it on weekends and holidays. My tolerance for alcohol rose rapidly and I began to drink people under-the-table, people who were older than me and who had been drinking much longer. I became proud of my reputation and laughed at those who could not keep up with me. Within a year I was able to nip on the wagon with Jim, and often it was my bottle we drank from.

Meanwhile, mother had gotten tired of getting out of a warm bed to let me in every night; she finally gave me a key of my own. I took advantage of that by staying out later each night and drinking more. I was no longer afraid she would notice how drunk I was, and many a night I just made it to my bed before I passed out.

By that time, though, my drinking had started to cost me more money than I could spare. I soon found I could not steal very much from Jim, he was too alert. But I stole from our customers every chance I got. Still, I was always broke and borrowing on my next pay to give mother my earnings for the week. I had to find a way to get my hands on some extra cash.

One evening, the owner of a restaurant where I ate quite often, asked if I could get him ten gallons of range-oil, and I quickly agreed. I knew I could siphon the oil from a storage tank in the barnyard. Although I would have to hand-carry the two five-gallon cans four blocks, it meant seventy-cents for my own pocket, twice as much as my whole dinner cost.

It was almost ten o'clock and pitch black as I
sneaked into the yard with the two empty oil cans. To
my utter amazement, Jim was there siphoning oil from a
storage tank into the small tank on his wagon. Jim
told me he had been stealing oil for a long time, and
that he had a duplicate key for every lock in the
barn. He told me he returned many nights to supply
his wagon with uncounted goods. We began to work
together at night sometimes as well as days. My money
problems disappeared, but my drinking increased.

I worked for that company, with Jim as my boss,
for about eighteen months. I never did earn a
promotion while there, but I didn't care. Things were
working out well for me just the way they were.

Meanwhile, I continued to work long hours, and
to drink heavily. There were many times I drank too
much and could not make it home. Those nights I would
crawl, unseen, into the hayloft and pass out until the
next morning. Even though I drank almost daily during
the last six months I worked for that company, I
managed somehow to avoid getting into serious trouble.
However, I was never out of my work clothes. I didn't
own one piece of dress clothing and saw no reason to
buy any. It seemed the only way I could feel
comfortable was to be working or drinking with the men
in a barroom. I hated Sundays when people went to
church, all dressed up, with their families; so I took
to cleaning the barn and feeding the horses on the
pretext of earning extra money. The truth was I did
not know how to function outside of a work
environment. Regardless of how much money that went
through my hands, I was always broke because of my
drinking.

I WAS FIRED AGAIN

My career with that company came to an abrupt
end unexpectedly. One bitter cold night in the middle

of February 1939, just one month before my nineteenth birthday I was arrested on a charge of grand larceny. However, I was not alone. Jim and I were both in the barnyard late that night stealing oil and other products as usual. We were both very drunk and evidently very noisy. Someone must have heard us and called the police.

One minute we were alone in a darkened yard, the next minute there were two police cars, four cops and plenty of lights all around us. The police must have come up the street with their headlights out because we hadn't seen or heard a thing until they were on us. We were caught red-handed, arrested, handcuffed and taken to the police station. There we were locked up for the night and our employer was notified.

It was four o'clock the next afternoon before we heard from anyone. Bail had been set that morning at five thousand dollars each but there was no one to vouch for us, let alone put up that kind of money. We were not wise to the ways of the court system and knew nothing of a bailsman. I had no idea what might happen next or that we could do anything about our predicament; we didn't know we had certain rights and the police did not tell us we had any. So we waited. Late that afternoon a lawyer representing the company we worked for came into the police station. He spent over an hour behind closed doors with several important looking people. Finally, Jim and I were brought in from our cell and made to stand in front of a huge man seated behind a large desk. We were told we were going to be released with all charges dropped. It seemed the company did not want the publicity that prosecuting us would bring. However, the lawyer told us we were not to set foot on the company property again or we would be arrested for trespassing. And if that did happen, there would be no mercy shown a second time. We agreed to stay away from the place, and ten minutes later, much to our surprise, we found ourselves out of jail and walking down the street.

I LEFT HOME AGAIN

When we left the police station around six o'clock that evening, Jim and I headed right for the nearest barroom to celebrate our good fortune. I didn't want to go home and face mother just then anyway. By midnight, when the bar closed, I was drunk enough to face anyone, so I left Jim and headed home. Usually mother would be asleep at that time of night and I could slip quietly up to bed. However, that night she was waiting for me in the darkened house. When I could not get my key to work in the door, she surprised me by yanking the door open, and pulling me in by one arm --- all that in one swift motion. She had moved so quickly she caught me completely off guard, and as a result, I landed in a heap on the floor at her feet. Mother was in a terrible rage, and she started lashing me around my head and face with the dog leash. At the same time she was screaming,

"You dirty, drunken son of a bitch, I'll teach you to shame me. I'll kill you before I'll let you disgrace me in front of everyone."

However, I was just drunk enough to fight back that night, and all the fury I had kept bottled up for so long exploded. The alcohol helped me to overcome my terror of her, and I burst into action. I jumped up, shoved her hard against the wall, and tore the dog leash out of her grasp.

"Who the hell do you think you're beating," I shouted at her. Tears of rage were running down my face as I continued, "I am not Jake, you know. You will never beat me again mother, I will kill you first," I ranted.

My words had shocked even me; it was as if I was hearing a stranger's voice, but I knew it was mine. For just a moment mother had been stunned by my unexpected charge, and that gave me a slight advantage. But I had torn a bit of flesh off of two of mother's fingers when I pulled the leash away from her, and her hand was all bloody. When she saw the blood, a scream of rage escaped her lips as she leaped at me with her bloody fingers hooked like claws. I was afraid she was going to rake my face with her sharp nails. Instinctively I jumped back and kicked her in the shin and she fell to the floor screaming obscenities at me. I was blinded with rage by then and I tried to choke her with the dog leash, but I was not aware of what I was doing. However, mother was too strong for me to hold down, and before I knew what was happening, she and Jake, who had come racing down the stairs, had thrown me out the front door onto the sidewalk. I heard the door slam and lock behind me even before I could pick myself up.

The struggle had sobered me enough so that I realized I had attacked mother. I became frightened then because I began to think of what had happened to Erma when mother felt she couldn't handle her any longer. I didn't want to be called an incorrigible and get locked up, so I got out of the neighborhood as fast as my legs would carry me.

Though I had been warned to stay away from the barn where I used to work, I could think of nowhere else to hide, so I sneaked into the hayloft and buried myself deep into the hay for the rest of the night. But, fear of what would happen to me if I got caught there did not allow me to sleep. And so about five o'clock that morning I left there and walked the streets until daybreak.

For the next four or five weeks, the ten-cent all night theater in Boston became my nightly residence along with several other homeless men and women. In fact, that was where I slept on the night of my nineteenth birthday. Emotionally I was in a terrible state. I felt completely alone, lost and worthless. I felt guilty and ashamed for putting my hands on my mother and I wished with all my heart I had not done that. I cursed the alcohol that had turned me into a monster. Again there was that awful feeling in the pit of my stomach that something

144

terrible was about to happen, and because I could not identify what it was, I was filled with a nameless fear. However, I covered up those bad feelings with a sharp tongue and an arrogant attitude.

Regardless of where I was sleeping, I had to go out job hunting once more. While looking for work as a helper on an ice truck, the only work I knew, I found that everyone knew I had been fired as a thief, I couldn't get a job anywhere in the ice business again.

Finally, I answered an ad for a dishwasher in a large restaurant and I was hired. The job paid nine dollars a week and one meal per day for six days work. I knew then I had a good chance to survive if I took care of my new responsibilities. I made a solemn promise to God, who I didn't believe in, and to myself, who I wasn't sure of, that I would never drink again as long as I lived; and I meant that with all my heart.

MOTHER DEMANDED THAT I COME HOME

I stayed sober for six months that time and took good care of my job. Nice things began to happen. With my first week's pay I rented a room near my work, and I started sleeping in a bed again; it felt wonderful. Then I bought a few pieces of clothing each week, and soon I began to look decent going back and forth to work. Three months after I began working in that restaurant I was promoted to the position of counterman. There I had direct contact with the customers and I loved it. It paid three dollars more per week than a dishwasher too so I felt proud. But, I was living in fear, I could not trust myself not to drink. Way down deep inside of me was the feeling that I could not stay sober long; that sooner or later I was going to pick up a drink again. Even back then I knew it was the first drink that started me on a binge. To combat that possibility I began to stay in my room and read in my off-hours. I read book after book as the weeks rolled by and I began to feel almost normal, but I also began to hate the sight of a book.

Four months after I started working in that restaurant, mother came into my life again. I thought I had seen the last of that monster when she slammed the door on my back months before. But there she was, standing in front of the counter glaring at me, and I knew she had not picked the restaurant I worked in by accident.

Fortunately, the day she came in had been an exceptionally quiet one with only a customer now and then to wait on. In order to pass time I had begun to polish the big coffee urn. I was engrossed in my work, with my back to the counter, when I sensed that a customer had strolled in. I spun around to see what the person wanted and I found myself face-to-face with mother. I was dumbfounded and could think of nothing to say. But, as usual, mother was never at a loss for words; she was always in charge of the situation.

"Well, aren't you the smart one?" she snapped at me. "What the hell do you mean by running away from home like that? You know I need your help to run the house."

Her voice was harsh and her manner tyrannical. I could hardly believe my ears. She had thrown me out bodily, and yet she was accusing me of leaving home. Without waiting for me to answer, she continued,

"There is no need for you to be paying room rent to a stranger when you have your own room at home. You are my son, and with your father gone you have to help me. So help me, Freeman, I will have you arrested if you don't come home when you get off work today."

Just as she said that, the store manager happened to come behind the counter for something and he heard her last few words.

"What is the problem, Freeman?" he asked.

I had no choice then but to introduce him to my mother. Immediately mother told him how much trouble she was having trying to raise her children without a husband. She let him know what a selfish boy I was by running away from my responsibilities. She was so convincing I could not help but think of the old saw, "An outside angel, but a house devil" --- it fit her perfectly!

My boss advised me to go home and help my mother as any good son should. He even hinted I might not have a job if I didn't do the right thing by my mother. Then he said,

"Look, it is very quiet in here today, why don't you go with your mother now and get your personal problems straightened out. There is enough help here to take care of the counter. Go ahead, I'll see you tomorrow."

Going home on the subway, with mother carrying my clothes, and holding me by one arm, I felt crushed and humiliated. The resentment I felt toward my boss was intense; she had everyone on her side, I thought. But the fury raging inside me toward mother was all consuming. I really wanted to kill her that day. Throughout the entire trip I had to listen to an endless string of complaints, and how badly money was needed to keep the wolf away from our door. Mother was treating me as though I had never left home. Not one word was said about our terrible fight, and she never even asked me how I managed to survive the past few months. Then, the anger I felt toward her, the anger that I dared not let her see, turned in on myself for being a coward. I was furious at myself for not being able to tell her to go to hell; I hated myself for what I was.

HOME AGAIN

Back home things were exactly the same as they had always been. Jake was still sleeping on the sofa all day; our room still smelled terrible, and there was no food in the cupboard as usual. Added to those unpleasant facts, I then had the extra expense of twenty cents a day for carfare on the subway going back and forth to work. Then too, the additional half hour travel time each way, during rush hours did nothing to cheer me up.

After being late for work a few times I was placed on the evening shift from four o'clock until midnight. The manager told me he expected me to be on time on that shift or else. From then on there were several hours from the time I woke up around nine o'clock in the morning until I had to leave for work at three in the afternoon. To kill time and to stay out of the house I began to drink at the corner barroom. Strangely, there seemed to be a degree of control at that time. I would drink only beer or wine, start for work half-drunk, but be almost sober by the time I got there. Then I would go straight to work without speaking to anybody. As I created no fuss, nobody paid any attention to me and I was getting by. However, at home I was most uncomfortable living under my mother's dominating influence. Finally the day came, when I had to get out of that house or go completely insane.

I LEFT HOME FOR GOOD

From the moment I got out of bed at nine-thirty that morning, the day felt strange. The sun was hidden behind heavy, gray storm clouds making the day cold, dark, damp, and miserable. Besides, I had drunk too much, and eaten too little the day before. As a result, my stomach was upset and my nerves were raw. I felt at odds with everybody and could not even drink a cold glass of beer after I bought it.   I was able to get to work on time, but by six o'clock I had to leave for home I was so ill.   Riding home on the subway, I thought I would have to get off the train before I got to my stop, but luck was with me, my stomach stayed quiet, and I made it without incident.   The ten blocks to my house seemed twice as long as they actually were and I was glad to see the front door.   Even before I was inside I could see, in my mind's eye, my comfortable bed, and saw myself lying on my belly, suffering in quiet contentment.   However, the scene that greeted me as I stepped through the door made my blood run cold, and my illness vanished immediately.

Mother had Jake backed up against the pantry door next to the kitchen stove.   In her raised right hand she held a large bread knife in a viselike grip.   Jake was holding onto both of her upraised wrists, and he had his left knee buried deep in her stomach.   With all the strength he could muster he was struggling to keep mother from stabbing him.   Lisa, who was then only ten years old, was backed against the opposite wall near the kitchen table, and her face was a frozen mask of fear.

Mother and Jake were locked in that position in silent combat and I don't think either of them knew I had come through the front door.   It seemed that fear had given Jake extra strength, but even with that, I knew he could not hold mother at bay for long.   One look at the rage on mother's face and I knew she was beyond listening to reason.   I had to act immediately.

Jumping behind her, I grabbed her wrist in both hands, the wrist she held the knife in, and as strong as I was, even with Jake holding her other wrist, it took all of my strength to pry her fingers open and get the knife away from her, but I did.   As soon as I had the knife, I opened the cellar door and threw the weapon into the blackness.

When I turned my attention back to the kitchen I found that mother and Jake had parted, and mother was holding her right wrist in her left hand. Staring at her hands, her eyes wild with anger, she screamed at me,

"You bastard, you almost broke my fingers. Who the hell do you think you are, coming in here and assaulting me like that!"

"My God mother," I answered, "you have had the police here several times already because of problems in our family. You wouldn't want them to come here again because you stabbed one of your kids, would you?"

"He is my kid," she shot back at me, "I can kill him if I want to, and I can kill you too if you get too goddamed smart."

Everything seemed to stand still for a minute at that point. I felt awkward and didn't know what to do next. Jake started to move slowly toward the stairs to get to his room, and mother made a lunge for him. When she did, I stepped between them and told Jake to go on upstairs.

"I want you to get out of my house," mother raged at me, "If you don't go now I will call the police and have you taken out."

"I can't go and leave Jake here with you, at least not tonight," I answered.

"If you love the son of a bitch so much why don't you take him with you," mother hollered. "He is no good to me, and neither are you!"

A half hour later Jake and I had packed a few pieces of clothing and left home. It proved to be the last time for both of us. In a nearby rooming house we rented a room, and true to his habit, Jake wet the bed more than once during the night. The next morning we were told not to come there again, and the rent we had paid in advance was kept to cover the cost of cleaning up after us.

Then I had another problem. As much as I liked my job, I did not dare report to work for fear that mother would have the police after us. Besides, my boss would have stuck up for mother anyway --- "Kids don't have a chance in this world," I thought. I had no choice but to leave the city, and find work elsewhere. Mother could not have me arrested if she could not find me, I reasoned.

It only took me five days to find another job. I was hired as a dishwasher in a diner thirty miles outside of Boston. Jake was still with me; I did not know what to do with him, but I felt responsible for his welfare. I don't know why, he would not look for work. Instead he would come to the diner where I was working and hang around all day. I would feed him and ask him to leave but he wouldn't. My boss didn't like it and threatened to fire me if I could not leave him at home. We finally came to a compromise --- he could sit on the empty crates in the backyard if he kept out of sight. Then too, he could not stop wetting the bed, and we kept getting kicked out of our room because of it. After losing our third room, I refused to allow him in my room with me. He slept in empty houses after that, but I still took care of him. I fed him every day, and kept him in spending money. Every time I heard of a job opening I would give him carfare so he could apply for the work. I found out, time after time, he didn't even go and ask about the job. When I tried to talk to him about that, he would sit sullen and sulk, but would not answer me.

Being responsible for Jake was a heavy burden. Supporting the two of us on my small salary left me no money to drink with, and so there was another sober period in my life even though it was not of my own choosing.

Christmas of 1939 came --- it was a lonely time for us, but I was able to lessen the pain by working long hours throughout the season and not thinking about it. February of 1940 Jake turned nineteen, and by then he was as big as a man. He was only five feet six inches tall, but he was fat. He weighed one

151

hundred eighty-five pounds. He always looked dirty, and it was about that time I became acutely ashamed of him. I was going crazy trying to think of what to do with him or about him. I had wished many times I had left him with mother.

It was sometime around Jake's birthday that year, we had another unexpected jolt handed to us. My mother's landlord, just by chance, came into the diner for a bite to eat. He had no idea I was working there, but he seemed glad to see me. He told me mother had shocked the neighborhood by selling her furniture and moving. She had taken Lisa, the baby, with her, but she had left Eileen to fend for herself. The landlord said mother had told him she could not afford to keep the house going any longer. She had been offered a live-in job as a domestic and when the employer had agreed to let her bring her ten year old child with her, she took the job.

Once again I was dumbfounded by mother's behavior. Eileen would be seventeen on her birthday that year and she was developing into a beautiful young woman. I thought that would be a time in her life when mother would want to watch over and guide her closely. I could not understand how anyone could be like my parents were to their children. First dad had walked away without a backward glance, and it looked as if mother had decided to do the same. Even though I had no reason to doubt our landlord, I had to find out the truth for myself before I could believe it.

On my next day-off, Jake and I rode a bus back to our old neighborhood. We found Eileen at her friend's house, and she confirmed everything. She told us that without any warning, mother had just told her that she was going to close up the house. "You are hardly ever home anyway," mother had said to her, "you are big enough to take care of yourself from now on." Eileen said if her girlfriend had not taken her in, she did not know what she would have done.

"I hate that woman so much," Eileen said, "I

152

hope I never see her again."

It was to be six years before I saw my mother again and I really didn't miss her.

March 12, 1940 --- my twentieth birthday came and went without any fanfare. I told no one and I pretended it didn't matter when even Jake forgot to mention it. We were getting along, but just barely. I wanted to kick Jake out of my life but I kept dreaming about him freezing to death in an empty house, or starving because nobody cared. If anything like that did happen, I knew I would blame myself, and feel guilty. At those times I could not look Jake straight in the eyes, I felt so ashamed for my selfish, evil thoughts.

However, it finally became a question of survival, and as much as I hated being cruel, I had to make the separation. One Monday morning I had been on the job only about two hours, when my boss came bursting into the kitchen. He had Jake by the back of his collar and the seat of his pants. As big as Jake was, my boss was throwing him around like a rag doll he was so angry. He pushed Jake hard in my direction and Jake landed on the floor at my feet. My first impulse was to protect Jake, but one look at my boss and I stayed where I was.

"I caught that son of a bitch stealing two cases of canned goods out of the cellar storeroom," my boss shouted. "It is not the first time he has been in there either, he had been seen by a neighbor coming out of there more than once. Since you two have been here there have been plenty of goods missing."

He was so angry that his words were tumbling over each other and I could hardly make out what he was saying. But I was so frightened of him by then, I kept my mouth shut.

"You take that brother of yours and get the hell off of my property --- you're fired," he hollered.

I felt humiliated, hurt and angry. I wanted to kill Jake at that moment, but I didn't say a word. I thought, "What's the use, I can not say anything I had not said before". It took only a few minutes for me to change my clothes, then we left the diner and went down the street toward my room. When we came to the empty house Jake was sleeping in, I asked him to wait for me there.

"Jake, you sit on the steps here and I will go and pack my clothes," I said, "I know where I can get another job not very far from here, we'll be OK."

Then I went to my room, packed all my clothes, and sneaked out the back way. I walked a mile or more before I would allow myself to get on a bus that was headed back into Boston. At last I was free of Jake, but not really. Every once in a while, for a long time, I would dream about him; then for days afterward I would feel terrible for deserting him.

As soon as I arrived in Boston, I rented a room for the night. And after putting my clothes away, I went out for a few long-awaited drinks. The freedom of not having Jake to care for was a wonderful relief and I wanted to celebrate a little. I only wanted a couple of glasses of beer, and I promised myself I would drink no more than that. However, as I had done so many times before, once I got started, I drank all evening, went into a blackout, and came to about midnight, only to find myself in jail once more.

Being tossed in jail that time appeared at first to be a stroke of good luck. Armand, a neighborhood friend, one whom I had worked with on the ice-wagon, had also been arrested for being drunk, and by chance we were thrown into the same cell. When the alcoholic haze had cleared enough so that I recognized him, I was overjoyed at seeing a friendly face in that forlorn place.

We spent hours telling each other of the things that had happened since we last met. I told him all about Jake and of how I was out of work because of him. Armand, in turn, told me that his father had died just the month before, the result of years of heavy drinking. We were so excited over seeing each other we did not sleep all night. Instead we reminisced about the adventures we had together while selling ice.

About six o'clock in the morning, much to our surprise, we were let out of jail, and a police officer told us to "Get lost!" Six other men had been turned loose with us, and one of them, a very old man, told us they always kicked the drunks out early in the morning to avoid the nuisance of hauling them into court. That was a break we hadn't expected, and we took advantage of it by getting out of that neighborhood fast.

"Why don't you come and live at my house until you get back on your feet?" Armand asked. "With my dad gone, there will be plenty of room and my mother would be glad to take you in. Besides, my sister Irene always liked you."

"Sure, why not!" I answered.

It sounded like a good idea to me. So after picking up my clothes from the rooming house I went home with Armand.

Moving in with Armand's family turned out to be both a circus and a nightmare. Armand's mother, Mary, was a slender, pretty woman, but she drank constantly; beer and wine were her favorite drinks, but she would drink anything, with anybody, and she was nearly always drunk. She had a boy-friend who was a truck driver, and when he was not on the road he was with Mary, and he would be drunk too. It was no secret that Joe had been Mary's lover for years, long before her husband, Jerry, had died.

Armand and I were drinking anything we could get our hands on, and we managed to get a hold of plenty. Bobby, Armand's only brother, was just fifteen then, but he could drink as much as any man. I found out he had been drinking beer and wine since he was ten, when his father got him drunk on his birthday. All the years I knew him, Bobby was drunk more often than he was sober. Armand had two sisters --- Irene, who was sixteen and as pretty as a picture, and Betty, who was only fourteen, but rapidly developing into a beautiful young woman. Irene and Betty would not drink, but they did everything else. They were wild.

It was party-time every day in that house. There was always liquor of one kind or another available. Even when there was no food someone would show up with a bottle. There were many fights among the constant flow of guests, and not a few among ourselves. The neighbors called the police on us more than once.

Whenever Joe was around he and Mary were together, and they never stayed home. It was not unusual for them to be gone three or four days in a row. Sometimes during their absences we would run out of food with no money to buy more. In order to survive we took to stealing groceries from the local stores, and over a short period of time we managed to get ourselves barred from several of them. A few managers wouldn't let us in their stores even when we had money to spend.

Those were crazy days all right, but I loved the excitement. There did not seem to be any restrictions placed on any of us; we did whatever we wanted to do. Needless to say, under those circumstances, I didn't look for work very hard. I was too afraid I would miss some of the fun. That was probably the same reason why Armand only worked once in a while, and Bobby not at all.

However, there is always a price to pay for everything, and I paid dearly for my lack of responsibility. During the year I lived at Armand's house I managed to get myself arrested six or seven times. Either I had been fighting with someone or I had become a public nuisance, forcing somebody to call the police. There was one time in particular I almost got a serious jail term for my shenanigans. It seemed that in a drunken rage I had smashed all the kitchen furniture to smithereens. Everyone became terrified of me that day, and Irene had to call the police. Again I was hauled off to jail without knowing anything about it, and was released only because Armand's mother would not press charges against me. The police had to let me go.

It was that episode, more than any other, that deepened my fear of alcohol. I began to realize, as never before, I had no control over my behavior once I began to drink. I did not want to drink that way, but I kept getting drunk in spite of my good intentions. Nevertheless, as concerned as I was, I could not visualize a life without alcohol, because the feeling of euphoria it created within me was so valuable. And so I would push all those annoying thoughts aside because thinking about them only added to my confusion.

The last time I was arrested in Armand's house, Armand and Bobby were arrested with me. We had been having a knock-down-drag-out fight among ourselves and we scared the devil out of Irene and Betty. The police were so aggravated about the whole thing they threatened to send us to jail for a long time and to have the children taken away from Mary, but they never did.

It always surprised me that Armand's mother didn't say much to us no matter what we had done. Even when I smashed her furniture she was not overly angry about it. Of course I would be full of remorse whenever I created any damage and I would promise to replace or repair whatever I had broken. Even those promises were only halfheartedly carried out though, if at all; and still Mary did not press me. Her reactions were so different than my mother's would have been, I thought it was because Mary was a kind and loving parent. But I know better today.

On my twenty-first birthday, the day I legally became a man, we had a big party at a friend's house. There were no balloons, no cake and ice-cream, no decorations around the room; those things were for kids, but there was plenty of booze. Our host, Nick, had stolen the key to his father's liquor cabinet which was well-stocked.

The party started about ten o'clock that morning, and it was a wild noisy affair by noontime. Evidently, it continued to get out of hand from then on because the police arrived the first time around three and told us to quiet it down. They were back again by five o'clock and had words with a few of us about our behavior. We told them what they could do with their badges and billy-clubs, and as a result I found myself in jail again along with four of my pals. We were all pretty drunk by then and took the whole thing as a big lark. Although we knew we might have to pay a small fine to get out of the mess, a couple of my friends had some money with them and they said they would pay for those of us who couldn't so we were not too concerned.

However, we were in for a rude awakening; we found ourselves in much more serious trouble than just Drunk and Disorderly. All five of us were charged with Carnal Abuse, among other things. The charges against us stemmed from the fact that there had been a fourteen year old girl at our party, a girl who had run away from home four days before. When she was questioned by the police about where she had spent her time during those four days, Audrey told them she had stayed at Nick's house. That proved to be a possibility because both of Nick's parents worked and he was an only child. As a result, Audrey had the run of the house all day while the parents were out working, but she had to retreat to Nick's room in the evenings. Nick's father said later they knew nothing of their son's guest. Audrey told the police she had slept with Nick every night she had been with him, and that they had made love several times. The police reasoned, as we were Nick's friends, and had been to his house often, each one of us had probably been to bed with her as well. At the very least, they said, because we had given her alcohol, we had contributed to the delinquency of a minor --- another serious crime.

They say the wheels of justice grind slowly, and maybe they do most of the time. However, things happened fast for us that evening. Within two hours we had been taken into a courtroom and arraigned. Bail was set at ten thousand dollars on each one of us. My four friends all had concerned families, and so before ten o'clock that night every one of them had been bailed out of jail and taken home. I had no one to turn to and so I stayed in jail and waited.

It took six weeks before our case came before a judge. Meantime, I ate, slept, and socialized with murderers, rapists, thieves and gangsters. My one cell-mate was a sixteen year old boy who had raped and murdered a fifteen year old girl. He was revolting to me with his strange sexual suggestions. The many cartoons he had drawn on the walls of our cell were weird, and they were all of a sexual nature. He wrote a hundred or more poems on those walls also, the kind of poems one would find written on the walls of third-rate men's rooms throughout the city. What shocked me most though, was the fact he had murdered and mutilated a beautiful girl. I had seen her picture, and yet there wasn't an ounce of remorse in him about the heinous act. In fact, he never mentioned the crime, nor did he defend himself with even a weak explanation. Although he was much smaller a boy than I was, and never gave me cause for personal concern, I was afraid of him. I believed he was insane and gave him a wide berth.

All during those long miserable weeks I was afraid most of the time. None of my friends had come to visit me, not even one of the boys I had been arrested with. I felt alone and lost. The atmosphere I found myself in was so foreign to me I experienced a sensation of being in another world altogether. Emotionally I was a wreck. Whenever I found myself alone in my cell I would come apart at the seams.

During those times I wept, I prayed, I cursed God one minute and pleaded with Him the next. I would make a bargain with God on a Monday, then tell Him to go to hell the very next day. Then the day after I would deny His existence altogether. I cursed my friends for not coming to visit me. I cursed their families for taking them home and leaving me. I cursed their lawyers, the judges in court, the guards in our prison, the other prisoners, everyone. I guess I did about everything a scared, lonely, desperate young man would have done while waiting for that awesome day in court to arrive. Nevertheless, through all of the emotional turmoil, in every single situation I found myself, I always knew it was my drinking that had caused the problem. Or to put it more accurately, I believed the problem really was I had not learned how to drink like a gentleman. And, in spite of my many failures, the thought persisted that it was just a matter of time, that someday, somehow I would learn how to handle my liquor and life would be wonderful.

When the day of our trial did arrive, I was brought into the courtroom in handcuffs like a dangerous criminal. To make matters worse, I was wearing the same clothes I had on when I had been arrested. They had been washed a few times in the jail laundry and they were clean, but I had no others and I was ashamed of that. My discomfort was made more acute when I saw my friends in suits and ties, with members of their families with them. Two of them even had a lawyer at their side.

Our trial lasted for an hour and a half and then it was all over. We were found not guilty on the Carnal Abuse charge, but were placed on probation for two years. One year for being drunk and disorderly and another for giving Audrey liquor.

We learned much later Nick's father had paid out a lot of money for that not guilty decision. He had to get all of us out of trouble in order to save his son's neck. For many weeks afterwards, I shuddered whenever I thought of what might have happened to me if Nick's father had not been the concerned father he was.

Freedom never felt as good to me as it did that day. I walked all the way home to Armand's house, about three miles, even though I could have ridden a bus for just a dime. I wanted to enjoy being able to walk more than twenty feet without bumping into a wall. As I walked my mind seemed very clear and as I thought about my life and my future, I knew I had to move away from Armand and his friends. I knew I would never be able to stop drinking nor would I ever be able to generate a desire to amount to anything as long as I was submerged in that family.

Jail had been a blessing for me in a way. No one had come to visit me and because of that I concluded no one cared about anyone but themselves. I became determined to change my ways; I was tired of partying all the time and of not thinking about the future.

I MOVED FROM ARMAND'S HOUSE

Two days after I got home, Mr. Sullivan, my probation officer, came to see me. He explained to me what being on probation meant and what would be expected of me. Mr. Sullivan was a man in his late forties and he proved to be a kind man. He took a genuine interest in me and I felt comfortable talking to him. As a result of that, I told him of my fears about not being able to stay out of trouble if I stayed where I was. I told him of my desire to find a job and get away from Armand's house. As he left that day he promised to see if he could help me in any way. I thought at the time he was just being polite when he said he would try to help, but he had really meant it. Two weeks later he was back to see me with information about a job he thought I might be interested in. It seemed someone was looking for a maintenance man in an apartment building and Mr. Sullivan knew I was handy with carpenter's tools. One interview and I knew I wanted the job. Not only did it pay eight whole dollars a week, but there was a nice, big sleeping room, furnished, that would be available to me free of charge. I could live right on the premises and have a chance to start all over again.

Less than a week after the interview I was told the job was mine if I wanted it. I sensed Mr. Sullivan had put in a word on my behalf and that made me feel good. I was walking on air as I moved my few meager belongings from Armand's house, with high hopes of a brighter future. There was no one at home to say goodbye to that day and I was glad there wasn't. I especially didn't want to see Irene. Many years were to pass by before I saw any of that crowd again and I found I wasn't sad about that at all. For just a short while I had missed Irene but even the memory of her faded rather quickly as I became absorbed in my new life.

It was near the end of May 1941, when I finally wrenched myself away from Armand's family and began my new employment. Springtime had always been a special time of the year for me. It seemed to signal the rebirth of everything. I hoped that particular year I too would be able to experience a transformation and a renewal. The weather had been exceptionally warm and sunny during the past month and that added a great deal to my already cheerful mood. During that time, and for a couple of months afterwards, I felt all was right with the world and I was going to be all right regardless of what might happen.

I liked that job immensely from the very first day. Every time I repaired a broken window, changed a trap under a sink, or opened a stubborn locked door I would be filled with a sense of accomplishment and pride. I enjoyed helping the tenants and they all seemed to take to me easily. A few of them were generous with their tips whenever I did something extra for them.

May gave way to June, and June slipped away fast. July was on us before I knew it and still I was oblivious to everything but my work. By the time

August arrived that year, I had begun to feel I had conquered my drinking problem at last. I was sure I was not going to drink again --- ever. It was with pride that I went to Mr. Sullivan's office each month to make my report. Evidently Mr. Sullivan had developed a lot of trust in me because when I saw him in September on my regular report day he told me I didn't have to come in town anymore. He said a phone call to his office would be sufficient and I was elated.

Meantime, the local newspapers were carrying headlines every day about the war in Europe. Hitler was creating a hell of a problem for Russia, Poland, Hungary and especially for England. The United States was under tremendous pressure to join the fray and shoulder some of the burden. Although we supplied millions of dollars worth of war machines, food, and hospital equipment, we managed to stay out of the actual fighting, at least until the end of 1941. However, as frightening as all that news was, I was too busy worrying about myself and how I was going to fare to be upset over things happening across the ocean to people I did not even know.

Nevertheless, everyone became aware of the seriousness of the situation by the number of young men in fresh uniforms who began showing up on our streets. Every week they seemed to have more than doubled their ranks. It was not unusual for me to meet school chums and neighborhood friends in brand new Army or Navy uniforms heading for the nearest train station on their way to camp. They appeared to be alive as never before, all excited over their coming adventures. I must admit I experienced a bit of envy toward them as I saw how glamorous they looked. Regardless of how attractive those uniforms appeared I was just beginning to get my life straightened out and did not dare think of anything else at the moment.

I MET VERONICA

One day, Mrs. Sloan, a tenant on the sixth floor, called saying she had blown a fuse and did not know what to do. So up to her apartment I went with my box of tools. My knock on the door was answered by a young woman I had never seen before; she was beautiful. The moment our eyes met strange things happened inside of me. First, my heart leaped into my throat, then my legs turned rubbery and my hands began to tremble. No girl had ever affected me that way before and I was unnerved by my reaction. However, I was able to stammer something about being the maintenance man and that I had come to repair a blown fuse.

"Come in", she said, "the fuse box is in the kitchen." I didn't tell her the fuse box was in the kitchen in every one of our sixty-four apartments. Instead, I just thanked her and headed for the kitchen with her right behind me.

"My name is Veronica," she volunteered, "what's yours?"

"Freeman," I answered.

I hoped she didn't detect the tremor in my voice.

"My mother and I come to visit Mrs. Sloan often," she said, "Mrs. Sloan used to live next door to us on Hazel Street for many years and she is mother's close friend."

"Where is Mrs. Sloan now?" I asked.

"Mother and Mrs. Sloan just went to the corner store for a moment; they will be right back," she said.

Veronica was, what some people call, a little on the heavy side, but she had beautiful auburn hair that

164

she wore long and straight with bangs across her forehead. Her face was round and gentle looking and it was made more attractive by her large dark eyes that were framed by long curved eyelashes. But with all of that, the most attractive thing I recognized at once was her shyness. Even when she spoke it was in a subdued, quiet tone of voice. She presented a sharp contrast to the loud household I had just come from.

Veronica stayed in the kitchen and talked to me all the while I was working on the fuse problem. Needless to say it took me three times longer than it should have to locate the bad fuse and change it.

I liked Veronica at once but did not dare let her know that. However, when I met her for the second time, about a week later, even though I was sick to my stomach with fear, I asked her for a date and she accepted. We went to the movies one evening and ate popcorn out of the same box. By the time the popcorn was gone, the movie was over and I walked her home, I considered Veronica my girl. Because I wanted her company and her respect so badly I did not dare tell her about my past. Especially so because I really believed all of that sordid life was behind me and never again would I be involved in that kind of behavior. Time was to prove me wrong again soon enough, but at least for a while I was blind enough to feel safe and happy in my new world.

For more than six months, I worked hard, kept away from alcohol and spent most of my spare time with Veronica. She never asked me about my family or anything about my past. Needless to say, I did not volunteer any either.

JAKE SHOWED UP AGAIN

One evening, late in October, we were walking along the river bank, as we had done many evenings when we had no money for a movie. It was a little chilly that particular evening, so when we strolled near the beach area we were not surprised to find it nearly deserted. We were standing there, side-by-side, overlooking the water and enjoying the peacefulness of the whole thing when someone tapped me on the shoulder.

Startled, I spun around and found myself face-to-face with Jake. He looked terrible. He was fatter than I had ever seen him. The suit he was wearing was much too large for him. His onetime white shirt, his suit, and even his heavy overcoat were so dirty I was shocked. He had a pair of white shoes on that were dirty, all shrivelled, and curled up at the toes. He had not shaved for weeks and his beard was thin and scraggly. His hair was uncut and matted. One side of me wanted to reach out and help him, but another side of me was humiliated and angry because now Veronica would know about him.

"Hi Jake, what's going on with you?" I asked lamely, not knowing what else to say.

"Nothing," was his reply. Once again his one word answer forced me to make another response.

"Where are you staying now?" I asked, hating myself for becoming involved with him, but not being able to do anything different.

"Over there," he said, pointing to an abandoned factory across the river. It was a building we had played in a few times when we were kids. I knew there were rats, and God knew what else, in that monstrous structure and I shuddered when I pictured Jake curled up in a corner all night in pitch darkness.

"Are you working?" I asked.

"No," was his quick response. Then he added, "Freeman, could you lend me fifty-cents? I haven't eaten in three days and I'm starved."

Although he had said not a word about me

deserting him, his eyes and my conscience spoke loud
enough. I felt guilty and blamed myself for his
plight.

"No, Jake," I said, "I don't have any money, but
I don't live far from here. You can take my key and
get some rest while I walk Veronica home. Then we can
talk and see what we can do."

"Ok," he said, as he took my key and my address.
I was so glad to get him out of Veronica's sight I
thought of nothing else. After he had gone, I told
Veronica just enough about him to cover my
embarrassment, nothing more. That may have been a
serious mistake in light of the things that happened
between Jake and Veronica about eighteen months later.
But that is getting ahead of myself again.

Usually when I walked Veronica home I would sit
with her on her porch swing for an hour or more.
However, I was too uneasy about Jake being in my room
to spend much time with her that night. I felt that
about twenty minutes was long enough to be considered
gentlemanly and so I took my leave about ten o'clock.
It was about sixteen blocks from Veronica's house to
my apartment building and I made it in about fifteen
minutes. When I got to my room, Jake was not there
but he had left his mark on everything. He had left
my key in the lock and my door wide open, anyone could
have walked in from the hallway. Several of my shirts
and my two suits were gone, as was a wristwatch and my
only tiepin. A small bank I had on my dresser was
also missing. There had been only sixty-eight cents
in that bank, but when one considers a man earned
about a dollar a day back then it was a substantial
loss. I knew the suits would not fit Jake because of
his enormous size so I guessed he intended to sell
them. He had taken underwear, socks, and even my
extra pair of shoes were gone. He missed nothing.
The closet door was left open, bureau and dresser
drawers were pulled out, a few old pieces of clothing
were scattered around the floor --- the place was a
mess. I was shocked. I could not believe Jake would
do that to me. Evidently, enough time had gone by so

that I had forgotten Jake was not predictable and probably not even responsible for his behavior. I was deeply hurt and as angry as a man could get. It was to be three years after that incident before I saw Jake again and that was good for both of us. However, I swore I would never help him again as long as I lived and I almost kept that promise.

I GOT DRUNK AGAIN

My sobriety lasted almost seven months that time, and when I did take a drink I had not planned to. I was extra tired that day and when a tenant offered me a drink I took it without thinking. After I left the tenant's apartment I knew I had to buy a bottle for myself. I paid top dollar for it at that hour of the night, and I had to give the bootlegger a couple of drinks out of it as well. As tired as I had been at eleven o'clock, the fatigue vanished completely after a couple of drinks and I stayed out until dawn. Then, with only two hours sleep I was up and on the job as scheduled, but my head was killing me.

That was the beginning of my drinking again, and as one would expect my life started to slide backward as well. I didn't get in trouble with my probation officer at first because I was on schedule with my phone calls. I managed to keep the worst of the drinking from Veronica by staying away from her on those nights when I had too many. Needless to say, she began to see me less and less as time went on. The job was not much of a problem because I worked alone most of the time. Even when the manager stopped to see how things were, I was usually in the middle of a repair job and he did not stay long. It was not hard to hide my drinking from him, or maybe he didn't want to see it. However, I was spending more money than I could afford on liquor and I had a hangover most of the time. The feeling of futility that engulfed me during the next few weeks was incredible. The thought became clearer than ever before --- "I cannot stop my drinking and stay stopped." I had known for a long time one drink would start the roller-coaster ride again, and yet I had talked myself into believing that this time it would be different if I was careful. I had read somewhere that insanity could be summed up simply as "A person doing the same thing over and over again and expecting different results." That was exactly what I was doing --- at least as far as my alcohol consumption was concerned. Was it any wonder that suicide looked attractive to me then? I believed each member of the Carpenter family was crazy, each in a different way, but crazy just the same; and that included me.

PEARL HARBOR DAY

December 7, 1941, was a Sunday. I had been out with some friends that Saturday night and this particular Sunday was typical of any Sunday-after. My first concern upon opening my eyes was how to make it until one o'clock, the time the barrooms open, without shaking to pieces. However, as hard as it was, I made it. At 1:10 P.M. I walked into a local bar where I knew several of the patrons. There were about forty people in that bar all huddled around the radio. That was about thirty more people than usual for that time of the day so I knew something important had happened or was happening.

Above the hubbub of men's voices I could distinguish the radio announcer's voice clearly.

"Ladies and Gentlemen, I repeat, Japan has attacked the American Fleet at Pearl Harbor, thousands of American sailors have been killed, the Navy all but destroyed." He went on and on with the details that are familiar to the world today. There was no paying for drinks that day; the bartender would not hear of it.

Everyone of the men were talking about joining the service as soon as the offices opened in the

morning. To a man they all wanted to "Get those b----
--s and make them pay for what they had done." As for
me, I was excited because a war would give me a good
reason to stop worrying about being a decent person.
I reasoned I could drink all I wanted to now because
the whole damn world was going to hell anyway.

I began to drink openly then but I managed to
take care of my job, at least well enough so I had no
flack from my boss. However, Veronica was on my back
constantly about my drinking, probably because I would
show up at her house drunk while in a blackout and say
nasty things to her and her mother.

Then, two days before Christmas,
three of my friends and I were arrested
for starting a barroom brawl. I couldn't
remember going into a barroom nor
anything about a fight. It seemed one
minute we were all talking and laughing
in the car, and the next thing I knew, it
was three hours later and we were in jail.

Mr. Sullivan, my probation officer, had been
notified as a matter of routine and that really
frightened me. I knew I could be in serious trouble
with him. I was furious at myself for drinking so
much, for risking my job and my freedom. Again, I
tried to figure out what was wrong with me, and again
I came to the conclusion that I was crazy. After a
while though, I turned my mind off because I did not
dare think of what was going to happen to us when we
were brought before the judge. However, the next
morning when we were ushered into court, it was
Christmas Eve and I think the judge was feeling
magnanimous because he let us off with a modest fine
and a stern warning. He even allowed us plenty of
time to pay the fine.

Later on that day, I was back on
my job, congratulating myself for getting
out of that mess so easily when Mr.
Sullivan came by to see me. He was angry,
and did not hesitate to let me know it.

170

He laid the law down in no uncertain terms.

"Freeman," he said, "you were told you could not drink alcohol as long as you were on probation, that you were not to be in the company of a person who was drinking, in fact, you were even warned to stay out of places where alcohol was served. I thought you were sincere when you told me you wanted to change. Evidently I was mistaken."

"Mr. Sullivan," I pleaded, with genuine sincerity, "I honestly do want to stay sober and keep this job. Please give me another chance and I will prove it to you."

We talked for a long time about the consequences of breaking my probationary agreements, and as we did, I watched his anger subside. Mr. Sullivan seemed to be really interested in me and was concerned about my future. He made me feel comfortable in his presence and the time flew by. Finally, he stood up to leave, and as he did he said,

"Freeman, I believed you once, and I am inclined to believe you this time, but I must admit I am skeptical. However, I will not make out a report on you today; but I will not put up with any more of your foolishness. If there is one more incident of this kind I will revoke your probation. If I do, you will find yourself behind bars for a long time. Do I make myself clear, Freeman?" He paused then waiting for my response.

"Yes, Mr. Sullivan, I understand," I answered humbly.

Then, as Mr. Sullivan started toward

the door, he said,

"Incidentally, Freeman, no more
reporting by telephone. From now on I
want to see you in my office at ten
o'clock in the morning on the first and
third Thursday of every month."

"Yes sir, and thank you for giving
me another chance. You won't be sorry,"
I said.

Mr. Sullivan didn't answer as he
slipped past me going out the door, but
his clear, steady gaze spoke volumes.
I knew he was not a man to be toyed with.

For the next eight weeks, things ran smoothly,
but then I drank again. That particular time though,
I could not use being overworked as an excuse. There
had been no undue tension on my job, I wasn't angry at
anyone, things were going well. In fact, the tenants
had been so generous with their gifts at Christmas I
could hardly believe my good fortune. The problem was
one of boredom, I guess. I had become fed up with
spending so many hours on the porch swing necking with
Veronica. I had become tired of reading every evening
when I wasn't with her. I craved excitement. I
needed to experience the feeling of euphoria alcohol
gave me. I had been fighting to stay away from the
corner bar for about a week, when a tenant offered me
a large glass of wine and I downed it without a second
thought.

That was the beginning of ten months of mental
torture, emotional turmoil, and physical hell. I was
drunk most of the time. When I wasn't drunk I was
nursing a horrible hangover.

Blackouts were frequent. My twenty-
second birthday came and went without any
fanfare. It was just another day for me
to enjoy feeling sorry for myself and to
drink more. The little money I had managed

to save disappeared quickly. Veronica did
not see much of me in those days. When
we did meet I could not look her in the eye
even if I happened to be sober enough to
focus mine, because of my feelings of guilt
and shame.

On the days I had to report to Mr. Sullivan's
office, I would manage to get sober and cleaned up
enough to hide what was really going on, but I would
proceed to get drunk the minute I left his office.
Always, on those occasions, I would smugly
congratulate myself for being smart enough to fool
even my probation officer. For more than four months,
I managed to keep up the charade, but everything came
to an abrupt halt in July of 1942.

I WAS FIRED ONCE MORE

The holiday of the Fourth that year was just one
more reason for me to drink with abandon. After all I
reasoned, everyone who was worth anything gets drunk
on the Fourth! Even when the bars closed at midnight
a couple of my friends knew of a private club that
stayed open until three in the morning and we didn't
hesitate to join the crowd that was already there. It
was after four by the time I staggered home and
flopped into bed.

Much to my horror, I woke up two hours later, to
find I had wet the bed in my drunken stupor.
Instantly I was up and working feverishly to clean up
the mess least anyone should see it. The bedspread,
sheets, and blanket were not a big problem; they only
had to be washed. However, the mattress was a
different story. Even when I turned it over there was
a spot, about the size of my fist, clearly visible
where the urine had gone all the way through. The
feelings of disgust I used to experience when Jake wet
his bed, came flooding over me again, only that time
the disgust was directed at myself. Needless to say,
my hangover that morning was one of the worst I had

173

ever endured.

Somewhere along the way I had learned a few beers the next morning would lessen the pain of the headaches, and calm the shakes. When there was no beer available, I soon found whiskey was just as effective, but I always had a hard time keeping the first drink or two in my stomach; many times I had to drink three or four shots before one would stay with me. For a long time I had been able to use alcohol as a way of nursing myself back to normal after a binge, but it didn't work for me that day. Instead, the three bottles of beer I had hidden in my room, rather than calm my nerves, stimulated a desire for more alcohol. I knew then I would have to replenish my beer supply even if it was a Sunday and all the legitimate places were closed. I also knew I would pay the bootlegger whatever he asked. Nothing was more important to me than getting more to drink. I realized I was a slave to alcohol, and I would follow it wherever it took me regardless of the cost. That insight had been so clear, and it had burst on me so suddenly it scared me. So much so that the memory of the moment will always be with me. Without any difficulty I can recall the whole scene whenever I want to. I can see it now.

I was standing in front of my dresser in my underwear. The room was stifling hot as there was no air-conditioning back then. I had just finished the last bottle of warm beer, when it struck me that another drunk was coming on and I was powerless to stop it. The fear and frustration that came over me was all-consuming. As I looked at my gaunt and disheveled reflection staring back at me from the mirror I began to talk to myself ---

"Freeman, you stupid son-of-a-bitch, you've done it again. You are a slave to alcohol. You will never amount to anything. Why don't you kill

174

yourself? Why don't you finish the job
right now and end this misery once and
for all?"

With those ugly thoughts churning in my mind I
went about like an automaton getting washed and
dressed. I was still in that black mood as I slipped
out the door in search of a bootlegger to get more
booze.

An hour later, I was back with three quarts of
beer under my arm and one more in my stomach. By
then, my dark mood had completely vanished and I was
feeling on top of the world.

I was glad it was a Sunday because that meant I
would have nothing to do unless an emergency came up.
Other than that, all I had to do was be there. I
couldn't even keep that obligation. The barrooms
opened at one o'clock that day and I was one of their
first customers.

Three hours later my manager came in looking for
me. When he saw how drunk I was he fired me right on
the spot. That gave me more reason to feel sorry for
myself and drink more. I had intended to be in there
for only a short time, instead I ended up spending the
day and evening. I even helped the bartender cleanup
after closing time and he gave me a couple of bottles
of beer to take home with me.

For the next three nights I slept in an old car
in a junkyard nearby. Each day I had continued to
drink, but I couldn't shake the fear and anxiety that
had engulfed me over the loss of my job.

Then too, I was worried about Mr. Sullivan. The
last time I had reported to him he had looked at me
suspiciously and had asked too many questions. I had
become very uncomfortable under his gaze and I was
sure I could not bluff through another interrogation
from him even if circumstances had been normal. There
was no doubt in my mind that my boss had reported
everything to him, and I reasoned he probably had a

175

warrant out for my arrest already. Needless to say, I was terrified of the prospect of going to jail, having been there more than once already. I figured I had nothing to lose by running away from the neighborhood and taking my chances with the law. I retired to my bedroom, the old car, with a firm decision to get out of town the first thing in the morning.

Thursday morning dawned hot and humid. The temperature was near eighty degrees at six A.M.. The humidity must have been as high. To make matters worse it had rained all the night before forcing me to keep the car windows closed. When I woke up I felt as though I was suffocating. My clothes were stuck to my body, and they were wet clear through with a combination of sweat and humidity. And because I had not been able to take a bath or even change my clothes for the last three days, I felt dirty from head to foot. Needing both a shave and a haircut I looked anything but neat. I was very aware of my appearance and knew if I didn't find some way to clean up, I not only would not be hired for any job, but I might even be stopped by the police just on general principles. If that happened my freedom would have been short-lived.

I was racking my brain trying to think of who I could turn to for help when I thought of Erma. After she and Ed had married in September of 1938, they had lived in our neighborhood for about a year and then they had moved away. I had heard they had moved to Lynn, a city about twenty miles outside of Boston. I reasoned that twenty miles would be far enough away from Mr. Sullivan for me to feel safe. Although it had been almost three years since I had seen Erma and Ed, and chances of finding them were slim, I had little choice because I had no one else to turn to. I had no address, no telephone number; I didn't know where Ed was working or if he was still out of work. I didn't even know if they were actually living in Lynn. But I had to get out of town fast, and so Lynn was as good a place as any and I might even find Erma if I was lucky.

Working my way from barroom to barroom I finally hit pay dirt. At seven-thirty, nine hours after I began my search, I found a barroom where Ed was well-known.

The bartender said he hadn't seen Ed for a week, but he was sure he lived somewhere nearby. Then one of the men at the bar heard us talking, and he volunteered the information that he knew both Ed and Erma.

"I don't know what street they live on," he said, "but I can direct you to a restaurant where Erma works."

Forty minutes later I stepped through the door of the restaurant into an atmosphere of intense heat, cigarette smoke and burned hamburgers, smoke from a too-hot grill behind the counter provided its share of pollution. My eyes began to smart and I could hardly breathe, the air was so heavy. There were a half-dozen scruffy teenagers hanging over the counter drinking coca-cola and talking loudly. There was no one behind the counter, but I could hear voices coming from the kitchen, way in back. I sat on a stool as far away from the other customers as possible, partly because I did not want to become engaged in conversation with them, and partly because I was extremely conscious of my unsightly appearance.

About five minutes passed, and then the swinging door, leading into the kitchen, was suddenly kicked open and Erma burst through with a tray of coffee cups in her hands. She didn't see me at first and I hardly recognized her --- she had changed so much! However, I was so relieved at seeing her, I was not as shocked at her appearance as I might have been under ordinary circumstances.

Erma was unkempt and overweight. Her dress and her apron were both filthy. She was wearing her hair in two braids, as a teenager would, but it looked greasy. Even the two small ribbons tying the braid-ends were frayed and dirty. Her stockings were bobby socks, another favorite of teenagers of that era. Her shoes were too large for her and they were turned over at the heels. Then, to add to her misery, when she talked, I noticed she had lost most of her teeth and the few she had left had turned black. To make matters worse, she seemed to be unaware that anything was wrong with her appearance, or at least she acted that way.

"Erma," I said, "how about a cup of coffee for your favorite brother?"

"Freeman," she screamed, "where the hell did you come from? How long have you been here? How did you find this place?"

She had come running from her end of the counter as she threw the questions at me one after the other. When she got in front of me she reached over and grabbed me by the neck in a bear hug. She was so excited over seeing me she almost pulled me over the counter with her. I was embarrassed by her open display of affection, and gently backed out of her grasp as soon as I could without hurting her feelings.

"Hi, Erma," I said sheepishly, "I really didn't have any trouble finding you once I decided to look you up," I lied. I did not want her to know how desperately I needed her help.

"What brings you out this way?" she asked. "Is anything wrong?"

"No, Erma, there is nothing wrong," I answered. "I just wanted to see you, that's all."

"Well, you look like hell," Erma said. "You look as though you have slept in your clothes for a week."

"I just lost my job and I am looking for work," I said. "I haven't slept for a couple of nights because I don't have money for a room. I was hoping that you and Ed could put me up for a day or two until

178

I collect my thoughts."

"That won't be a problem," Erma said, "but Ed is not here. He left last week to check out a job in Philadelphia, and I don't expect him until I see him."

By that time I was so exhausted I just wanted to end the conversation with Erma, find out where she lived and get myself into a bed. I was just about to tell her how I felt, when she handed me a key that I assumed was to her house.

"I don't get through work until three o'clock, Freeman," she said, "but you can take my key and get some rest while you are waiting, you look like you could use it."

"Gee! that would be swell, Erma," I said. "Do you live far from here?"

"Only eight blocks straight down the street," she said, "I can walk it in ten minutes."

"Thank you Erma," I said, as I stood up to leave, "if you don't mind I will go now because I really don't feel good."

"OK Freeman," she said, "I got a lot of work to do here anyway. I'll see you about three-thirty and we can talk over coffee."

Then she said something that really floored me.

"Please be quiet when you open the door," she said, "I don't want you to wake the babies."

"What babies?" I asked.

"Oh! you didn't know about Eddie and Albert?" she said. "Eddie is almost two years old now and Albert is six months. I had both of them at home, no damn hospital for me," she continued. "I wanted to let all of you know, but Ed would not let me contact any of my family. Just the same, I thought you knew

179

somehow."

"I'm sorry, Erma, I didn't know," I said, "but who is taking care of them now?" I asked.

"Nobody," she said, "I don't earn enough to pay a baby-sitter and Ed never gives me any money."

"My God, Erma, do you mean to tell me those two infants are home all alone?" I asked.

"Sure they are," Erma said, "once I put them to bed for the night they can't go anywhere. Even if they wake up they can't climb over the sides of their cribs."

I was appalled at how unconcerned Erma seemed to be. I knew if I had a couple of babies at home alone I would never be able to concentrate on my work. I would be a wreck worrying about them.

"One more thing," Erma said, "when you go in the front door, close it quickly so my pets won't get out."

By that time I was too overwhelmed by the sudden turn of events to be very concerned about her pets. I just answered,

"OK Erma, I'll be careful, I won't let any of them out."

I should have asked her about those pets. I would not have been so surprised when I got to her place and slipped through the door a half hour later.

The neighborhood I had to walk through was spooky. There were more abandoned houses than I had ever seen before. More than half of the streetlights had been broken by youngsters throwing stones. Several one-story factories took up a large section of the area along the railroad tracks. Even some of those buildings were empty. With many of their windows missing they looked sinister, and I was glad

when they were behind me. In the short distance I had
to travel I had seen three gangs of young teenagers
roaming the dark streets apparently looking for
mischief. And even as street-wise as I credited
myself for being, I became uneasy about my safety. I
wondered how Erma could walk those streets day after
day, especially after three in the morning.

Exactly eight blocks later I found myself at
Green Street, and the third house on my right was 28,
Erma's home. It was pitch-black as I stepped inside
the hall door. I felt my way along the wall, tripped
over the bottom stair leading to the apartment
overhead, and finally got hold of the door-knob.
Feeling for the lock I guided the key carefully into
it and slowly opened the door. I breathed a sigh of
relief as I saw that Erma had left a dim, night-light
burning in the kitchen. Quickly I stepped through the
door and closed it silently behind me. For about a
minute I stood there with my back to the door and
tried to get my breathing back to normal.

The apartment smelled horrible. The familiar
odor of stale urine hit me full in the face, but I
could also smell baby's dirty diapers and cat-dirt.
Because of the summer heat the odors were much
stronger than usual, therefore more insulting to my
nostrils. Even in the faint light I could see many
dirty dishes on the table, and there were lots more
piled in the sink.

As I stood there in one spot, not wanting to
venture any farther into the place, I became aware of
the silence. The only sound was the tic-tocking of a
clock in some other room. Its ticking was magnified
by the lack of other noises. There wasn't even
traffic noise coming from the street. It seemed that
the whole neighborhood had gone to sleep. I became
very uneasy and wanted to bolt out of there. I didn't
want to look in on the babies, because I was afraid
that I might find them dead. I would have left right
then, but I had nowhere else to go, so I decided to
look for the room Erma said I could use.

Somewhere from the front of the house the faint meowing of a kitten came to my ears. Immediately following that, there was a loud commotion that sounded to me as though one of the babies had fallen out of bed. Before I could even move to investigate, however, a huge white rabbit came through the door and hid under the sink! A second white rabbit, just as big, came hopping slowly behind the first. Then, from the blackness of the next room, very close to the door, a cat made a spitting sound as though it was facing an enemy. Suddenly, there was a flurry of motion, and a big tiger cat came racing through the door. Something must have scared it badly, because its hair was standing up all over its back and its eyes looked frightened. The cat raced twice around the kitchen as though the devil himself was behind it. Then, when it couldn't find a place to hide, it vanished into the front part of the house from which it had come. Every nerve in my body was alert by that time, as I didn't know what to expect next. A moment later I heard a strange noise I couldn't identify. It was something like the sound a dumb person might make if he tried to speak, but it was very low and guttural. Another sound, just as weird, joined the first, and created an eerie harmony. By the fact the noises were getting louder, I knew whatever it was, it was coming toward the kitchen. Mixed feelings of amazement, relief and then anger flooded over me as two big ganders lumbered through the door! The noises I had heard were coming from deep in their throats. Without hesitation they both waddled up to me, evidently, to see who I was or if I had anything for them. "My God!" I thought, "Erma must have a menagerie here! I wonder if there are more."

The collection of animals at final count was three kittens, one cat, three rabbits, two ganders and one duck. Their trademarks were all over the floors in every room. I began to feel sorry for the landlord, whoever he might be, as I thought of the damage his property would sustain over a long period of time. However, I didn't get a chance to think of him long because just then Eddie, the oldest boy, woke up screaming and I felt that the circus was then complete.

I really didn't want to, but I had no choice; I managed to change the baby's diaper and find him a bottle without Albert waking up. With Eddie on the bed alongside of me we both fell asleep.

I didn't know when Erma came in or when she took the baby from my room. Nevertheless, I was grateful she let me sleep until 3 P.M. that day. As she didn't have to be in to work until seven that evening, we had plenty of time to catch up on each others comings and goings during the past three years.

Fortunately, Ed had a few clothes in his closet that fit me, and although they were somewhat seedy-looking, they gave me a chance to get my own washed and back on again. With that done I began to feel some degree of control creep back into my life. Especially so, because I had been able to stop my drinking completely once I had located Erma.

I JOINED THE ARMY

Erma suggested that I join the army as thousands of others were doing. "That's a good idea," I thought, "that will solve all my problems".

The very next morning I was one of the first men at the local draft board, but I was drinking my morning medicine. They wouldn't talk to me, they called me a drunk and threw me out. I learned I had to stop drinking in order to get in the army. That was the pressure I needed. I stopped drinking.

The withdrawal was horrible, but I stayed in my room for three days, shaking, ate nothing but soup, and came through all right. However, I was too anxious, and reported to the draft board before my shakes had disappeared completely. As a result, during the physical examination, they claimed I had a heart murmur and rejected me. I was classified 4F, a disgrace, a failure, a reject, an unfit person. Thinking about that made me mad as hell; after all I had been through, I knew I had "grit". Then, getting into the army became an obsession. I began going to bed early every night, eating regular meals, and taking long walks every day.

My body mended, my nerves calmed down, and three weeks later I went back to the draft board.

However, that time I used a phony address in Cambridge so I could go to a different draft board than the one where I had been rejected. I was banking on the confusion that was present within the whole draft system and I was right. I said nothing about my earlier experiences, and I passed the physical. But there was one more hurdle to jump over.

The officials wanted a copy of my court record from Boston, or a statement from the records department that I had none. That meant they would learn of my probation and the bench warrant. It also meant that Mr. Sullivan would hear of my request and be on top of me in an instant. I had thought I would never have to see Mr. Sullivan again and I dreaded to think of facing him, but I had come too far by then. I had told too many people I was a soldier already, I had no choice. I telephoned Mr. Sullivan's secretary and told her I would be in his office at ten the next morning, the time she had said Mr. Sullivan would be there.

That meeting proved to be the most uncomfortable two hours I had spent in a long time. Mr. Sullivan's greeting set the tone for the entire meeting. He stood up upon my entering his office and shouted at me,

"Freeman, tell my why I shouldn't call a cop in here and have you dragged to jail in handcuffs as you deserve!"

I told him several lies, about my past five months and why I hadn't been in to see him. He questioned me on every detail, I squirmed a lot and lied some more. He knew I was lying and I knew he knew, but I was committed to brazening the whole thing through. I was either going to jail or into the army, and at that point I didn't care which. Finally, Mr. Sullivan ended the meeting rather abruptly, as though he had gotten tired of playing a game.

"Freeman," he said, "it is wartime and the army needs men; maybe they can straighten you out, but I doubt it. I will release you from probation but only for you to go into the army. I will be glad to close my records on you. Is that what you really came here today for?" he asked.

"Yes sir," I answered, "and again I ...." I was going to thank him, but he anticipated my intention. He held up his hand for me to stop as he said,

"Freeman, don't thank me, you don't mean a damn word you say. I'm not doing this for you, I'm doing it for the State of Massachusetts and the United States of America; however, I believe that the army is getting a dud. And if you don't end up in the guard-house I'll be surprised."

A half hour later, still chafing from the remarks Mr. Sullivan had made about my character, I was walking down the street toward the subway with a release in my pocket. I felt that nothing could stop me at that point. I was on my way! I felt a new excitement that day, because that small voice inside me told me I had made a smart move by going into the army. "You need some discipline in your life," it said, "someone to make a man out of you. The army will do that and maybe a bit more."

By three o'clock that afternoon I was back in the office of the draft board with all the necessary papers. The clerk looked them over for what seemed to be an exceptionally long time. Then, placing them in a folder he said,

"Everything looks in order now. I want you to

be here at eight o'clock Saturday morning, December 19, 1942, ready to leave for camp. Bring only three changes of underwear and the clothes on your back," he said, "because you will be issued army clothes as soon as you get to camp, and you will have to send your own things back home."

Saturday morning I was there at seven, and there were about ten other men ahead of me. I learned from them we were going to be taken to Fort Devens, Massachusetts; our army career was to begin there. By eight o'clock there were forty more of us, standing in the parking lot, freezing, waiting for further orders.

Then at eight twenty-five, an army captain came out of the building with four sergeants at his side. One of the sergeants explained to us what a formation was, and then barked an order to "Faaall...in." What a circus that was! But as clumsy as we were, he marched us across the parking lot to four small army buses.

About eleven o'clock that same morning we pulled through the gates of Fort Devens. It was not a very attractive place in mid-winter, and I found it as cold as a walk-in refrigerator! Quickly we were ushered into a large room that resembled a gym. The oath of allegiance was to be administered there. We really looked like a group of misfits and I thought, "No one could win a war with this bunch!" Again we were put into formation, but by then there must have been five hundred of us from all over the Boston area.

A colonel, a major, and two lieutenants, in full-dress uniform stood on a raised platform in front of us. They were going to swear us in. Fifteen minutes later I was a soldier.

The next day was a Sunday, so the only thing we really had to be concerned about was making our beds and getting to meals on time. That wouldn't have been so bad if we had not had to stand at attention, in formation, for thirty or forty minutes at a time. We were always cold; not one of us was dressed for the icy blasts that were constantly blowing across the field we had to stand in. My first day as a soldier was anything but encouraging!

We had been told from the beginning we would be issued a uniform as soon as we had taken the oath. That turned out to be an impossibility. The supplies from the manufacturers could not keep up with the demand. Every morning we marched a mile to the supply room, hundreds of us, looking for army clothes. What had come in the day before would be issued on a first come, first served basis. By eleven o'clock everything would be gone, and those of us who had not been served would be back again the following morning to try our luck.

All that week we made the pilgrimage to the supply room every day, arriving earlier each morning. Friday was Christmas day, but it was business as usual, so to the supply room again right after breakfast. That was my lucky day, or unlucky, depending on the way you may see it. Lucky because I was issued clothes, unlucky because none of them fit! Well, I shouldn't say none of them fit; the underwear was near enough to my size to satisfy my need, especially so because I was tired of being sick to my stomach from the cold. I would have settled for anything that day. However, when I found everything else was a size or two too large, I put up a gallant effort to get them changed. As the discussion between the clerk and I got louder, the supply sergeant came over to me and said,

"Look soldier, it is going to be easier for you to change clothes that don't fit, than it would be to get clothes if you have none. Take it from me, you had better latch onto these clothes and be thankful you got them."

I could see he didn't want to take them back, and the uniform looked so warm, especially the overcoat, that I stopped arguing and filled my duffel bag. Nevertheless, for the next three weeks, the time it took me to finally exchange them, I was the warmest, yet the funniest looking soldier at Fort Devens!

In order not to feel the pain of loneliness too keenly during the holiday season I volunteered to help the cooks in the kitchen. And because I had a background in restaurants they gladly accepted my offer. Working in the kitchen I was able to duck a lot of formations and rollcalls. I liked that. It taught me the army was not much different than civilian life, a person could use an angle to his advantage if he had one. It was also in the kitchen I learned there were more bottles of whiskey, and more cases of beer, in the army than anywhere else! In fact, I discovered that a soldier could buy beer in the P.X. (Post Exchange) regardless of his age.

However, the wounds I had received from my last bout with alcohol were so raw I had no difficulty turning down all offers to join the fun. Nevertheless, I did feel left out, and I did take a lot of ribbing from my buddies for being a sissy. Regardless of how much they teased me though, I handled their banter with little rancor, and stayed sober.

It was in the middle of January 1943 when my first shipping orders came through. Fort Devens had only been a receiving depot for new recruits. Our basic training, an intensive six week course in soldiering, was to be given at one of several locations scattered throughout the United States. There were training camps especially designed and staffed for just such a purpose. Soldiers were shipped, by troop trains, in groups of five hundred or a thousand, to whatever location that could accommodate them. Six or seven hundred men were in the group I shipped out with. As it happened with many of the troop movements in the early days of the war, ours too, turned into a fiasco. If I had thought I had seen the ultimate in confusion during my neophyte days, I was mistaken. However, that mistake was about to be corrected during the next three days as we traveled across the country.

THE BIG MOVE

My first adventure in massive troop movement began on a bitter cold Wednesday morning. At five-thirty a bugler blasted reveille into the speaker system, waking everyone within a mile of his horn! Although I had heard that call every morning since I had arrived, I could not get used to it. Besides, it seemed louder than ever that morning. Then, to add insult to injury, the sound of the bugle had not faded from our ears before the door was thrown open, and a corporal burst into the barracks in a blast of cold air.

"Rise and shine, you lucky people," he hollered the minute the door closed behind him.

When he had everyone awake and up he hollered,

"Listen men, you have exactly twenty minutes to shower, dress, strip your bed and be ready for breakfast. Roll your mattresses up the way they were when you first came in here. You won't be sleeping in that bed again. Dress in Class A uniform," he continued, "you are going to leave this beautiful camp today. Now get with it," he ordered. "And don't miss roll call or you will land in the guardhouse."

When the corporal had finished his litany of instructions, he spun on his heels and marched smartly out the door. Immediately the men sprang into action, and I wondered if they were as eager as I was to get out of this icebox of a place.

Late that evening we were all on a train heading south not knowing where we were headed.

We traveled for four hours and then were shunted to a siding to await a passing express. We were there for an hour and a half before the special train went

189

whizzing by and we were allowed to move on. That same maneuver was to be performed several more times during the three nights and three days we spent on that train.

About four o'clock in the morning of our first day we picked up our kitchen or mess car. It was nothing but an old boxcar with three field ranges to cook on, bolted to the floor. At least we were going to have hot food on the journey we thought, and we would have had plenty if we hadn't taken a day longer than we were allowed to make the trip. Nevertheless, food was not our only concern; space became a critical issue soon after we started.

FIRE

Thursday morning was beautiful. The sun was shining high in the heavens by eight o'clock when the cooks called "Chow time!". Although it was still bitter cold, the sun added a certain charm to the day, and in spite of the fact I had a semi-sleepless night, sitting almost straight in that hard coach seat, I felt really refreshed and excited.

Scrambled eggs, bacon, hash browned potatoes, orange juice, toast and coffee were the only items on the menu, but we could have all we wanted. I marveled at how good the food was considering the crude equipment the cooks had to work with.

During breakfast our excitement increased considerably when we learned we were somewhere in the state of Connecticut, and heading south. There began a sort of a speculation game as to our final destination and we were all seriously embroiled in it. It was a good pastime. Miami Beach, Florida, was mentioned again and again but none of us thought we could be that lucky.

Suddenly, in the middle of our fun, a cry went up in the car ahead of us, "Fire!" a voice screamed.

190

"This goddamed car is on fire!" Instantly there was the beginnings of panic, and just as quickly our corporal took over.

"Pull that emergency cord and shut up," were his first orders.

Forty people pulled on the cord at once and pulled it right off the wall! However, someone must have gotten to the engineer, because the train came to an abrupt stop and at that instant I smelled the smoke. There were a lot of orders shouted up and down the train, and one could hear plenty of curses. But within five minutes we were all out of the train standing in the cold. Many of us had not had time to get our jacket or coat, and we felt the bite of the cold immediately.

Fortunately, we were only a mile or so from a small town, and within minutes a fire truck was on the scene to assist us. With their expertise the fire was confined to the underside of the coach and they had it out in minutes. However, enough damage had been done so the car could not be used. It had to be left behind. One of the brakemen explained, that because of a lack of grease, we had developed a hot-box. He said the axle had gotten so hot it set fire to the old grease and dirt that was packed in all the cracks and crevices of the car.

After the fire was out, and everything was under control, the engineer had to get rid of the useless car. He accomplished that by unlocking the last car and leaving it on the track. That placed the disabled car on the end of the train. Then he took the whole train some miles away until he found a siding. Dropping the damaged car there he came back to us, hooked up to the car he had left and we were on our way once more. However, things were not the same as they had been.

The sixty men from the abandoned car were divided among the other six cars. The car I was in had no empty seats so the ten men from the disabled car had to stand in the aisle with their bags stuffed wherever they could find room. It was a difficult task for anyone to get to the toilet at the end of the car and back again. Then too, three hours had been lost due to the fire, hours no one expected to make up.

When the cooks called us for chow later that evening, we began the round trip to the mess car for our food. The extra men in the car made the maneuver an almost impossible task. With a mug full of coffee in one hand and a full mess kit in the other, it was a difficult job getting back to our places. It seemed the train jerked and swayed more than ever during that meal, causing us to bump into seats on one side and passing soldiers on the other. There wasn't one of us that didn't lose some of our meal running that obstacle course. Then the food we lost became an additional hazard. It was almost impossible for those soldiers to eat standing up while balancing a tray and holding their coffee mugs between their feet.

The next twenty-four hours were uncomfortable and boring. We spent as many hours on a siding, waiting for other troop trains to pass, as we did traveling. The time became so monotonous even the insane struggle to get food at mealtimes created a welcome diversion.

Mile after torturous mile we continued to creep southward. One after another the states slipped past. Soon Pennsylvania, Maryland, Virginia, and North and South Carolina were left behind. The temperature continued to climb as the miles disappeared under our wheels, and the heavy clothes we were wearing became intolerable. A few of the men were brave enough to strip to their waists, in defiance of the corporal's direct order to keep up their appearance as soldiers. Finally, when it looked as if a showdown between the corporal and the troops was inevitable, the corporal took his tie and shirt off, to the cheers of everyone in the car. None of us wasted any time following suit, and our spirits rose dramatically. Our elation was short-lived though, because the temperature continued to climb. As it did, the odor of unwashed bodies grew stronger, and we began to curse the army for it's lack of foresight!

At dinnertime that evening the corporal unsealed the orders he had been carrying all along. Those orders confirmed our destination to be Miami Beach, Florida.

Forty-five minutes after the corporal had opened our sealed orders we pulled in back of a huge one story building that looked as if it had been a factory at one time. Double army bunks were lined up in straight rows throughout the building with just a narrow pathway between each row of bunks. There must have been enough bunks for a thousand men to be bedded down. We had arrived at a temporary holding area, and would be leaving there Monday morning for our final destination, Miami Beach.

A few phone calls made by the corporal and we found out we could be fed. However, we would have to march, in formation, almost two miles to the mess hall. They told us they would not wait all night for us. If we wanted to eat we had to leave immediately. I could not go even if I had wanted to. I was too hot, tired and weary. Fifteen other men were as exhausted as I was, and chose not to go either. But the rest of the men, over six hundred of them, went marching down the street in cadence toward the mess hall. That left the latrine, with its several shower stalls, to us, and I wasted no time getting cleaned up and in my bunk. I was dead to the world as soon as my head hit the pillow, and even the noise of the men returning from chow did not disturb me.

The next morning we were not obliged to get up for breakfast. Lunch and dinner were also optional. I took advantage of that free time and slept until 1:00 P.M. without any difficulty. The rest of the afternoon I spent rearranging my duffel bag. We could not unpack but I could get out my suntan uniform and pack up my heavy olive drabs. The temperature was in the low seventies that day and I felt like a brand-new person in my light summer clothes. In fact, after my long sleep I was refreshed and felt excited as I walked down the street looking the neighborhood over; I could hardly believe that I was in Florida.

It was after nine o'clock by the time we got back to our area from breakfast the next morning. To our surprise there were fifty or more army buses waiting for us. Six of them were assigned to our company. Evidently all of the soldiers who had been on the train with us were not going to the same place.

At four o'clock that afternoon the buses pulled into an area of the street that had been blocked off by three long, wooden horses. The entrance to the area was guarded by about twenty military policemen, whose uniforms looked brand-new. They were very tall men, every one of them, and they were dressed to impress all who happened to see them. Their helmets were metal, but they were painted with a high-gloss white paint. The big black letters M.P. stamped on the front of them were visible from a good distance. The helmets were so shiny I thought they must have waxed them that morning. Their suntan uniforms looked as though they had just come from the cleaners, they were so neatly pressed. The black boots they wore came up well over their ankles, and they were polished to perfection. Their pants legs were folded neatly and tucked into the tops of their boots. Then there was a wide, white, webbed belt around their waists, and another, hooked to it, that went across their chests and over their left shoulders. A black armband, about five inches wide, with the white letters M.P. stenciled in the center of it, decorated their left arms and boldly declared their authority. A forty-five caliber revolver swung in its holster on their right hip, while a black, highly-polished, billy club was hooked on the left. A pair of white gloves finished off their ensemble. They looked both magnificent and ominous standing at attention, feet wide apart, and their hands clasped behind their backs.

As my eyes took in that whole scene, a feeling

of excitement flooded through me. The military policemen, the thousands of soldiers, and the hectic activity going on all around me, brought home, with force, the exciting and terrible fact we were really at war. Even the vague knowledge that I may be killed, or maimed, did not dilute the strange acceleration and joy I felt by being in the midst of it. There was no time to enjoy being a spectator though, because we were ordered off the buses the minute we stopped at the curb.

Our bus driver volunteered the information that we were on Collins Avenue, one of the nicest sections of Miami Beach. He also told us several hotels in the area had been taken over by the military and that we were going to be housed in one of them.

"This is where the army is going to make soldiers out of you," the driver said, with a sinister laugh. It looked as though the army didn't intend to waste any time either.

As fast as we got off the buses, we were lined up in formation right in the street. Then, when the last man had both feet on the ground, the six buses drove away. We were left standing in the street, with all of our bags, just waiting to see what would happen next.

"At ease, men," our corporal shouted, "the smoking lamp is lit."
He meant that anyone who smoked had permission to do so. About fifteen minutes went by with everyone milling about talking to each other, and most of us smoking. The sun was high, the temperature about sixty-five degrees; the day was beautiful, and the atmosphere was electric.

In the excitement of the moment we didn't hear the army jeep until it was almost on top of us. All of a sudden it came speeding down the street, seemingly from out of nowhere, and screeched to a stop near the center of our ranks. A captain and a sergeant jumped out, and the jeep disappeared around

195

the nearest corner. The corporal who had been in charge of us since we left Fort Devens, walked up to the captain, saluted, and turned our papers over to him. We didn't see that corporal again, and I assumed he had gone back to Massachusetts.

Our new sergeant stepped forward then, and addressing the troops, he shouted,

"Company --- atten--tion!" dragging the last word out and cutting it off abruptly. His order was repeated by the corporal in charge of each section until we were all standing as stiff as boards.

"My name is Harry Simpson," the sergeant shouted.

"You will call me Sergeant Simpson as long as you are here. We plan to make soldiers out of you sad looking bums, and by looking at you I can see we have our work cut out for us. You will hear more about that later, I can promise you. Right now though, I want to introduce you to Captain Lewis. He will be your Commanding Officer." The sergeant took a step back then, and the captain took his place.

"Men, I want to welcome you to the United States Army Air Force," the captain shouted. He had no trouble making himself heard up and down the ranks. I think it was the clear air around us that helped his voice carry so distinctly.

"You are all capable men," he said, "that's why they sent you to us. You are capable of much and I am going to expect much from you. The United States Army Air Force is a proud outfit. You should feel honored you were allowed to join us. However, let me warn you right now. I will not let any one of you disgrace this fine organization in any way. I will not put up with any foolishness. You are soldiers now and I insist you act like soldiers."

He paused for some moments, and then added,

"I have said all I wanted to say to you for now. I am going to turn you over to Sergeant Simpson here for your basic training. If all goes well you will not see me again. I advise you to make sure you don't land in my office, because if you do it will mean you have caused Sergeant Simpson some problems. I can assure you, you won't be with us long if you let that happen."

"Sergeant Simpson, front and center," he shouted, and the sergeant almost fell on his face in his eagerness to comply. In a fraction of a second he was standing in front of the captain. He clicked his heels and executed a snappy salute at the same time.

"Sergeant," the captain said, "take these men, get them assigned to their rooms and make sure they get to chow on time. I heard they have had a hard time getting fed these past few days."

"Yes sir," the sergeant said.

Then he took one step backward, offered another salute, and turned on his heels to face us. His actions seemed to be a signal to the captain, for he too spun on his heels, but in the opposite direction. I watched his back as he walked across the sidewalk and disappeared into one of the hotels.

The captain had left a deep impression on me, with his medals and his bars. I was terrified of the authority and the power he represented, and I made a solemn promise to keep as far away from him as I could. But the next minute I became furious at myself for being such a damn coward. I berated myself with a mental lecture. "A hell-of-a-fine soldier you're gonna make. If you are scared of your own officers, what the hell do you think you will do when you are called on to face the enemy?"

Again I was able to push my personal thoughts aside because the sergeant was speaking, but I could not get rid of the fear. My stomach was knotted up, my skin was crawling, and my knees were trembling ---

it was that bad.

The eyes of all the men seemed to be glued onto the door the captain had gone through.

"All right men," the sergeant shouted, "there will be plenty of captains for you to look at from now on. Right now I want your complete attention. The hotel directly behind me, the one the captain went into, is our hotel. There will be four men to a room. I will call out your name and a room number. When I do, I want you to pick up your bags and get in there. You may not have time to unpack, but don't worry about that. You will have the whole evening to yourselves after dinner. You had better unpack then because you won't have time tomorrow. At eighteen hundred hours, six o'clock to you, you will hear this whistle." He blew it then in order for us to recognize it.

"When I blow that whistle you will have exactly ten minutes to get down here and into formation. You will not have eleven minutes, you will not have ten and a half minutes, you will have _ten_. Do you understand me, soldiers?" he screamed.

"Yes sergeant!" we shouted in unison, and at the sound of all those voices, a feeling of pride and excitement flooded through me again.

"How much time will you have to get into formation when you hear my whistle?" he asked.

"Ten minutes, sergeant!" we responded.

The sergeant seemed satisfied we were not a bunch of dummies, and he began to call names and room numbers in rapid succession. As each name was called, the soldier grabbed his bags and ran for the hotel door. Within forty-five minutes there wasn't a man left on the street.

We had just enough time to stake our claim to a bed before the sharp blast of the sergeant's whistle sounded throughout the hotel. No one dared to keep the sergeant waiting!

Ten minutes later, four abreast, we began a march that lasted twenty minutes and covered ten city blocks. It was a strange feeling to be marching down the street, with the sergeant calling cadence, and traffic moving past us in both directions. Then too, there were more civilians than soldiers walking along the sidewalks. We felt more like soldiers in a parade than soldiers training for war. The looks of admiration that some of the civilians cast in our direction made me feel proud to be their protector.

As our march continued, I became aware of how hungry and tired I was. At that point I wanted nothing more than to eat and crawl into a soft bed. On and on we marched, block after city block, and still we saw nothing that even looked like a mess hall.

Just as the troops began to grumble openly among themselves, the sergeant, unexpectedly and without warning, gave a sharp order, "Com - pany - halt!"

I was near the front of the formation, on the sidewalk side, so I had a chance to look around. The sergeant was standing in the street facing us, and to our right I saw the front door of a large cafeteria restaurant. With more than a little explaining the sergeant was able to get across to us how we were to proceed into the restaurant to get fed. He also showed us the area in back of the place where we were to congregate as soon as we had finished our meal. I was surprised to find the cafeteria could seat about six --- or eight hundred people at a time, and they fed soldiers and civilians alike. The only difference was the fact that the military had a large section of the dining room reserved, and we had to eat in that area only. Then too, I was most impressed by how orderly a fashion we were able to execute that whole maneuver. There were over two hundred soldiers in our company that night, and we were all fed and on our way back to our hotel in less than an hour and a half. We ate three meals a day in that restaurant all the time we were there, and we always had good food and efficient service.

Back in our room, I managed to get unpacked and even wrote a letter to Veronica before I went to sleep. Somehow the meal and the march back had shaken off my tired feeling. The other three soldiers in my room were in a good mood, and one of them proved to be a funny character who kept us laughing all evening with his impersonations of movie stars, including the Three Stooges. My sides were aching as I slipped into bed that night, but as tired as I had been before dinner, I could not get to sleep for hours.

I FOUGHT TEMPTATION

All during our stay at Fort Devens, we new recruits were not allowed off base, neither were we permitted to buy beer at the Post Exchange regardless of our age. I felt safe in that environment, and thought it would be that way as long as I was in the service. Even when we arrived at Miami Beach we were told we would not have any time for anything but our training. We soon found out we were too tired in the evenings to want anything but rest anyway. Nevertheless, it quickly became common knowledge that liquor was always available. Any soldier who wanted whiskey or beer, and was willing to pay the price for it, could get as much as he wanted.

Before we had been in our hotel a week, we had learned that members of the permanent cadre had developed a bootleg system that was most efficient, and operated quite openly twenty-four hours a day. Of course, a fifth of whiskey cost two dollars more than it would have if purchased at a liquor store, and the markup on a case of beer was about the same. More than one noncommissioned officer's private room was well-stocked with booze, and trading was usually brisk. However, because I was not thinking about alcohol, and didn't want any, I had no idea it was so accessible, nor that there was drinking going on all around me. My ignorance was shattered completely however, on our first payday.

That evening, my three roommates wanted me to share the cost of a case of beer with them, and have a party. I declined their offer, claiming, in a sanctimonious manner, that I didn't drink. They ignored my attempt to get into a discussion on the evils of alcohol, and bought a case of beer without my help. The three of them drank all evening, they became so loud and boisterous I couldn't get to sleep. A couple of times they began to taunt me for not drinking, but I ignored them and they went on to other things. During the evening, soldiers from other rooms dropped in, each with his own bottle of beer clutched in his hand, and each added his bit to the noise as well as to my discomfort. Then, about midnight, a corporal stuck his head in our doorway and told us to break up the party and get to sleep. An hour later he was back, and insisted on lights out. The party was over.

I was really shaken by that experience. It was not that I had wanted to drink; my commitment to sobriety was still as strong as ever. However, I felt betrayed. I thought the army officers would not stand for drinking among the soldiers, and therefore I would be safe from temptation. Then, when I learned that was not the case, I became anxious because I didn't know if I could trust myself to keep up the struggle. And, because I wouldn't join the party, I felt that strange isolation from my roommates I had felt all of my life whenever I was with a group of people.

As uncomfortable as I had been, I managed to get through the evening all right. In fact, there was even a twinge of satisfaction in it for me. Early the next morning, as I watched my three friends getting ready for the drill field with their bleary eyes and their aching heads, I felt smug.

But the experience did something else to me. It made me acutely aware of all the liquor that was floating around. It seemed that once I became conscious of the drinking that was going on among us, I could sense its presence in a group even when I couldn't see it. Then, it was shortly after that party I began to notice a distinct change in my personality. It didn't take much for me to become angry and lash out at anyone whom I felt had crossed me. I developed a negative attitude toward anyone in charge and was placed on company punishment more than once just for being mouthy to a corporal or a sergeant. It was an odd experience for me, because I was conscious of feeling rage but could not explain to myself where it was coming from, nor who I was angry at. Even knowing my belligerency would bring trouble down on myself, there were times when I could not hold it back.

During those uncomfortable days, I was kept somewhat safe from temptation by our strenuous schedule. Our crash course on soldiering consumed almost every minute of every day. However, I found I had to stay away from my roommates in the evenings because I felt ill at ease around them. Nevertheless, I was able to lose myself during much of my free time by writing of my love to Veronica. It was around that same time though, the letters I had been getting from Veronica, the letters I had always looked for with so much anticipation, began to decrease in number, and the content of those letters began to cool. Where I had been getting one almost every day, and sometimes two, by the end of January they had dwindled to two or three a week. In the beginning, when I noticed changes in the tone of her letters, I tried to ignore them. If anything, mine became more ardent. I told her, over, and over again, she was the only person in my life and that my love for her made army life bearable. A large portion of those letters were romantic mush, right out of the movies, but a good deal of the things I had written were true. She was the only important person in my life at that time. I had no family to write to as other soldiers had. I didn't know where the members of my family were then, and I don't believe any of them knew of my whereabouts. Although I began to sense I might not be

202

as important to Veronica as I had been, I still considered her my girl back home. And because she had never mentioned she was seeing someone else, I assumed she considered me her sweetheart. Therefore, I was stunned when, two days after Valentine's Day, instead of a Valentine, I received a "Dear John" letter from her.

VERONICA MARRIED JAKE

A "Dear John" letter is one in which a wife asks her soldier husband for a divorce, or a girlfriend breaks off an engagement, or a friendship. The letter I received from Veronica was slightly different though. She didn't break our engagement; there really had never been one. She didn't even address our friendship. She just made an astonishing announcement. I don't remember anything that was in the letter except the first few lines. The letter read:

"Dear Freeman:
For several days now I have been trying to find the words to tell you something that may hurt you, but I could not help what happened. I guess the only way to tell you --- is to tell you. Your brother Jake and I have fallen in love and are getting married next month...."

There was much more in the letter but I couldn't read on. I read and reread those few lines to make sure I understood correctly what she had written. I don't think I could have been shocked more, even if I had been struck by a bolt of lightning. I hadn't known that Jake was even in Veronica's neighborhood, never mind him seeing her! I wanted to kill them both, Veronica more than Jake! I knew Jake had no respect for loyalties, nor did he honor anything that was noble. In other words, I understood Jake. I wanted to kill him, but I was not surprised by his treachery.

However, I was insulted that Veronica would even go out with him. She had seen the contrast between us. I had shared some of my frustrations over his past behavior with her more than once, and she knew of my despair over the prospects of his future. The few times Jake had been in her company, while I was there, he had done nothing but tell dirty jokes, and make lewd remarks to every girl that passed our way. He was loud, vulgar, lazy, and dirty. I was enraged that Veronica would let him sit on the same porch swing with her that we had enjoyed so many evenings on together.

I seethed with rage and resentments. I thought about nothing else. It got so I couldn't concentrate on my training instructions during the day, and in my sleep at night, I dreamed of Jake's dirty hands caressing Veronica. The one thought that persisted though, the thought that kept returning to my mind again and again, was how those two must have been laughing at me all the while that I was writing, so seriously, of my love. My mind just would not let me rest. Then, when the sergeant refused my request for a leave of absence, I began toying with the idea of going home and beating the hell out of Jake anyway. However, one look at the number of military police scattered all over the area and I gave up that idea quickly.

By the end of the second day I was an emotional wreck, and I was fighting with everyone. The sergeant gave me hell a couple of times for goofing up on the obstacle course. Then, on Friday, I was in front of him again for getting into a fistfight with another soldier on the rifle range. As he gave me the assignment of scrubbing the hotel lobby floor with a toothbrush, he said,

"Freeman, take my advice and get out of your room this weekend. If you don't put a little fun in your life you won't make it through basic training."
I didn't answer him, but I knew he was probably right.

That evening, as I was scrubbing the floor, I

came close to hitting another soldier for laughing at me. The fellow who had made me angry apologized for being rude and invited me to go out with him on Saturday night. As it turned out, a group of soldiers had gotten together and rented a bus to take them to the dog races in Miami. There were a few empty seats available, and it would only cost me two dollars if I wanted to go with them. I had never seen a dog race, and I had sixteen dollars left from my pay, so I agreed to go.

I DRANK AGAIN

My spirits were higher than they had been in days when I joined the men waiting for the bus the next evening. Some of the bitterness I had felt toward Veronica and Jake had faded from my heart by then, and I was in the mood for some fun. After all, the sergeant himself had said I needed a break. Almost every soldier had a bottle of liquor on that bus, or so it seemed. I was able to refuse their offers for a while, but I could feel my determination weakening. And when a corporal held up a fifth of Southern Comfort, and said,

"Here Freeman, take a slug of this. You won't get drunk on this stuff, nobody does. It's too sweet."

I said, "OK", and took a long pull right out of the bottle. It was sickeningly sweet all right, but it was alcohol, and I loved the feeling it produced. There was that familiar warm feeling in the pit of my stomach, then my face felt flushed, my legs and feet got comfortably warm, as they always did when I drank, and I felt an overall excitement that was marvelous. I also felt my resolve to stay sober drift right out the window of the bus, but I didn't care! That insatiable desire for more alcohol had me in its grip once again. I wanted more alcohol, and I wanted it right then. However, so as not to embarrass myself in front of the men, or take the chance of being called a

205

pig, I drank very little from the bottles that were being passed around, but every nerve in my body was screaming for more. By the time the bus got to the race track, I was desperate for a drink.

We arrived at the track too early for the first race, but in plenty of time to drink lots of beer in the glittering tavern. Just around the corner there was a liquor store, still open, and there I bought a pint of whiskey for two dollars and twenty-seven cents. I thought with the whiskey, and all the beer I could buy over the bar, I would have enough booze for the evening. In view of what happened I guess it was more than enough.

Although we spent hours at the track, I never saw one dog race, I was too busy drinking and talking. The alcohol had loosened my tongue considerably, and I told anyone who would listen, about how my brother had moved in on me and stolen my girl. The more I drank, and the more my fellow soldiers sympathized with me, the more enraged at Jake and Veronica I became. Several of the soldiers had said they wouldn't have let their brother get away with a thing like that if they were me, and their words made me feel foolish for not doing something. Later that evening, about ten o'clock I guess, I was pretty drunk when one of the soldiers, a very big man, screamed right in my face.

"What the hell kind of a man are you, Freeman? If my brother did that to me I would have killed the bastard!"
I was furious at him, and at myself. I couldn't let anyone get away with telling me I was not a man. I decided to show everybody. Pass or no pass I was going to hitchhike home and kill Jake, and maybe Veronica too for good measure. I stormed out the door, into the cool night air, and right into a blackout.

At seven o'clock Sunday evening I woke up in a military jail for the first time. The army had taken the entire top floor of one of the hotels on Collins Avenue and turned the rooms into cells. They had

206

removed all the regular doors and replaced them with iron-barred doors. Every window that was near a fire escape was covered with an iron mesh, and there were military police all over the place. There were about twenty other soldiers being held prisoners, most of them just for being drunk and disorderly, and through a couple of them that were in the same room with me, I learned I had been brought in about three o'clock in the morning. They said I was as drunk as hell and fighting the MPs every step of the way. I also found out from those men that we were only four blocks up the street from my own hotel. That got me to thinking about my sergeant then, and I became terrified wondering what he might do to me for missing bed check.

Monday morning, about ten o'clock, I was taken back to my hotel under guard. It was humiliating to be walking down the street, in wrinkled clothes, with a military policeman on either side of me. Then, when the MPs turned me over to the sergeant, I was surprised at his cool reception. I had seen him fly into a rage at a soldier who couldn't keep in step, or scream at another man who was a minute late getting into formation. Being calm was not natural for him and that had me worried.

I WAS KICKED OUT OF THE AIR FORCE

Then after the police had gone, the sergeant kept me sitting in his office for an hour without saying a word to me. I felt most uncomfortable, and wished I was anywhere else but there. Even being locked up, away from everyone's eyes, began to look attractive. Just before noon the captain came through the front door and headed for his office. He didn't even look in my direction. A minute later the sergeant disappeared into the captain's office, and about five minutes after that I was called in. I looked calm on the outside, as I stood at attention in front of his desk, but every nerve in my body was

207

trembling I was so afraid. Even my kneecaps were jumping and I was glad I was wearing enough clothes to hide in.

"Private Carpenter, you are a troublemaker and a fool," the captain said. "We don't want your kind in our organization. I am placing you under house arrest until we can transfer you out of here. That means you are confined to your room except for meals. Is that clear, private?" he asked.

"Yes sir," I answered.

"Dismissed," the captain said, as he turned and picked up the telephone.

I knew he was through with me, and a feeling of relief swept over my entire body. The experience had left me so weak, though, that I just wanted to lay down and rest for a while.

"Do you really think that you were lucky?" the sergeant asked, as soon as I came back into his office. Without waiting for me to answer, he continued,

"You won't think yourself so lucky when you wake up on a troop ship headed for the front lines in Europe. Now get up to your room," he said, "and don't let me see you again until I send for you."

"Yes sir, sergeant," I said, and I went up those stairs three at a time. I wouldn't let on to anyone, but what the sergeant had said about me going to the front lines had me worried.

Word had gotten around quickly that I was an undesirable, and was being kicked out. As a result, my three roommates stopped talking to me, and acted as though I wasn't there. I think that was the hardest part of the ordeal for me --- to be treated as though I didn't exist. Every morning they flew out of the room to make reveille on time and left me there. In the evening they came bursting into the room, full of excitement from the day's activities. It was an experience I shall never forget. Three days of that kind of treatment, with absolutely nothing to do, drove me to the brink of insanity. I began to believe they had forgotten all about me, but I was afraid to ask anyone about my status, especially the sergeant. On the fourth day a corporal came into my room and told me to report to the sergeant's office at once. With excited anticipation, I bounded down the stairs and right up to the sergeant's desk. As soon as he saw me, he said,

"Good news, Freeman, you are being transferred to Camp Kilmer in New Jersey for reassignment. I want you dressed in class A uniform, have your gear packed, and be back in my office by thirteen hundred hours, ready to leave."

I flashed a quick look at the wall clock and saw it was ten thirty in the morning. I had only two and a half hours to get packed and eat lunch.

Back in my room I packed two duffel bags and a civilian suitcase before I had all my stuff packed. It was a difficult job carrying all that baggage down to the sergeant's office but I was there ten minutes ahead of time.

As I sat in the office, with my bags at my feet, a feeling of sadness stole over me as I watched my company going out to the drill field after lunch. I felt left out again, and the feeling caused a lump in my throat. However, I was too proud to let anyone know I was hurting. I knew if I told anyone how I felt, they wouldn't have believed me anyway. They would probably have said something like,

"Well, if you don't want to be left out all the time, why do you always keep goofing up?" And because I couldn't answer that question, even for myself, I had to keep everything bottled up.

As usual, it was over an hour before I was picked up at the sergeant's office to begin my journey to New Jersey. An army bus, driven by a corporal, took me and about twenty other soldiers to the railroad station. We immediately boarded a train headed north, and in less than a half hour we were on our way.

However, it was noon on Sunday, the last day of February, before we pulled into Grand Central Station in New York. Even the trip itself was an exciting experience, because two-thirds of all travelers were service men. Army, Navy, Marines, and Air Force were all represented. One could see officers of every rank in the moving throngs. Enlisted men from every branch of the service were as numerous as nervous ants, and just as active! All kinds of military police were everywhere, watching everyone, and occasionally checking an enlisted man's papers. Many foreign services were represented as well. There were Canadian airmen, English sailors, Australian soldiers, and many others I could not recognize. Everyone seemed to be on the move, and it looked as if no one could get to where they were going fast enough. The excitement I had felt in the air when I arrived at Miami Beach, now appeared to be everywhere. It was especially high in New York.

CAMP KILMER N.J.

Camp Kilmer was many different things to different people. First, it was a permanent military installation; it had been there for a long time. Then, when the draft began gathering young men by the thousands, Camp Kilmer became a processing center for those men, the same as Fort Devens had been of service to me. Next, as the war progressed in Europe, our generals began looking to Camp Kilmer as a demarcation depot for replacements, as their own men were killed or wounded. And lastly, there were those soldiers who, for one reason or another, found themselves between assignments. Those men needed a place to stay for a while until they were given a new post. All those added functions put a strain on the small camp.

210

Overnight they had been called upon to accommodate four or five times as many men as they had serviced before. Their barracks were soon overflowing, and still the men kept coming. In order to house those extra men, a small city of quonset huts sprang up. The camp doubled its size in a very short time, and kept on growing.

What a come down, I thought, as I walked into the hut I had been assigned to. From a comfortable hotel room on Collins Avenue in sunny Miami Beach, to a cold, dark tent on a muddy dirt road somewhere in New Jersey, at the tail end of a bitter cold winter. As I sat there, on the edge of my cot in that empty hut, I began to feel sorry for myself all over again. I felt that being kicked out of the Air Force was too steep a price for me to have to pay for what I had done. After all, I had seen others do things I considered were much worse, and they seemed to have gotten away with it. Nevertheless, after a short period of time, I began to realize, like it or not, I was stuck in that godforsaken place, and I had better make the best of it. The one good thing I found in that entire experience was, that for the time being at least, I had been relieved of my rage at Veronica and Jake. I had so many things concerning my own survival to worry about I forgot almost everything else.

As I sat there alone, with my chin resting in both hands brooding, the potbellied, coal-burning stove in the center of the tent began making sharp crackling noises. When I looked closely at it, I saw it was becoming red all around its middle, it was getting so hot. Quickly I closed all the drafts, and shoveled more coal into it to cool it down. The immediate attention the stove had called for brought me out of my slump a little. I was able to see my surroundings more clearly then, but what I saw did nothing to cheer me up.

As I looked around, I noticed the tent was about thirty-feet square, and it had a dirt floor. The walls were not much more than four feet high, but the center pole was all of ten feet. The potbellied stove

211

was a small, round, black-iron thing that gave off
more than enough heat. There was coal in a scuttle at
its side and all the wood needed in a huge pile
outside. The stove was placed about six inches from
the center pole and it had a six-inch stove pipe going
straight up through the roof. Our four windows, one
in each wall, were rectangular holes about eight by
twelve inches. They had pieces of screening sewn over
them to keep the insects out, and they were covered by
a flap on the outside which could be laced down in bad
weather. An electrical cord with a lightbulb on the
end of it had been inserted through the roof alongside
the center pole, to give us light. I soon found there
was no off-and-on switch! One had to screw and
unscrew the bulb to get it to work. Four iron cots,
each with a thin mattress and a lumpy pillow, were the
only pieces of furniture in the place. The cots were
set, one against each wall, as far away from the stove
as possible. Evidently, I was the first occupant of
that particular hut, because there was no clothing or
anything else to indicate otherwise. I immediately
moved my things from the bed near the door to the one
against the back wall. I figured I would be warmer
there if others kept opening and closing the door. As
it turned out later, that proved to be a good move,
especially on a windy day.

After looking the interior over carefully, which
didn't take long, I stepped outside to check things
out. Five minutes later I was back, digging into my
duffel bag looking for my heavy winter overcoat. With
my coat buttoned to my chin against the bitter cold I
went out again. That time though, I was much better
prepared to stay long enough to see everything there
was to see.

I noticed the door I had stepped through as I
left the tent had been made of heavy plywood. An
inexpensive barn-latch had been installed where a
doorknob should have been. A large hook-and-eye on
the inside of the door secured it at night from
prowlers but there was no way to lock it from the
outside. Then I saw a wall, about three feet high,
also made of heavy plywood, that went completely

around each and every tent. A maintenance man told me the plywood walls were necessary because of the high winds that sometimes went whipping through the area.

As I remember it, the tents were setup in blocks of one hundred, or close to that number, with unpaved streets running north and south, east and west between them. The canvas the tents were made of were of different shades of army brown, olive green and gun-metal gray. One could see an attempt had been made to keep each block of tents the same color, but the whole area looked ugly just the same. Still I guess it was better than sleeping in our two-men pup tents. There must have been two or three thousand tents in that area, and it became a beehive of activity as men flooded in daily.

It began to get too dark for me to see much more, and I was surprised to see it was almost six o'clock when I looked at my watch. Then, as I turned to go back to my tent, I spotted a sign that said "Latrine" and there was an arrow on it pointing to an old, brick, two-story building. I wasted no time heading for the relief it promised. The warm air that engulfed me as I stepped through the door was most welcome, and I leaned my back on the door for a few minutes just soaking it in. However, there were too many men coming and going for me to stay there long. I followed a couple of soldiers who looked as though they knew their way around, and they led me down a long corridor, around a couple of corners and right into the latrine.

The bathroom was a very large room, about twenty-five feet long and twenty wide. It looked as if someone had knocked out a couple of partitions to create one large room out of three smaller ones. There were fourteen toilets along one wall, one next to the other, with nothing between or around them. There were always five or six men sitting on those toilets whenever I went in there, but they didn't seem to mind the lack of privacy. A few could actually read a newspaper while sitting there. However, I felt very uncomfortable each time I had to use one.

Continuing my observation of the room, I saw there were ten or twelve urinals along the back wall, but many a time they were not enough to accommodate the crowd. The washbasins were on the wall directly across from the toilets, one for one. Each washbasin had a square mirror bolted firmly to the wall above it, and just beneath the mirror there was a narrow glass shelf that served to hold our toiletries.

Across the corridor from the latrine there was another room about the same size. The room had a sign over its door that said "Shower Room". I poked my head through the door and counted four shower stalls, one in each corner. Ten men could take a shower at the same time in each stall they were that large. Then there were six large laundry tubs, three along each of the longer walls. Three of those tubs were in use that evening, and because of that I noticed each tub had a washboard hanging on its side for our convenience.

During the next three weeks I was to learn that the latrine building was always nice and warm, and there never was a shortage of hot water. The whole place was always clean, because each one of us had to take our turn keeping it that way. We learned that if the sergeant wasn't satisfied with the job we had done, he would make us clean it all over again the next day, so we made a serious attempt to do it right the first time. All in all, that community hall was a building that served us well, and we appreciated having it most of the time. However, it was an inconvenience to have to get dressed warm enough, in the middle of the night, to walk across the cold, dark yard, just to use the urinal for a minute or two.

By the time I had looked everything over to my satisfaction, I began to realize how hungry I was. My watch told me it was five minutes before seven, way past my regular dinner hour. I was trying to figure out which one of the many soldiers I should ask about chow, when a loud, brass bell began to clang incessantly outside. I thought at first it might be a fire alarm, so I watched the other men to see what they would do. Immediately they all began heading for the front door without saying a word. Automatically I began to drift along with them, simply because I didn't know what else to do. Then, as I stepped through the door, I heard a loud voice, from way up the street calling,

"Last call for chow, anyone who hasn't eaten yet, last call. Last call for chow, let's go, let's go."

Soldiers were running toward that voice from all directions. They were blending into a formation that was already a block long. I ran up to the corporal who seemed to be in charge and told him I hadn't eaten since morning, and that I didn't know where I belonged.

"Fall-in rank, soldier," he snapped, "you will have most of your questions answered after you eat."

"Thank you, corporal," I said, and tried to force my way into the middle of the formation.

However, none of the soldiers would give me an inch of room, so I was obliged to go to the extreme end of the line. I wasn't on the end very long though, because more and more soldiers kept falling-in behind me. About two or three minutes after I had found a place for myself in the formation, we began to move. We marched over a mile, into the main part of the camp, right to one of their large mess halls. There, we came to a halt, and as usual, waited!

Less than five minutes went by before the mess hall door was thrown open, and a huge black man stepped out onto the small porch to look us over. He must have been at least six-foot four, and his waist was all of forty-eight inches. He had a huge stomach. By the stripes he was wearing one could easily see he was a master sergeant. The four hash-marks on his sleeve told me he already had more than twelve years in the service, and I suspected he intended to stay in forever. But, it was the four rows of ribbons, and the cluster of medals he was wearing that impressed me most. He must have been everywhere, and done everything, I thought. Then I began to wonder how he had landed in this out-of-the-way place, taking care of soldiers that nobody else wanted.

The sergeant stood there, with his hands on the porch railing, slowly turning his head, first to the right, then to the left, in order to survey his charges. He stood that way for such a long time we became uncomfortable under his steady gaze and started to shuffle our feet and grumble under our breath. Then, when he finally did speak, he shouted, and his voice sounded as though it came from deep inside a sturdy barrel.

"All right men, all of you who have been assigned to a table can go in now, the rest of you stay right where you are." His voice carried easily to everyone's ears.

As soon as he had finished speaking, there was a mad rush. Three-quarters of the formation tried to squeeze themselves through the mess hall door at the same time. Then, about five minutes later, when most of the men had managed to get inside, the sergeant turned his attention back to us.

"Corporal, bring your men to attention, and dress up those ranks," he hollered.

Then he came down the four steps from the porch, and took a position next to the corporal in front of us.

"Forward march," the corporal hollered over his shoulder, and we were on our way again. Around the building, and right into the mess hall we went.

Six long tables had been reserved for us new men, away from the main part of the dining room. Each table could accommodate ten men, and we filled four of them completely. The food was served family style, by other soldiers, and within minutes after sitting down, we had all the hot food we could eat. Twenty minutes later there wasn't a scrap of food left on anyone's plate. We were stuffed, and ready to go back to our tents. However, we were not allowed to do that. Just before we had finished our meal, the corporal had come over to our corner and told us not to leave until he was ready to march us back.

"Besides," he said, "the sergeant wants to talk to you about our camp and why you are here. He wouldn't like it if some of you were missing and he had to repeat himself later."

It was after eight o'clock before the sergeant finally showed up.

"Which one of you poor excuses for a soldier wants a discharge because you don't like it here?" he shouted.

Everyone became deadly silent. He stood there, all six-foot four inches of him, hands on hips, and glaring at us. There wasn't one of us brave enough to answer him. A full minute went by before the sergeant was satisfied that he had us completely cowed.

"Good," he finally said. "We may be able to make soldiers out of you after all."

Then he walked slowly between the tables, looking intently at each one of us. When he could catch someone's eyes he would hold the look until the other person turned away. He tried to catch my eyes a couple of times but I was afraid of him and would not look in his direction unless I knew his attention was elsewhere. For some unknown reason I was terrified of the strength he exuded and wanted no part of him. When he had finished his personal inspection he walked to the front of the room again, and took a stand with his back to the wall. We waited for his next move with bated breath, not daring to attract his attention. Finally, after what seemed like forever, he spoke to us again,

"For your information, you men are in Camp Kilmer, New Jersey, and you are here for reassignment. You wouldn't be here if you had not screwed-up in some way where you were. Because there is a war on, they decided to give you one more chance. However, if it was up to me I'd kick your ass out right now. I don't think you're worth the effort, I don't think you have the guts to be a soldier. What do you think of that?" he asked.

Again no one dared to answer him. I felt ashamed to be addressed in that manner, by that self-assured, arrogant, pompous soldier, but I knew he hadn't earned his medals by sitting in his barracks, or guzzling booze in a barroom. I had the feeling he didn't like being stuck in that place any more than we did. I was extremely angry at myself for getting into that mess, and I promised myself I would become one of the best soldiers they ever had. Unfortunately that turned out to be another promise I could not keep.

The sergeant gave us only a minute to recover from his verbal assault before he continued his prepared speech, in a mechanical fashion. Listening to him, I had the feeling he had given that lecture to hundreds of new arrivals, and he was tired of it. Nevertheless, like the staunch soldier he was, he continued to discharge his duties faithfully.

"You won't be here very long," he said, "within ten days or so you should be on your way to your new post. Some of you will be going overseas, right to the fighting front. While you are here you will keep your bags packed and be available at all times, that means twenty-four hours a day. That's because, the minute your shipping orders come through, you will be expected to respond instantly. Keep your living quarters neat and clean at all times because I make my inspection rounds daily. The only duty you will have will be to help keep the latrines and shower rooms clean."

The sergeant paused then, a long pause. No one moved because he didn't move. Again I began to feel uncomfortable under his influence and I believe he knew we were ill at ease with the silence. After a few minutes, he unexpectedly hollered,

"Let me warn every one of you, now, if we go looking for you at any time and can't find you, you will be court-martialed. If that happens you will either land in the guardhouse, or be discharged from the army. Either way, your military career will be over. You will be disgraced."

It was nine forty-five when I got back to my tent, only to find it full of soldiers. Three of them had been assigned to my tent, the other four were their buddies. All seven of them were drunk, and they had brought three cases of beer with them. They were having such a good time that I could not refuse to join them when they offered me a bottle of beer. I was drunk by the time I went to bed that first night.

Even though I had a hangover, I made reveille on time, but I was desperately in need of a drink. No one in my tent went to breakfast that morning, instead we finished the few bottles of beer that had been left from the night before. But those few beers had been only enough to whet our appetites, and so, by nine o'clock we were worse off than when we first woke up.

We learned that it was only two miles into the nearest town, where we were told we could buy more beer. Between us we had enough money to buy a case, but no one wanted to break restriction by going after it; they were too afraid of the consequences if they got caught. I was more afraid of my hangover, I needed more beer to ward off the shakes, so I offered to take the risk. Then, thinking I would ride to town on a local bus I had seen running around the camp, I left our tent in high spirits. However, when I got near the bus-stop I saw two MPs had been stationed there, and they were checking every soldier's pass. Because of them I didn't dare chance that route. But still I couldn't give up the opportunity to get more beer either, so I struck out to walk to town. The hike was not bad going in. I made it in about thirty minutes. But carrying a full case of beer made the trip back a difficult one. Even though I drank three bottles, the case seemed to weigh a ton before I got halfway back. Then too, I had to keep ducking the beer behind bushes whenever I saw a military car go by, just in case there might be MPs in it. Regardless of the hardships though, I was back by noon and we partied the rest of the day.

All the time I was carrying the beer, hiding it behind bushes, and even when sneaking it into the tent, there was a part of me that was looking on as though he were a bystander. I could hear his admonishments faintly, but very distinctly, "You damn fool, Freeman," he said, "don't you know you could be arrested for this?" Then he went on, "Come on, Freeman, what the hell is the matter with you? Don't you remember what happened the last time you got drunk? How do you know what will happen this time if you keep drinking?"

It was like having someone at my side watching my every move, and I felt very uncomfortable when he talked to me. However, he could always be silenced with a good slug or two of beer. Then, in spite of what the sergeant had said about being court-martialed, I was drunk most of the time I spent at Camp Kilmer. There seemed to be an atmosphere permeating the entire camp that engulfed the noncommissioned officers as well as the enlisted men. Everyone appeared to have adopted the attitude:

"To hell with everything. Eat, drink and be merry, for tomorrow you may be dead".

No one seemed to be in charge, we were left to fend for ourselves most of the time. That kind of freedom gave us plenty of time to kill, and many of us spent those hours getting drunk. I was amazed at how much drinking that was going on, and I was shocked at the amount of liquor that was openly being passed around. Just as it had been in Miami, many of the soldiers who were stationed at Camp Kilmer were bootleggers, and they never seemed to run out of stock. Nobody seemed to care whose liquor it was either, nor who had paid for it. If you were there you were automatically invited to drink with everyone else.

My twenty-third birthday came while I was in Camp Kilmer, but I didn't pay much attention to it. I was partying every day anyhow, one day was the same as the next to me. However, I paid dearly for my continuous drinking. During the entire three weeks that I had to wait there I ate very little and threw up about half of the food I did eat. I became a nervous wreck, especially during the few times I couldn't get anything to drink. Most of my fingers were bleeding as I had started to bite my nails again. Fortunately though, I never missed reveille, even if I had to crawl back into bed as soon as roll call was over, a time or two.

Meanwhile, orders kept pouring out of headquarters, and soldiers were being shipped all over the world. The pace was hectic and constant. Every day, hundreds of tents that were full of men in the morning, would be empty by nightfall. Then, within a couple of days, they would be full of soldiers again. Some of them would be brand-new draftees in for their basic training. Others were like myself, just waiting for reassignment. Shipping orders seemed to be coming for everyone but me. And I hated the waiting, the not knowing. Then, even the men in the same tent with me were pulled out.

About ten o'clock in the morning on March sixth, a Saturday, one of the men in our tent received his orders and he was gone by noon. That same evening the second man was suddenly called to headquarters. He left an hour later in a convoy of twenty-five army trucks with about two hundred others. That operation was clothed in secrecy, but later, word trickled down from headquarters that they were going to an outfit in Europe to replace men who had been killed or wounded in the fighting. That news really frightened me because it made me realize that the sergeant had not been kidding when he said some of us would be sent right to the front. However, I had learned by then that a little drinking could dull my thinking, and my fears would not be so overwhelming.

When the convoy pulled out that evening, with our friend Ralph aboard, Harold and I were the only two left in our tent. Then, two days later, Harold was assigned to the motor pool at Camp Kilmer. He told me he had been a mechanic in civilian life, and he welcomed the chance to practice his trade. That afternoon I helped him pack and get his baggage in the jeep that was to take him to his new quarters. As he was going out the door for the last time, he called to me over his shoulder,

"Freeman, look under my bunk. There's something there I can't take with me. You can have it."

Immediately I was on my knees rooting in the dark under his bunk. I pulled out a half a case of beer, and I felt as though I had just been given a Christmas present. However, I had been sober for the past two days and I didn't want to get a binge started. So I pushed the beer under my own bunk for another time.

A couple of days later I was walking back from the mess hall when it began to rain. Until then the day had been beautiful. The temperature had climbed quickly to fifty-eight degrees that day, and the sun had been shining brightly. Then too, there had been a soft gentle breeze blowing that brought with it all the smells of an early spring. It looked as though it was going to be one of those near-perfect days that we get so few of. I wasn't too concerned when it first started to rain. It had begun with very light sprinkles anyway, small drops that disappeared as fast as they fell. However, as I had put on my lighter suntan uniform that day, I decided to head for my tent without delay just to be on the safe side. It turned out to be a good decision because within the next hour it was raining so hard I couldn't see three feet beyond the tent door. The sound of the rain on the canvas was rather hypnotic, and I just sat there for a while enjoying the strangeness of it all. I was amazed that the tent didn't leak a drop for all the water that was pouring down on it. With nothing to do but sit on my bunk and wait out the storm, it soon became boring and dreary. I was nursing a bottle of beer from my supply when suddenly the door burst open and a soldier jumped in. Truthfully he scared the hell out of me. We both had a good laugh though, when we realized he had jumped into the wrong tent by mistake. He was bunked in the one next to mine.

However, he had a fifth of whiskey with him, so we began to spike my bottles of beer with his liquor. We talked and laughed as the afternoon flew past, and by dinnertime we both were pretty drunk. He left me then to get his dinner, but I couldn't eat, so I fell asleep on top of my blankets.

I slept through the whole evening without anyone disturbing me, but woke with a start when a truck backfired as it went past my tent. By then, the fire had gone out in the potbellied stove, and I was chilled to the bone. I felt terrible, the early symptoms of a hangover were all present. My tongue was thick and dry, my mouth felt as though it was full of cotton, and I felt as though I was going to vomit. Shakily I got to my feet only to find that my head was pounding as though it was going to burst, I was trembling from head to foot, and my hands were shaking so badly I could hardly tie my shoes. I needed a drink in the worst way just then, but there wasn't a drop left in any one of the twelve bottles on the floor. I had money in my pocket, so I could buy beer in town if it wasn't too late. My faithful watch, the only thing about me I could depend on, told me it was five minutes to eleven. I had fifty minutes left before the bartender would publicly announce,

"Last call for drinks." I was pretty sure I could walk the two miles in thirty minutes if I hustled. That would still leave me fifteen or twenty minutes to buy a few drinks. I reasoned that even if I only had time to buy two or three

223

quick beers, the walk would have been worth
it considering the alternative. I felt
sure I couldn't live through the night
without more alcohol.

However, there was one serious problem I
couldn't avoid. It was still raining as hard as it
had been all afternoon. The streets were like
miniature rivers by then, and there was mud
everywhere! It was one of those nights that was not
fit for man or beast. Regardless of the weather, I
needed a drink. And so without thinking twice, I was
out the door and down the street.

Two minutes later I was soaked from head to
foot, but being stubborn, I would not turn back. My
small hat and raincoat were no protection whatsoever.
The rain was pouring down my face so hard at times I
couldn't see a thing. Soon the water had found its
way under my collar, and in minutes my clothes were as
wet as if I had no raincoat on at all. Luckily, I was
wearing ankle-high boots, otherwise I would have lost
them in the mud. Nevertheless, the walk had warmed me
considerably and I knew I would make it. I kept my
eyes glued on the faint light coming from the store
windows on Main Street some distance away, as though
they had me hypnotized. In that way, I was able to
put one foot in front of the other block after block.
Then, to add to my misery, the voice of my inner
companion began to berate me as soon as I left my
tent.

"Freeman, you're crazy. You can't see two feet
in front of you and yet you keep going on. Every time
you step off a curb, you land in a puddle of water
over the tops of your boots. And the horrible part is
that you are doing this because you need a drink.
You're a rummy, Freeman, a no-good drunk. Worse than
that, you're really stupid. Remember, when this is
over, you will have to walk back again. Suppose they
were looking for you while you were gone? What will
you do then? Besides, how do you know if the barroom
is even open? The bartender may have closed early

because of the weather if he wasn't doing any business. Even if he is open, he may think you're drunk enough already and refuse to serve you."

I did make it to Main Street in exactly thirty minutes that night. The barroom was still open, and I had time to buy three glasses of beer before the last call. The bartender was a pleasant fellow, and probably because I was the only customer, he gave me a free beer after closing time and we talked for an hour while he cleaned up. Then, even though it was against the law, he sold me two bottles of beer to take with me when I left. I think he felt sympathetic toward me because I had to go back out into the rain. Nevertheless, because of him, the return trip was much more pleasant than the trip in. Although the rain was as heavy, and I got just as wet as before, the voices were finally quieted. Then, when I sneaked into my tent without finding an MP waiting for me, I felt smug. I figured I had beaten the system once more.

MY ORDERS CAME THROUGH

It was about two o'clock in the morning when I finally got back from town. I was wet, and the tent was cold. I had to do something about both. I wasn't sleepy because I had slept all the evening before, so I set about getting my fire going again. By three A.M. the fire was going nicely and the tent had warmed considerably. Then, about a half hour later, I was able to bank the fire for a few hours. Only then was I comfortable enough to drift off to sleep for a while. Seven o'clock reveille found me in formation where I was supposed to be, but I was somewhat the worse for wear. However, the rain had finally stopped, and everything smelled as though the world had just been given a bath, it looked as though it was going to be a beautiful spring day.

When my name was called and I answered, "Here" the sergeant told me to report to the information desk in the headquarters building right after breakfast.

ANOTHER OPPORTUNITY

I couldn't eat much that morning, but I drank several cups of strong black coffee, and I felt less shaky as I stood in front of the information desk forty minutes later.

"Can I help you, soldier?" the clerk asked.

"My name is Private Freeman Carpenter," I answered. "I was told to report here this morning for instructions."

The corporal sorted through a stack of yellow-colored papers and pulled one out to read it. When he was satisfied he had the correct one, he handed it to me and said,

"Take this order upstairs to a Sergeant Harrison in section E. When you get to the top of the stairs, turn left and you will see section E is well-marked."

"Thank you, corporal," I said, as I quickly headed for the stairs.

As I was walking, I glanced at the papers in my hand, and my heart beat quickened. Most of the print was too small for me to read while I was walking, and I wouldn't even try, but way down near the bottom of the page, in big bold letters, were the words,

"Destination: Dow Air Force Base, Bangor, Maine". At least I wasn't going directly to the front. I had gained a moment's reprieve, I thought.

Sergeant Harrison was a wounded soldier in a wheelchair, and despite the fact he had lost his left leg, above the knee, he was pleasant and efficient. He went about his work in a consistent, methodical manner and I could not help but admire the way he wheeled himself from desk to desk as he performed his various duties. Especially I respected his pleasant manner.

"Private Carpenter, I'm Sergeant Harrison," he greeted me, his right hand extended to shake mine.

"I'm glad to meet you, sergeant," I said, as I took his hand. His grip was as firm as I expected it would be, but I was surprised at how warm his hand was.

"Look, private," the sergeant said, "there's a problem here. We have six men, including yourself, to send to Bangor, Maine. We are opening a new base there and you men are to be the advance cadre. There are two clerks, one ambulance driver, and three cooks being sent from here. Other men will be sent from different parts of the country to make up an entire regiment. You came here for reassignment and so you are now assigned to the Combat Engineers attached to the air force. Bangor, Maine, will be a training ground for you. The problem we have is that we have no noncommissioned officer to send with you. As you are the oldest man in the group, we have decided to put you in charge. It will be a chance for you to redeem yourself after that little fiasco in Florida."

I was absolutely speechless. I didn't want to take charge of anyone! I figured I had enough trouble trying to be responsible for myself, never mind anyone else! However, I had no choice in the matter. I wasn't asked how I felt about it, or if I would accept the responsibility. I was told that I was in charge.

"I can't promote you," the sergeant said, "but I can make you an acting corporal. If you handle yourself well, and discharge your responsibility properly it will not do you any harm."

"We don't want your records to be lost," the sergeant was saying, "so I'm going to entrust them to you. Please wait here and I will get them."

Five minutes later he was back. There were seven large, brown manila envelopes in his lap. I

227

could see six of them were very thick and sealed. Not only that, there were official-looking stamps on top of the seals as well. A person could not get into those records without destroying the seals or the envelope itself. My first thought on seeing them was, "They really don't trust me after all. All that talk about trust is bull". The seventh envelope was flat and unsealed. As a matter of fact, the flap was not even closed. Sergeant Harrison handed the whole pile of envelopes to me. They were heavy.

"Here are the records for each one of you, yours included. You are not to let anyone open them, nor let them out of your sight. The top envelope has your train tickets, meal vouchers, and travel orders. When you arrive at Dow Field, Bangor, Maine, you are to report to Lieutenant Richard Redkin. He is the Commanding Officer of B Company, Combat Engineers. You are to turn these records over to him no later than Saturday, March 20.

Only after he had given me all those instructions did he take me to the room where the other five men were waiting. One by one he introduced us to each other, but as usual, I immediately forgot everyone's name. With the introductions out of the way, the sergeant had more instructions for us. Addressing us as a group, the sergeant said,

"You are to be back here by fourteen hundred hours with all of your belongings. A command car has been ordered to take you to the train station. Your train leaves for Grand Central Station in New York City at fifteen hundred hours. At Grand Central Station, it will be up to acting-corporal Carpenter here, to get you to Bangor, Maine, as quickly as connections will allow. That means you all should stay close together because it would be easy to get separated, and Carpenter has all the tickets; you can't even get fed without him. Now take off," the sergeant said, "and good luck to all of you."

I was back in front of headquarters by 1:15 P.M. and anxious to be on my way. At 1:30, two of the five

228

showed up with all their gear and ten minutes after that a third man was delivered to us in a jeep. Two more men, and our group would be complete, I thought, as the command car pulled to the curb. However, those two proved to be a thorn in my side throughout the whole trip. The corporal driving the command car started bugging me to get started at about two minutes before two. I held him until three minutes past before the last two men came running down the street with their bags banging against their legs. During the last few minutes that I waited, not knowing where to look or what to do if they did not come, I got to thinking of my frustration whenever I tried to force my brother Jake into being responsible. I remembered that even my mother and father could not get him to cooperate with us. All those feeling of impotency I had felt back then were with me that day and I wanted to kill those two characters for making me feel so helpless. On the other hand, I didn't want them to know how easily they could get me upset, so I said nothing. Then, as soon as the command car pulled away from the curb, those two renegades reached into their bags and brought out a bottle of whiskey. Without even trying to hide the bottle, they proceeded to drink in front of the open window. I tried to protest in a joking sort of way but they ignored me. Not knowing what else to do about the situation, I let the whole thing drop. By the time we got to the train station, a half hour later, all five of my charges were high, and I was wishing I was. Although we made a lot of noise, and caused many a person to look at us with a jaundiced eye, we managed to get on our train in time and at three o'clock were headed north to New York City.

I had wanted to stay sober and discharge my duties, but the closer we got to New York the sillier the men were acting. It was like having a bunch of kids to take care of. I was embarrassed to be seen with them. Every effort on my part to quiet them down only invited them to use me as a butt of their jokes. When we pulled into Grand Central Station, at twenty minutes after five that evening, I was furious at them, and I let them know it. I was afraid I would lose control of them completely when I went to the ticket window to make the arrangements to get to Bangor, Maine, so I threatened to go to the MPs if they didn't stay where I told them to. That cooled them down some, but it didn't last long.

The ticket agent told me the next train going right through to Bangor, would not leave Grand Central Station until 11:50 that night. If I took any other train going east we would have to change in Boston and then again in Portland. I decided to wait for the later train and hope for the best. When the men heard we had more than five hours delay, they wanted to roam around Grand Central and see the sights. I agreed if they checked their bags and promised to be back at the train gate at eleven o'clock. I was glad to be free of them for a while because I wanted to buy a few beers for myself without them knowing it. In the nearest bar I met a couple of soldiers from Cambridge, Massachusetts, my hometown, and they helped the evening pass very quickly.

At five minutes to eleven I headed for our meeting place, but I could not resist the temptation to buy a pint of whiskey as I passed a liquor store. I knew I could easily hide that small bottle in my clothing. Three of the men were already sitting on a bench when I got there, but the two rebels were unaccounted for. At 11:15, when I could not contain my nervousness any longer, I sent two men, one in each direction to check the nearest bar. I gave them strict orders to come right back whether they had found their buddies or not. The waiting was torture for me, and I was glad I had a bottle to nip on. At eleven thirty one of the men returned to report, "No luck." Five minutes later the two missing links showed up together, on their own.

"Where the hell have you two been," I practically screamed at them. "You were told to be back here by eleven o'clock."

"What's the big deal, corporal?" one of them

asked. "We knew the train wasn't going to pull out until eleven-fifty. We still have almost fifteen minutes left."

"That's not the point," I shot back at him, "I am in charge of you, and you are obliged to carry out my orders exactly as I give them to you."

"You're a jerk, corporal," the self-appointed spokesman said, with a sneer on his face. "You worry too much."

I had a strong urge to punch him right in the mouth I was so angry. The battle to control myself was intense and I could feel myself losing it. However, the spell was broken when the gate to our train was thrown open, and a conductor hollered,

"Train boarding now for Connecticut, Massachusetts, Portland and Bangor, Maine. All aboard."

I still had one man missing, and that concern tore my mind away from the smart aleck, at least for the time being.

"Let's get aboard the train," I said, trying hard to pretend that I was still in charge.

"What about Ralph?" one of the men hollered.

"He will either get here or be left behind," I said. "What the hell more do you expect me to do?"

With that we struggled aboard the train, and found it was a pullman car. The beds were already made up for the night, and they looked inviting. It had been a long, hard day.

Just a few minutes after we got aboard, as I was stuffing my duffel bags in an overhead rack, our man Ralph came in. He was pretty drunk, and had to be helped with his bags, but he made it with about two minutes to spare. I was so relieved to have our cadre in tact once more I didn't say a word to him.

As the train slowly pulled out of the station, I took one more big drink from my bottle for a nightcap, crawled into my upper berth, and was dead to the world in a matter of minutes.

However, I was not to rest long. Around four o'clock in the morning I was rudely shaken by one of my men. It seemed the conductor wanted tickets and he could not get me up. My mind refused to function at first, but I kept forcing myself to focus on what I needed to do. It took a lot of deliberate concentration, but soon I had dug out our papers and handed the tickets to the impatient conductor. He tore off one portion, and handed the remainder back to me saying,

"Take good care of these. They will ask for them after you pass through Boston."

While I had been rooting for the tickets I was conscious that our train was at a dead standstill. Everything looked pitch-black when I looked out the window --- we seemed to be in the middle of nowhere.

"Where are we?" I asked the conductor, as he was getting someone else's tickets.

"We have just crossed the Connecticut State line," he said. "We are on a siding waiting for a troop train to pass before we can go on."

Hearing that I thought, "My God, at this rate of travel we'll never get to Bangor by the twentieth!" Then I began to worry about what "they" would do to me if I didn't meet my deadline. I didn't care for this responsibility stuff one damned bit.

I LOST ONE OF MY MEN

After the ticket incident, I slept another three hours. The men were grumbling for breakfast then, so into the dining car we went. It was while we were waiting for our breakfast to be served that the troop train we had been waiting for --- for hours --- finally went speeding by, and within minutes we were moving again. Slowly and cautiously we moved northward along the rails, giving way to other troop trains every now and then. However, there were no lengthy delays such as we had suffered in the early morning hours.

Just after breakfast, one of my men complained of feeling sick, and said he was going to lie down. I didn't think much about that. I thought he had probably drank too much booze and he was just paying the price for it. I wasn't feeling too good myself, so I dismissed him from my mind, and went for a walk to stretch my legs.

Roaming restlessly through the cars, I stopped to watch a blackjack game that was in full swing. By then I had been able to get a little of my own whiskey into my stomach and my mood was lifted somewhat. I was fascinated by the sight of all the money on the card table. There must have been at least fifty dollars in silver and more than a hundred in one dollar bills. I even saw a few fives and a couple of tens. The game was fast, and exciting. The men were having a great time with each other. They were joking and laughing uproariously. Even when they lost a hand they took their losses in good spirit and played on. I watched them for about a half hour, enjoying their exuberance and wishing I could be as expressive. Then, one of the players dropped out of the game, because he had gone broke. To my utter surprise, one of the remaining players invited me into the game. Fearfully I slipped into the empty seat. I was curious to see if I could play with these boisterous fun-loving men --- and be able to hold my own. Twenty

233

minutes later, after I had won a few hands, I knew I was hooked. Gambling had found another advocate, and I had begun a new addiction. I loved the excitement of the risk, and the rush of blood to my head, especially when I won a big hand. An hour later I was fifteen dollars ahead and completely engrossed in the game when Ralph, one of my men, came racing through the car calling my name.

"Corporal Carpenter, Corporal Carpenter, where are you?" he was frantically shouting. By the wild look in his eyes I knew there was something seriously wrong.

"What do you want?" I asked, as I jumped up from my seat to meet him.

"Carl is deathly sick," he said. "He is holding onto his stomach and screaming. I think he may be delirious because he keeps babbling, and nothing he says makes any sense. Besides, he is as hot as hell. I found that out when I put my hand on his forehead a moment ago."

When we got back to our car, the conductor was standing over Carl's bunk looking down on him.

"We had better get an ambulance for this man, corporal," he said to me.

One look at Carl's contorted face, and writhing body, and I knew the conductor was right.

"How can we do that, sir?" I asked. My own fear had made me humble for once and I was willing to listen to anyone.

"I can have the engineer radio ahead and have an ambulance meet us in the next town," he answered.

"Go ahead and do that," I said. "We will cooperate in any way we can."

I was thankful that a problem I didn't know how

to solve had been taken out of my hands.

About thirty minutes later the train stopped at a street crossing where there was a police car and an ambulance waiting. With their lights flashing, they had a long line of traffic stopped in both directions. The ambulance crew already had their stretcher out on the street, and there were about a hundred people standing around waiting to see what was going to happen. I felt helpless, and I was grateful that there were people who knew what to do.

Even before the train had come to a complete stop the ambulance crew were on board. Immediately they administered a shot of morphine to the sick man, and I saw him begin to relax. By the time they had gotten him on the stretcher and were wheeling him out, he was sleeping peacefully.

The ambulance driver wanted papers on the soldier but I wouldn't give mine up. He finally settled for the man's name and serial number, but he insisted I sign an authorization form he had filled out on a clipboard before he would go. A feeling of relief swept over me as I watched the ambulance disappear over the rise with its siren wailing. With our sick friend in good hands, our train continued on its journey north. Because of the way events unfolded during the next few days I never did find out what had been wrong with Carl, nor what eventually became of him. I was so busy worrying about my own skin I had no time to be concerned about anyone else.

I LOST OUR RECORDS

With some of the money I had won in the card game, I bought a fifth of whiskey from the conductor. It seemed that everybody was a bootlegger in those days. I passed my bottle around freely then, I didn't care who saw me drinking. "After all," I thought, "I have a tremendous responsibility on my shoulders taking care of these kids. Anybody would drink if they were in my position". The two troublemakers were almost openly defying me by then, and it was only my free booze that was keeping them somewhat in line.

While we were eating dinner we arrived at South Station, Boston. The conductor reminded us we need not change trains, but he told us we would be tied up for about three hours before we began our journey to Portland, Maine, our next stop. All five of us were in a drunken silly mood by then, and we were not really concerned about time or place anyway.

During our wait in Boston, we roamed around South Station together. I didn't dare let those men out of my sight, I didn't want a repeat of what I had endured in New York. We were going in and out of every store we came to, pestering everyone and having a great time. Sometime between seven and eight o'clock that evening I slipped into an alcoholic blackout, and couldn't even remember getting back on the train. Later I was told that the two men who had given me so much trouble, had actually carried me on board and had put me to bed. I hated hearing that, because I did not want to be indebted to those two clowns! I knew I couldn't put them on report regardless of what they would do if they had saved my neck along the way.

Sometime in the early hours of the morning, the conductor came through our car collecting tickets. It was not the same conductor who had been with us before. That fellow had been a kind and friendly person. The new man turned out to be a nasty cuss. He hated soldiers and didn't hesitate to let us know it. When he couldn't wake me up, and my men failed to find our tickets for him, he called a couple of MPs, who had boarded the train in Boston.

They woke me up all right, and they weren't gentle about the way they did it either. Then they stood off to one side and watched me with amused expressions on their faces, as I frantically went through all my things looking for our papers. My brain didn't want to function, my eyes wouldn't focus,

236

and even my legs didn't want to hold me up. I needed a drink to steady my nerves, yet I didn't dare take one in front of the MPs. The fact that I couldn't find our records was sobering me up fast though.

When I had looked everywhere, and still didn't find our papers, I began accusing my men of deliberately sabotaging my command by stealing the records from me, just to make me look bad. That kind of talk only caused me more trouble though, because one of the men lunged at me, and probably would have punched me in the face if the MPs hadn't grabbed him.

At that critical moment a major stepped into our car. One of the MPs noticed him first, and he hollered,

"Atten - tion," as he himself became rigid and snapped the officer a salute.

"What's going on here, soldiers?" the major asked the MP as he returned his salute.

"We were just trying to help these soldiers find their train tickets sir," the MP answered. The major looked us over carefully, one by one, without saying a word. Meantime I didn't dare take a breath I was so terrified. After what seemed like hours of silence, the major finally said,

"At ease, men."

With that permission the air I had been holding in my lungs burst forth in a rush, and at the same time I felt weak in the knees. The fear I always felt in the presence of authority engulfed me, and I began to sweat profusely. The stern look on the officer's face did nothing to allay my fears.

"Which one of you soldiers is Corporal Carpenter?" the major asked. A flash of additional fear shot through me like a bolt of lightning when I realized that somehow he knew my name.

"Here sir," I answered timidly, and I was shocked to hear how my voice trembled! I was embarrassed too, because I knew everyone else heard the trembling as well, including the major.

"Were you placed in charge of these men?" he asked.

"Yes, sir," I answered.

"Were you given their records when you left your last station?" he inquired.

Again I had to answer, "Yes sir."

"Do you know where those records are now?" he continued.

"No sir," I said, "I have searched everywhere for them. I think someone stole them from me while I slept."

"No one stole those records, soldier," he shouted. "You left them on a chair in the dining car last evening!"

I realized immediately how he knew my name --- he had picked up our records! My concern then was why he did, and what he was going to do next.

"I watched all of you make fools of yourselves in the dining car last evening," he said, sweeping all of us with his eyes. "You are a disgrace to the uniform you have on," he continued. "I could have you arrested right now, all of you, especially you Corporal Carpenter. Did you know you could be shot for something like this during war time?" he asked.

I didn't dare answer him, but I don't think he expected an answer anyway. I felt like a worm under his verbal onslaught and I was wishing desperately for that unpleasant scene to be over and done with.

"We are too busy with the war effort to spend

any time on the likes of you," the major said.   "I
have decided not to have you arrested, only because I
don't want to be tied down prosecuting you. Instead,
I have confiscated your records," he continued, as he
looked me right in the eyes. I felt his steely eyes
burning a hole right through me.

"Evidently you can't be trusted even with a
simple command, corporal, and your men are no better.
I happen to know your commander at Dow Field
personally, so I will turn your records over to him
myself when I get back to base next week," he said.

While I was standing there, feeling very
uncomfortable, and mulling over everything that was
going on, the major was scribbling a note, using the
wall for support. Everyone else was standing just as
they had been, waiting for the major's next move.
When the note was finished, the major folded it, put
it in an envelope, sealed it, and handed it to me.

"If you don't lose this," he said, with a sneer
on his face, "give it to your company commander when
you report in.   I hope he throws you in the
guardhouse, it might do you some good."

Then, reaching inside his jacket, he pulled out
another white envelope.

"I am going to give you your train tickets and
your meal vouchers," he said, "you will need them if
you want to eat." He stood silent for a full minute
after giving me the train tickets; he kept looking
directly at me as though he was trying to decide what
to do or say next. Finally he said,

"Corporal, the least you could do now would be
to complete your mission like a soldier. I hope you
can do that for your own sake." Without waiting for
me to reply, the major turned his back on us and
slipped through the car door. He was gone just as
suddenly as he had appeared.

Almost immediately the two MPs moved toward the

door. They acted as though they too wanted to be away from that whole scene. I felt completely exhausted after that encounter. After all, I was in deep trouble with the military over my lack of responsibility, and could even spend some time in the guardhouse over it. I had been humiliated in front of my men, two MPs, and a handful of civilian passengers. I was in serious trouble with my men for accusing them of stealing the records from me, and I had a terrible hangover.

Dealing with first things first, I knew I had to square things with the men. Swallowing my pride was almost impossible, but I knew if I let too much time go by I would not do it, so I turned off my mind and opened my mouth,

"Look men," I said, "I'm sorry I panicked when I could not find our records. I had no right to accuse you of taking them. Even when I was saying it I knew you didn't. I was just scared. I'm also sorry I drank a little too much last night. I usually don't do that," I lied.

To my pleasant surprise the men were not very mad at me. The major had been so nasty to all of us that we now had a common enemy to focus on.

"That's OK corporal," Ralph said, "we knew you really didn't believe we stole your records. Let's forget it. It's finished as far as I'm concerned."

"That's OK with me, too," one of the rebels said. The other two just nodded their heads in assent and it was over.

"Thank you, men," I said, "we are going to get along much better from now on, I'm going to see that we do."

"That damn major didn't have to keep our records," Ralph said, "all he needed to do was to bawl us out and give our papers back to us."

There developed a lot of speculation on the major's character and what would happen to each of us when we arrived at Dow Air Base without identification. The common bond we felt brought us closer together and we began to function more as a group.

Noontime found us in Portland, Maine, and although my hangover was killing me, I hadn't taken a drink all morning. The experience of losing our records had made me very conscious of how dangerous to me my drinking had become.

We were still shaken by everything that had happened, so when the train stopped in Portland, we did not get off to stretch our legs. Instead we went to the dining car and had lunch. It turned out to be rather a quiet meal compared to the ones we had previously. We were a frightened, subdued bunch of soldiers that day, each with his own particular concern.

Forty-five minutes after we had pulled into Portland, we were headed northeast again, and I found the closer we got to Bangor, the higher my level of anxiety became. I knew it was because I was going to have to answer for my foolishness there, and I was afraid of the consequences. Anxious or not we kept going, and the miles continued to disappear under our wheels.

Nevertheless, we found ourselves sidetracked four more times to let troop trains, headed south, have the right of way. But we did get into Bangor at four o'clock.

BANGOR MAINE

Inside the station, behind a ticket counter, there stood a tall, thin man that looked to be about ninety-years old. His hair was snow white, very thick and it looked as though he hadn't combed it for days.

241

He wore a pair of heavy, thick glasses that seemed to have several layers of glass in them. The striped white and blue shirt, the shoe-string necktie, and the black vest he wore, opened, all helped to make him look like a character out of a comic strip. Regardless of his appearance though, he proved to be a friendly gentleman who was eager to be of assistance. He not only told us how to get to Dow field, he even came out from behind the counter, took us outside onto the street, and showed us where to catch the local bus.

Three miles, about twenty local stops, and thirty minutes later, the bus let us off at the main gate of the airfield. When we presented ourselves to the guards on duty, without any identification papers, they didn't know what to do with us. It took them over an hour to find out we belonged across the field in a section that was just being built. We could see the outlines of unfinished barracks about two miles away, on the extreme edge of the field, next to a wooded area that looked rather ominous.

Meantime, while they were trying to unscramble the mystery we had handed them, they allowed us to eat dinner in their huge mess hall. Then, when the meal was over we were driven to the new area in a jeep by one of the guards. He let us off in front of an orderly room that was empty and locked, and told us we were on our own.

"Where will we sleep, sergeant?" I asked as I noticed not one building was ready to receive occupants.

"You got your pup tents, don't you?" the sergeant asked.

"Yes, but it is too cold to sleep out here," I answered.

"That's what you think, soldier," he said. "You will use your pup tents often out here, you might as well start now and get used to it!"

Then he slammed his jeep in gear brutally and disappeared down the dirt road in a cloud of dust. In less than a minute even his tail-light could not be seen. We were at the end of the world, or so it felt like we were, and we were alone.

There was no electricity in the buildings, and it was getting dark fast. A loud thrashing in the woods right behind us scared us out of our wits, and in less time than it took to think about it, we had jimmied open a window and got inside the empty orderly room.

Evidently, we were the first men to arrive at our new headquarters. There wasn't another soul around as far as we could tell. There were no guards on duty in that forlorn area, and even Lieutenant Redkin, the officer I was to report to could not be located. I was glad about that though, for it gave me more time to come up with a story that might make some sense to explain my predicament when I stood in front of him.

It was getting too dark to see anything then, and we were becoming nervous about how to spend the night in that foreign environment. Looking the empty building over, we found a potbellied stove, set up and ready to go, in one of the back rooms. Scrounging around outside we found plenty of scrap wood that had been left by the contractors, and within half an hour we had a cheerful fire burning. The fire not only warmed the building, it also gave us some light to see by. That night we slept on the hard floor, fully dressed, with our duffel bags for pillows. Nevertheless, we were all tired and fell asleep quickly.

By seven o'clock Saturday morning we were all awake and hungry. I decided to walk the two miles to the mess hall with my men and go in as though we belonged there. I reasoned that they were feeding so many we wouldn't even be noticed. I guessed right, no one asked us who we were, and breakfast was great.

With breakfast over we went to report to the orderly room to find out if our commanding officer was around. No one could answer that question for us, but they said they were still looking for him. We were told to go back to our area and stay there. Then, when we complained about not having any bedding, a sergeant wrote out a requisition slip and sent us to his supply room. There, each one of us was given two blankets and a pillow. "At least it will be a little more comfortable to sleep tonight", I thought, "even if we do sleep on the floor again"!

When we got back to our area it was about eight-thirty, and we found the place a beehive of activity. There must have been at least two hundred workmen crawling all over the unfinished buildings. The echoes of so many hammers at work, in the crisp morning air, generated an excitement in all of us. I spent the day drifting from one work crew to another, just watching the men at work. I even helped some carpenters a couple of times, but almost everyone was afraid of either a problem with the union, or an insurance gripe if I should happen to get hurt, so I was kept out of many of the work areas. Nevertheless, I was offered a bottle of beer two different times, and one fellow had a gallon of port wine that he offered me a drink out of more than once, but I wouldn't take any. Each time I refused though, I had strong mixed feelings. On the one hand I was proud of my strength, but I also felt cheated in some way. The question was always in the back of my mind, "Why can't I learn how to drink alcohol like other men do"? And the other idea was forever present with the question, "Just you wait, I'll show everybody soon, I will learn how to handle my liquor some day, by God". Then too, I was always embarrassed whenever I refused a drink from anybody, I had the feeling that people could look at me and know I had a problem with alcohol, that I was less than a man because of it. In spite of all that though, Saturday was a good day for me. However, at four o'clock sharp everybody laid their tools down and went home.

Being left alone again, with nothing to do, we

made the long trek back to the mess hall for dinner. The excitement from the day's activities lasted all through dinner. It must have been contagious, because everyone in the mess hall that evening seemed to be friendlier than usual. We even got a ride back to our orderly room by a pleasant warrant officer with a jeep.

However, once back in our orderly room, a strange feeling of being let down crept over us. After all the activity I had witnessed throughout the day, the area looked and felt like a ghost town, it was so completely deserted. Nevertheless, it was easier bedding down that night because we knew enough about getting the fire going, and we had our blankets and pillows for comfort.

Early the next morning we woke up to a beautiful day, the more impressive to me because I had been city-bred most of my life. Although it was quite cold outdoors, the sun was a huge red ball that seemed to be hanging in mid-air on the edge of the horizon. The sky was a shade of light blue I had never seen before, and to add to the breathtaking splendor, there wasn't a cloud to be seen anywhere. And if anything more was really needed, there was the aroma of innumerable green trees, early wildflowers, and new shrubs, gently drifting over us from the woods just a few feet away. Being that close to nature reminded me of the few happy years I had spent in the country as a child. A feeling of wonder engulfed my soul, and I stood alone in the yard for some time just drinking in the marvel of it all. The magic spell was finally broken by my noisy buddies as they came charging out of the building heading for their breakfast. With some difficulty I was able to bring myself back to the present and join them.

Much to our pleasant surprise, while we were at breakfast, the workmen had returned to continue their building. I spent Sunday in much the same way as I had spent the day before, that is, until about three o'clock. It was then, that five army buses pulled into our area and more than two hundred soldiers piled out with all their gear. The first company of what was to become a new battalion of combat engineers had arrived.

When the noncommissioned officers in charge found that there weren't any barracks ready for their men, they immediately marched them a quarter of a mile into the woods and made them set up their pup tents. An hour later three large army trucks came rumbling into the bivouac area. Two of those trucks contained the cooking equipment such as field ranges, pots and pans, and plenty of food. The mess tent, and an officer's tent were in the third truck, and both those tents were up in less than an hour. One of the sergeants had taken command of my small group and ordered us out of the orderly room and into the bivouac area. We had no choice but to dig out our pup tents and set up with the others. It was very frightening sleeping on the ground, in the woods, but our blankets made a soft mat for us and with so many men around, it wasn't as scary as I first thought it might be. Still, every little noise woke me the first two nights. After that it was not too bad, but it lasted longer than I hoped it would. It was three days before the first barracks was ready for us and it was over a week before the last man had a bunk in a barracks. However, with the coming of that first company, the commanding officers began to show up and I finally got to meet Lieutenant Redkin.

He arrived on Monday morning the 22nd of March, while we were at breakfast. He came into the woods, introduced himself, and even had breakfast out of his mess kit with us. After the meal was over he asked the four sergeants, who had been in charge of the company, and myself, to report to him in the orderly room at ten o'clock.

We arrived on schedule, and found the orderly room was no longer bare of furniture. There were four desks, one in each room, a chair behind each desk, two long benches just inside the door, and even a couple of telephones. The lieutenant had his office set up in the room with the stove, the room we had used to sleep in. He was behind his desk talking into one telephone, while the other phone kept ringing persistently, when we all barged in. Quickly he ordered us to wait in the outer office until he called for us.

Using the benches to sit on, the four sergeants began to chat among themselves. They ignored me completely, and I felt uncomfortable in their presence. Withdrawing into my shell, I began to go over what I would tell the lieutenant about the mess I had made of my assignment. The full impact of my predicament hit me then. I realized I didn't know the full name of the soldier who had been taken off the train. I knew his first name was Carl, but because I had no records that is all I knew. More than that, I didn't know what the name of the hospital was they had taken him to, nor the town in which the train had stopped for the ambulance. I could not think of any way to explain that stupidity to my new commander except to tell the truth. However, I knew I would only tell enough of the truth to get by, and I would tell it in such a way that I wouldn't look like an imbecile.

By eleven o'clock the lieutenant had interviewed three of the four sergeants, and I was thankful he seemed to be saving me for last. Just the same, the waiting was torture. The last sergeant was called into the lieutenant's office at eleven-fifteen, and with his report given he was out the door by eleven-thirty-five. For the next ten minutes everything was deadly quiet in the orderly room. I could hear bulldozers in the distance, men were shouting orders to each other, and the echoes of hammers on wood filled the air. But, there wasn't a sound from the inner office, and I began to feel most uneasy. I was just beginning to wonder if the lieutenant had forgotten me, when he shouted my name.

"Private Carpenter," he hollered.

I almost tipped the bench over I jumped up so

quickly. On entering his office, I stood directly in front of his desk, at attention, and snapped him an excellent salute, as I said,

"Private Freeman Carpenter reporting, sir."

"At ease private," he said. As I relaxed somewhat, he spoke again,

"What's this I hear about you losing all the records that had been entrusted to you?"

"Well sir, I didn't exactly lose them," I answered, "A major took them from a chair in the dining car where I had left them for a short time."

"That isn't what I heard," he said, "why would a major take them and not give them back to you?" he asked.

"Maybe this note will explain sir," I said, as I handed him the envelope the major had given me. The lieutenant read the note quickly, then turned to me and said,

"Private, the major says that your men were so unruly, and your behavior was so unbecoming a soldier he recommends I court-martial you. What do you say about that?"

"We were a little rowdy, sir, but no more so than many other groups of soldiers we met," I answered. "We were all so excited about being transferred out of an unpleasant situation and anxious to get into the action we may have acted pretty silly in public and I am sorry about that."

"Do you know how serious your predicament is, private?" the lieutenant asked in a stern voice.

"Yes sir --- I do sir. I am sorry about how things turned out, and I am angry at myself," I answered. After a moment of deep thought, the lieutenant said,

"I need time to think about all of this. In the meantime consider yourself confined to the area until I send for you again. Report to the mess sergeant, you are going to be one of our cooks."

I was so relieved he hadn't asked me about Carl, the sick soldier, or that he hadn't thrown me right in the guardhouse I said

"Thank you for your consideration, sir."

"Private, you're dismissed," the lieutenant said. Not wanting to press my luck any further I spun on my heels and got out of his office as fast as I could.

For some strange reason, even though I knew I would be called in front of the commander for punishment, a calm settled over me. Every morning I was up at four o'clock working on the field ranges, cooking breakfast. Sleeping outdoors was making me feel healthy and alive. I soon learned that as a cook I was becoming popular with the men and I liked that. Then too, I found the desire to drink had disappeared. I had no trouble refusing the several drinks well-meaning buddies kept offering me. It was odd too, because every day new soldiers were arriving and many of them had plenty of booze with them. A new self-confidence was invading my being.

Three days after I had been assigned to the mess hall, on Thursday, March 25th, without any warning, the mess sergeant told me to report to the company commander. My days of waiting were over.

As soon as I stepped into the commander's office, I recognized the stack of folders on his desk. They were the records the major had confiscated from me the week before. Lieutenant Redkin was behind his desk, but he was engrossed in a pile of paper work. I became very uncomfortable as I waited. It was about ten long minutes before he put his pen down and looked up at me.

"Well Private Carpenter," he said, "we finally got the records for your men."

"I see, sir," I said, "I am glad they got here all right."

"They didn't get here, private," he said, "Major Crabtree brought them to me. He also brought me a firsthand account of what he had seen that day, and he told me why he felt obliged to pick up the records."

"I agree with the major when he says a court-martial would be the most effective way to teach you how to become a soldier."

"Having decided that a court-martial is in order in your case," he said, "I am obliged to tell you, you have a choice between a general or a summary court-martial."

"What would be the difference between the two, sir?" I asked.

"Well!" he said, "in a general court-martial you would have a high-ranking officer sit in as judge. There would be a panel of officers for a jury, and you would be represented by a military lawyer. Of course there would be a military prosecutor. A trial would take place, the charges read, the evidence presented, and your lawyer would defend you the best way he could. Then, if you didn't think the verdict of the court was fair, you could have your lawyer appeal to a higher court. It would be similar to our civilian courts when you have a 'trial by jury'."

The telephone rang just then and the lieutenant answered it with obvious annoyance. After listening for a moment he mumbled a "Yes" and hung up. Immediately he picked the phone up again and said,

"Sergeant, I told you not to put any calls through to me unless they were of the utmost importance. Please see that I am not disturbed again until I tell you I'm free."

Slamming the phone down almost hard enough to break it, he glared at me without saying a word. I became a little more frightened then, when I realized the lieutenant considered my situation important enough to cancel all of his calls in order to deal with me.

However, I had no time to think about that because the lieutenant barked, "Where were we, private?"

"You were just going to tell me what a summary court-martial was, sir," I answered.

"Oh yes," he said, "a summary court-martial is an informal affair. One officer would preside over the proceedings, in this case it would be me. There would be no prosecutor, and you would have no representation. It would simply be a case of pleading guilty to the charges and throwing yourself on the mercy of the court. The judgment of the presiding officer would be final. You would have no appeal."

When the lieutenant had finished, there was a heavy silence in the room that lasted for almost a full minute, and the temperature seemed to climb suddenly to a hundred degrees. I was beginning to feel sick to my stomach from the tension and I was thankful when the commander broke the spell.

"Do you have any questions about any of this, Private Carpenter?" he asked.

"No sir," I answered. "You made it all pretty clear."

My mind was traveling about ninety miles an hour over all the possibilities and risks of either court-martial. As afraid of authority as I was I didn't want to become a spectacle, nor did I want a circus created around me. I felt sure that was just what a general court-martial would become. I decided right there to take my chances with Lieutenant Redkin. I had just made up my mind when the commander said,

"Private Carpenter, have you decided which of the two court-martials you would prefer?" he asked.

"Yes sir," I said. "I would rather take the summary court-martial. I am guilty of dereliction of duty and I would like to get this over with as quickly and as quietly as possible."

"Very well," the lieutenant said. "Go back to work and I will let you know the date of your trial. There will be some preparation necessary, some paper work to be done first. In the meantime," he continued, "you are still confined to the area and I will be watching you closely."

"I understand, sir," I said, "and thank you sir."

"Dismissed private," the commander said.
And I almost ran back to my sanctuary, the mess hall -- the waiting went on.

I settled into a daily routine again, not daring to even think of the upcoming trial. I felt like a zombie living in kind of a trance. The urge to drink had completely left me and I considered that proof of the fact I could take it or leave it as I choose. A couple of times though, when I had been offered a drink and I had nobly said "No thanks," a touch of jealousy would shoot through me because "they" could party and I could not. Then, for a day or two I would be in a blue funk, and take it out on everyone around me.

Three weeks later, on a Friday, the mess sergeant told me I was to report to the lieutenant's office on Tuesday, April 20th, at ten o'clock in the morning for my court-martial.

"Wear your class A uniform," he said, "and for God's sake don't be late!"

All that weekend I was too nervous to eat, and

too restless to sleep more than three hours each night. By Tuesday morning, I was biting my finger nails and talking to myself out loud.

Nevertheless, I reported to the commander's office at ten o'clock sharp. My uniform was neatly pressed, my shoes were shined, and I looked a lot better than I felt. The lieutenant was waiting by the door for me and he was alone. He motioned me into his office and closed the door behind me. I waited until he had walked behind his desk before I came to attention and offered him a salute.

"At ease soldier," he said, as he returned my salute and sat down.

Picking up some official looking papers he read aloud,

"The Summary Court-Martial of Private Freeman Carpenter is now in session.

Private Carpenter, on March the eighteenth of this year, in the performance of your duty, and while you were an acting corporal in charge of five enlisted men, you have been charged with the following offenses:

(1) Dereliction of duty during wartime
(2) Conduct unbecoming a soldier
(3) Public drunkenness, and
(4) Endangering the safety of your men.

How do you plead, soldier?" the lieutenant asked.

"Guilty on all counts sir," I answered.

"Private Carpenter, it is the judgment of this court that you forfeit one-third of your base pay for a period of three months, and that you serve six months in the stockade on the main base of Dow Field, Bangor, Maine."

My knees turned weak, and my heart fell to the bottom of my stomach. I was going to jail again! I didn't know if I could survive six months of confinement! I had counted on my assessment of the lieutenant's nature, I had guessed he would be lenient if I was honest and remorseful. I had been wrong.

"Private Carpenter," the lieutenant said, "I am going to give you a break this once. I have been watching you work in the mess hall since you were assigned to that post. You have performed well. The mess sergeant has given me a good report on you too. He says you are not afraid of work and you do know how to cook. Because of that, and because you would be no good to me in the guardhouse, I am going to suspend both the fine and the sentence for six months. During that time if your behavior continues to be what it has been, I will drop the charges and clear your record. Do you think you can honor my trust and redeem yourself?" he asked.

"Yes sir," I said. "I can and I will. You won't be sorry for giving me another chance."

"Remember," the lieutenant said, "you are still confined to the area and will be for a long time. There is no need for you to ask for a pass, I would just refuse it."

"I understand sir," I answered.

"Very well, change your uniform and get back to work," the commander said. "The mess sergeant needs you."

I was ecstatic all the rest of that day and the next! I went to work with a new enthusiasm, being the first man on the job each morning and the last one to leave after dinner in the evening. I was determined to make the lieutenant proud of me and prove to him I was trustworthy. Regardless of my good intentions though, I could not keep up the pace I had set for myself very long.

During the week that followed, the other cooks were talking about going to town on the weekend, and a couple of them, not knowing about my restriction, asked me to go with them. Of course I told them I couldn't go, and I told them why. That proved to be a mistake because they began to tease me then, and I became the butt of many of their jokes. They were only trying to have a bit of fun with me, but being as supersensitive as I was then, I could not take it. I began to feel sorry for myself, and concluded that everyone, including the lieutenant, were treating me unfairly. I withdrew into my shell as I usually did under similar circumstances, and stopped talking to everybody. I began to work with a vengeance, taking my frustrations out on the pots and pans. A few times one or another of the men would try to talk to me, but I would snap at them angrily and soon they left me alone. Another whole week like that and I began to think of drinking again. I also began the same old reasoning; that I could handle my drinking differently if I was careful! "After all", I told myself, "you really have learned your lesson this time. You almost got yourself thrown in the guardhouse. You can't afford to take any more chances". The more I talked to myself the more convinced I became I could handle my liquor as other men handled theirs. I soon found a way to put my theory to a test.

Although I couldn't leave the base, I could go to the Post Exchange, and I found they served beer there. The next Friday evening I was in the beer hall mingling with all the other soldiers and trying to fit in somewhere. After the first drink or two I began to loosen up and to feel alive. I began talking and laughing with everybody. I had a good time all evening and did not get drunk, just high. However, the next morning at work, I realized the risk I had taken with my unpredictable nature and promised myself I would not do that again. I may have been able to keep that promise, at least for a while, but for my co-workers.

All during the following week they kept talking about the fun they had in town, and all the girls they had met. Their stories made me feel I was missing out on all the fun and I didn't like that. I began to feel my restriction was too severe for what I had done. "After all", I told myself, "I hadn't asked to be put in charge of those men, the duty had been forced on me". I began to wonder if I dare desert the army and take my chances of getting away with it. I thought about running away all that week, and the idea began to look very attractive to me. I might have acted on it too, if something else hadn't come along that offered a diversion.

Right after work that Friday evening a co-worker showed me a large hole that had been cut in the link-fence surrounding our base. That hole was being used by many a restricted soldier as a back door out of camp. We were in town drinking beer in a barroom by six o'clock that same evening. As time passed, we moved from bar to bar and met several local girls. We both got mildly drunk, had a good time and sneaked back into camp through the fence without getting caught. I was sure then I had found a way to make my army life bearable. I wasn't too worried about my restriction, I just told myself I would be careful and not allow myself to get into any trouble. There were several military police in town, but there were so many soldiers the MPs didn't bother anyone unless they caused a ruckus. I had promised myself that, not only would I not start anything, if there was even a hint of others starting something I would get away from them fast. I had it all figured out, or so I thought I had.

There were a few times I drank more than I should have but those times I guess I was just lucky. Once though, I had to make a sharp left turn to go down a side street to avoid meeting my commanding officer face-to-face. I shuddered to think of what would have happened if I hadn't seen him first.

Meantime, more soldiers kept arriving daily. Within a short time our battalion of four companies was complete. Our heavy equipment began to arrive before we were there three weeks. There were huge graders on flatbed railroad cars, and bulldozers on trucks. Everything we would need to build roads, bridges, and even airplane runways, was eventually sent to us. We were told we were there to learn how to operate those big machines, and we didn't have much time to do so.

As a result of our mission, we spent most of the six months I was there, deep in the woods, sleeping in our pup tents at night. We would spend two weeks on bivouac in the wilds, then return to base for one week to get cleaned up and refreshed. Then it was back to the woods again for two more weeks of training. In a short period of time we had bulldozed a road through the woods from one small town to another that was about seven miles long. Then, deep in the woods near the road, on top of a high hill, we built a runway two miles long that could accommodate large aircraft. It was an impressive piece of engineering even if no plane ever landed on it. Years later, I went back there and found the road had never been used either, and both the road and the runway had been reclaimed by nature. Only faint traces of hard-top here and there gave me a hint as to where we had done our work.

Even though we spent most of our time in the woods, that didn't stop some of us from getting into town on Friday or Saturday nights! The fact that we were forty miles into the wilderness didn't bother us at all. We would hitchhike rides in, and pool our money sometimes to hire a cab back. We always knew where the bivouac area was in general, but never where our tents were specifically. And so, it was not unusual for us to stumble around in the pitch-black woods, bumping into other tents and waking a lot of soldiers up before we found our own! Several of our buddies would be mad at us the next day for falling on their tent in the dark at two o'clock in the morning!

As I kept sneaking out of camp again and again without anyone challenging me I began to think I was very smart. That maybe I was above all those things that govern other people. As a result, I got bolder and bolder with my drinking. In a short time I was getting drunk as I always had, and it was not unusual for me to find myself back in camp, after drinking in town, and not know how I had gotten there, or when I had come in. The awareness of my blackouts scared me very much, but I pushed those concerns aside, not knowing what else to do about them. Then, I did something else that changed my life dramatically and almost got me thrown out of the army.

I GOT MARRIED

Bangor was not a very big city. There were only a handful of places that welcomed soldiers, and there was only one place large enough to accommodate the hundreds of soldiers that came in from Dow Field. That place was called "The Chateau". It was a redbrick building, two stories high, and almost a block long. It had a five-foot moat along one side, and many a soldier got wet by falling into it because he was drunk, or because someone pushed him in for a lark. Two wooden bridges, each about four feet wide, with handrails that were waist-high, led one over the moat and into the two large entrances. Once inside one discovered that the building was a combination bowling alley, restaurant, beer parlor, and dance hall. We soldiers spent most of our free time, and much of our hard-earned money in that place. It was there that many an army romance got it's start, for there were dozens of local girls there every night. It was there, on my first night in town, that I met Irene.

The first time or two that I met Irene I paid little attention to her. I had always been shy around girls, and anyway, I was more interested in my drinking just then. Besides, there were so many girls around I felt safe, as though I didn't have to be sociable to anyone in particular. However, Irene was there everytime I got in town and she seemed to be paying more attention to me than any other soldier. It wasn't long before I began to look forward to seeing her.

Irene was eighteen years old, five-foot five, one-hundred nineteen pounds, shapely, and very pretty. But it was her beautiful auburn hair that really caught my eye. Except for my mother's hair, before she had it cut, I had never seen such a full head of hair. Shoulder-length hair was popular with most girls then, but not with Irene. Her hair fell in loose casual waves down her back to her waist. It framed her whole face, and at times created the illusion that I was looking at a picture rather than a real person. We began to spend all the time together that we could. Of course I didn't tell her about my restriction and how I was risking my freedom by breaking it. In fact I didn't tell her anything about myself that might jeopardize our friendship. Another thing about Irene that I found comforting --- she never said anything about my drinking, even though I got drunk many times when we were together. That was all the more strange to me because Irene didn't drink much herself, one glass of beer usually lasted her all evening. However, there were nights when I didn't have any money to drink with, and those evenings were spent sitting by the river just enjoying each other's company. As the relationship became more intimate I began to rave about Irene to the other men in the mess hall. One day a corporal, who I guess got tired of hearing me, said,

"Freeman, why the hell don't you marry the girl if you are so stuck on her? If you don't, as soon as you get shipped out, she will find another soldier and forget all about you."

I had never thought of marriage, but I remembered how I had lost Veronica to my brother Jake not too many months before. I got to thinking that marriage was one sure way of keeping Irene to myself regardless of what happened to me in the army.

The very next Saturday, the last Saturday in May, I went to town as usual, had a few beers, met Irene, proposed marriage, and was accepted. I didn't go back to camp that weekend, I stayed in a hotel with Irene. We had planned to be married the following

Monday, but we found out it was not that simple. First we were told we had to get a blood test, and then we had to wait at least five days after we had filed our intentions. Besides, the Justice of the Peace said he would not be free to perform the ceremony until Saturday. The good news was that the authorities did not have to inform my commander because I was over twenty-one. But I did not dare go back to camp then --- I was afraid if I did, I would not get out again for any reason. So Irene and I hid out all week in an apartment that belonged to one of her girlfriends. Then, at four o'clock in the afternoon, Saturday, June 5th 1943, we were quietly married in the Justice's private home. Through it all though, I didn't feel right hiding so much about myself from Irene. I was afraid if I got arrested she would find out what kind of a phony she had hooked up with, and I might lose her.

But I was not the only one that was hiding things. Irene had a few secrets of her own that I got to know, one by one, as our relationship deepened. However, I was not prepared to hear the unpleasant news she unfolded the night before our wedding. That evening, after all the plans had been made, and our two witnesses had been lined up, Irene said she had something to talk to me about. She had such a strange, serious look on her face I became puzzled and nervous.

"What's wrong, honey?" I asked.

"Well," she said, "last year I was going steady with this fellow and I became pregnant. When he found out about it he deserted me and joined the army. My father threw me out of the house when he found out about it, and if my aunt hadn't taken me in I don't know what I would have done." She threw herself over on the bed then, and began sobbing her heart out into the pillow.

I was filled with compassion for her, and I began searching for some words of comfort but could

find none. I was speechless. After a few minutes
Irene sat up, and with tears flowing down her face she
said,

"Freeman, if you want to call off the wedding
before it's too late I will understand."

A strong urge to protect and take care of her
came over me, a feeling similar to the one I had years
before when I had looked into the face of my newborn
baby sister, Lisa. I took Irene in my arms, and
assured her I would not desert her as others had. I
promised her I would love and care for her. As I lay
awake next to her that night I felt a sense of power I
had never experienced before. I realized I had found
a beautiful woman who needed me in spite of my flaws.
We were married the next day.

Our marriage started off with several strikes
against it though. First there was my being absent
from my post while on restriction and probation. Next
was the fact that Irene knew almost nothing about me
and I knew as little about her. Then there was money.
I was only earning twenty-one dollars a month as a
soldier, and even that might be taken away from me.
Although Irene could earn a good paycheck at a local
shoe factory, she was out of work at the moment. The
night we were married, after we had paid the Justice
of the Peace a modest fee of five dollars, we had a
fifth of whiskey, and fifteen cents left to our name
to face the whole world with! Luckily we had rented a
large furnished room, in a private home, for three
dollars a week. We had enough money in the beginning,
between us, to pay for that room for three weeks in
advance. Then, Irene was able to borrow some money
from a girlfriend and we used that to eat on during
the following week. For the next seven days, except
for going out a few times to get a bite to eat, we
spent our honeymoon in our room.

Irene knew I was playing hookey from camp, but
she had no idea just how much trouble I was in, and I
didn't tell her. She seemed as glad to have me with
her as I was to be there, so we didn't talk of my

going back. However, I began to feel uneasy about my freedom and believed it was just a matter of time before I would be arrested. But when fifteen days had gone by and I had not been picked up by the military police, paranoia set in, accompanied by periods of anxiety. Any unusual or loud noise in the house made me jump, and many nights I would wake with a start thinking I had heard someone call my name. I became a nervous wreck in a short time, and I knew that for the sake of my sanity I was either going to have to run away from it all or turn myself in. I found I could not leave Irene, nor could I ask her to be a party to my desertion. The bottom line was that I really had no choice. Regardless of the consequences, I was going to have to surrender to the military.

However, I wanted credit for coming in voluntarily and I knew I wouldn't get that credit if I allowed myself to be arrested by the military police. It was common knowledge our company commander was a married man and that he had an apartment in town with his wife. I knew where his apartment was and I reasoned that if I turned myself in to him, he would have to admit I came to him for help. I got his telephone number from information and called his home. His wife told me he would be home that day for lunch at noon and I could see him then. Without telling her who I was or what I wanted, I told her I would be there at twelve-thirty.

Lieutenant Redkin was surprised to see me. It was written all over his face as he opened the door to my knock.

"Freeman, what the hell do you want?" he sputtered. "I thought you would be miles away from here by now."

"I did think about running away sir, but my conscience would not let me," I answered. "I want to turn myself in for being absent these last two weeks. I can't live as a haunted man --- I'd rather be in jail if I have to."

He invited me in then, and over a sandwich and coffee he began to ask me a lot of questions about myself before I joined the army. I found myself talking to him about my childhood, my parents, and about a lot of personal things. He made me feel most uncomfortable and so I was on guard and nervous. I felt as though I was going through an interrogation, and that the lieutenant was probing into things that had nothing to do with him and were none of his business. I deeply resented his questioning, but was too afraid of his authority to tell him so. Instead, I tried to tell him as little as possible and still satisfy his curiosity. Needless to say, I was less than truthful. We spent over an hour together, and in spite of myself I told him more than I had ever told anyone. I even told him about my marriage and of my dreams of making a life with my wife after the war was over. The lieutenant never asked me about my drinking and I was grateful for that. I wouldn't have told him the truth anyway. That was one area of my life I would not allow anyone to look at too closely, not even myself. Finally, after what seemed like an eternity, the lieutenant said,

"Freeman, I am not going back to camp until four o'clock. Why don't you go back to your bride and come back here at three forty-five. You can go through the gates with me and you won't be arrested."

"Thank you Lieutenant Redkin," I said, "but what happens to me if I get stopped by an MP? I have no papers of any kind."

The lieutenant bent over the table and on a personal notepad wrote me a temporary one-day pass. Handing it to me he said,

"This will cover you until four o'clock today, not a minute more."

Again I thanked him and could not get out of there fast enough. I felt great. As difficult as it had been, I had made the first step in getting my life back on track.

When I got back to Irene, I told her I might be
restricted for a short while but that things would
work out all right.   I told her our commanding officer
was a kind and understanding man.   I only wish I could
have believed all that bull myself.   I knew I was in
serious trouble and had no idea what was going to
happen to me.

In spite of my fears I was at the lieutenant's
door at exactly three forty-five.   The lieutenant's
wife ushered me in and asked me to wait in the living
room.   About ten minutes later Lieutenant Redkin stuck
his head in the door and said, "Let's go".

The ride back to base was a silent one, and I
had no way of judging what the lieutenant's intentions
were about my future.   He went right into his office
when we got back and he invited me in.   His whole
manner was different than it had been in his apartment
earlier.   There was no doubt then that he was the
commander talking to one of his subordinates, one that
he was not pleased with.

"Private Freeman," he began, "consider yourself
under house arrest from now on.   That means you cannot
leave this area even to go to the Post Exchange.   I am
relieving you of your cook's classification, the mess
sergeant doesn't want you in his kitchen.   As of this
moment you are a common foot soldier.   I want you out
on every hike that Company B goes on.   When they are
on the obstacle course I want to see you in the middle
of them.   If they are on the rifle range you had
better be there with your M1.   When you are not on
duty you had better be in your barracks.   I will
assign the First Sergeant himself to check on your
whereabouts every hour."   Then, he appeared to get
angrier as he said,

"Damn you soldiers who don't seem to realize we
are at war.   You don't understand that there are too
damn many important things to attend to.   We don't
have time to spend on petty disciplinary actions such
as this.   If I had my way I'd send you all back home
so the rest of us could address the war effort and

264

nothing else."

I felt small, embarrassed, and inadequate under his barrage and I began to shift nervously from one foot to the other. The commander seemed to notice my discomfort and he softened his manner as he said,

"Private, you're dismissed for now. Report to Sergeant Jones in Company B and tell him you are now assigned to him. I will send for you again to talk of your breaking probation."

As I walked over to the Company orderly room, I could hardly believe I was not behind bars. Then I got to thinking about all the things I had done in the last couple of months and of how monstrous I thought they were. To hear my company commander call them petty actions rankled me a bit.

Nevertheless, I reported to the sergeant as I was told, and the very next morning I went on a twenty mile hike in full field equipment, backpack, rifle and all. Halfway through the hike my knee started swelling and they had to leave me by the side of the road and send a jeep back to get me. The doctors examined the knee and recommended surgery to remove the torn cartilage, but I refused. They let me go with the warning that if it bothered me again I would have no say in the matter.

That weekend, some time in the middle of June, rumors had it that our whole outfit was being shipped to Europe, into the midst of the fighting. Dare I sneak in town to see Irene? Every soldier who had a wife or even a girlfriend in town was given a pass for the entire weekend. I went through the hole in the fence again and to hell with the repercussions.

Irene had gotten herself a job as a waitress in one of the local bars, and although I had to wait for her to finish work at midnight, we had a few dollars to eat on from her tips. I didn't dare take even one drink, so our weekend together was nice. However, it was over too soon and I was too nervous to stretch my luck. At five o'clock Monday morning I slipped back into camp while everyone else was asleep. I fell asleep in an empty bunk that was not my own just in case I needed a cover story for the sergeant. I didn't need one, no one had missed me. It seemed that even the soldiers who had to stay in camp had their own parties and gotten pretty drunk. There was a devil-may-care atmosphere pervading the entire base and it stayed with us the whole month until we were finally shipped out.

Meantime, I was able to duck a long march that had come up, by going on sick call with bad teeth. But I could not escape the brutal obstacle course a few days later, even though I tried.

By noontime that day we had crawled through a field laced with barbed wire, waded through a wet marsh a half a mile wide, and had even been dosed with tear gas. The gassing was a horrible experience, mostly because it caught us completely off guard.

We were marching two abreast along a country road when an army ambulance drove slowly by us. As I was on the outside, nearest the center of the road, I noticed a small rubber hose, about a quarter of an inch in diameter, sticking out of the bottom of the back door of the ambulance. Only about a half inch of the hose was visible but that was enough for me to see that a vapor was escaping from it. At first I thought the driver may be losing oxygen or some other innocent chemical used in rescue work. Someone hollered --- "Gas!" --- just as I felt the full force of it on my face. By the time I got my gas mask securely on, my eyes were blinded by tears, my nose was running profusely and my entire face felt as though a thousand needles had been shot into it. For a short time I was completely disorganized. Even when the --- "All clear" --- was sounded a few minutes later, I did not comprehend the call. The platoon sergeant had to take my mask off for me before I realized the raid was over.

Aside from that, I did a fairly good job of

keeping up with everyone until late in the afternoon. By then nearly all of us were exhausted, but we were encouraged to keep going knowing that the next exercise would be the last one for the day. It was a simulated attack on an enemy stronghold. At a given signal, two hundred soldiers, all screaming like banshees, went charging down the hill at full speed. With machine guns firing inches over our heads, and charges of dynamite blasting all around us to represent bombs, it could hardly have seemed more real. It was made extra difficult for us because we had our field packs on our backs, our steel helmets bouncing annoyingly on our heads, and our heavy rifles in our hands ready for instant use. When we had gotten about three-quarters of the way down the hill, I found myself trailing everyone, so I put on an extra burst of speed to catch up. It was at that point my kneecap jumped out of place and I went down as though hit by a sledgehammer. For a couple of minutes the pain blinded me and took my breath away. After the pain subsided I just laid where I had fallen and began to enjoy my collapse. Although the kneecap had snapped right back in place as soon as my weight was no longer on it, my leg swelled to twice its normal size and the knee was so sore I could not even stand on it. That afternoon, I was admitted to the base hospital. Surgery was scheduled for the following Monday.

Although I was anxious about the upcoming surgery, I liked everything else that came with being a patient. I had no duties to perform, Irene came to visit every day, the food was good, and the nurses were friendly and attentive. Nevertheless, any good feeling was dampened by the subtle gnawing fear I had in the back of my mind about going to jail for breaking probation.

Two days after my surgery, I heard that my entire outfit was leaving for Europe. I was temporarily assigned to the hospital, to be reassigned when I got on my feet. I was thrilled not to be going with them but pretended to be disappointed. Within the week, every soldier was gone from my old area and it looked more like a ghost town than when I had first seen it.

Eight days after the surgery, the doctor said I was ready to go back on duty. Two days later I was placed on temporary duty in the large mess hall on the base --- I was cooking again. The mess sergeant told me I would be with him until my reassignment came through. He also told me I could get a pass to go into town whenever I wasn't on duty. He didn't say a word about me being on restriction or anything, and that puzzled me. I was desperate to learn of my current status with the army, but I was afraid to ask, afraid of stirring things up.

For the next three weeks, Irene and I spent every night together. I couldn't drink because we had no money to spare, but I was glad of that. I liked my work and I was getting along good with the other cooks for a change. Besides, I enjoyed walking down the street with a genuine pass in my pocket, not worrying about being stopped by an MP. It was a good feeling.

Money was becoming an issue between Irene and me about that time. Because she was working she was the only one that had spending money most of the time. She did not begrudge spending her money, but she wanted me to apply for the allotment that was due her as a soldier's wife. My reason for stalling was the trouble I was in with my commander. I didn't feel I had any right to ask for anything. Even after my outfit had shipped out, and I was no longer part of them, I was still afraid to ask because it might stir up more trouble for myself. I couldn't explain any of that to Irene so I was forced to conquer my fears and ask my sergeant how I could go about applying for my wife's allotment.

Three days later, as a result of his guidance, I was in the orderly room sitting in front of an army clerk answering a lot of questions about my marriage and filling out a number of papers. When I realized the clerk had all of my records in front of him, I decided to take advantage of his friendly attitude and ask him what was in them. I knew I couldn't just come out and ask, it might make him cautious, and he would tell me nothing. So I invented the story that I had sneaked out of camp and married my sweetheart against my commander's advice. I was wondering if he had held it against me and put a black mark on my record. The corporal was silent for a few minutes as he looked over my papers. Finally, he looked up and said,

"No, Freeman, there's nothing in here about that."

I was tempted to ask him if my court-martial was recorded and what it said, but I didn't want to push my luck. Instead, I thanked him and took my leave. For some unexplainable reason, I had been given yet another chance to turn over a new leaf and make a success of my army life. Too bad I didn't know how to take advantage of the opportunity. But at least I was able to remain sober the rest of the time I was at Dow Field, and I stayed out of trouble.

During that brief, but peaceful period, Irene and I settled into a routine that made the war seem a million miles away. Irene had been able to change her working hours from evenings to days so we would both be free at the same time. A ticket to the movies on base was only fifteen cents and the pictures were always the latest. We spent many a quiet evening there. Some evenings, when we had enough money, we would bowl at the Chateau. I enjoyed the game, and to my own surprise became fairly good at it. That particular period was one of the best times I remember, but it was not to last long. The last week in August my shipping orders came through and I had to leave Irene behind.

It took two days for me to process out of Dow Field and pick up my transfer orders. Even though I didn't want to leave my wife, once I had my train tickets in hand I wanted to get started. The excitement of new adventures ahead beckoned me. Early on a Thursday morning Irene and I were at the train

269

station waiting for my train. By ten o'clock we had pledged our love to each other and said our good-byes. There was nothing more to say. I began to feel guilty because I was glad I was leaving, and I found myself becoming more uncomfortable as time seemed to drag slowly by. Because of that, I was relieved when, at ten forty-five my train finally pulled out of the station headed for Boston, New York, and points south.

My journey was to take me through Pennsylvania, Ohio and Illinois. It would end at an air base somewhere near Great Bend, Kansas, over a thousand miles from where I had left Irene. It was not to be a pleasant trip though, because of the number of people who were traveling at the same time. From Bangor, Maine to Boston, Massachusetts there had been seats for everyone, even a few empty ones as well. However, once in Boston, that all changed. Standing room only was the order of the day, and about eighty percent of those travelers were men and women in uniform. That made it unpatriotic for one to complain about any inconvenience. From New York on, we were jammed in so tightly that it was a hard job just to get to the toilet at the end of the car. Even then, if you had a seat, you lost it by answering nature's call, and I would dare anyone to try to get theirs back. As it turned out though, I didn't have to travel straight through, I had plenty of time to spare.

When I had been released from duty at Dow Field, and had been given my shipping orders, I had also been given what was called a delay-en-route. A delay-en-route meant that a transferring soldier was given time off between assignments. It was a customary practice then, and is still being utilized today. A delay-en-route helped to avoid schedules that would have been almost impossible to meet under the circumstances. The delay could be just a day or two, or it could be over a week. I knew of a couple that were longer than a month. My orders told me I had twelve whole days to get to Kansas and report to my new post. That meant I had eight or nine days I could call my own and spend where I wanted to. Of course that was another secret I kept from my wife. If I had stayed with Irene during those free days I probably wouldn't have gotten into so much trouble. Even at that, it wouldn't have been as bad as it was if my wife hadn't been so generous to me the day I left her at the station. As I was getting on the train that morning she gave me thirty-five dollars she had saved for just such an occasion. I am sure she intended her gift to make my journey easier, but she didn't know that free time and a little money had always been a dangerous combination for me to deal with.

Even before I had started my long trek to Kansas, I began to anticipate the fun and excitement of visiting new places and meeting different people. Of course, to me, fun and excitement always went hand-in-hand with drinking. I had never learned how to have one without the other. Nevertheless, I knew myself well enough to be leery of alcohol, although I would not admit that to anyone.

Even back then, I had realized I
couldn't predict, with any accuracy,
just where my drinking would lead me,
or how long I would be able to
maintain control once I had gotten
started.

Because of that, I promised myself I wouldn't drink at all, at least until I got to my new destination. In a way it was the same promise I had made a thousand times, a promise I was never able to keep. However, I was sure it was going to be different that time though. Because I had a wife to be concerned about, I didn't want to do anything that would disgrace her.

No ones intentions could have been more sincere than mine were the day I left Irene at the station. However, my resolutions had always weakened in the past, as time slipped by. It seemed I could remember the good times I had while drinking regardless of how fleeting they might have been, but I could not remember, for long, the horrible messes I got into because I had gotten drunk --- I was drinking again before we got as far as New York! To be somewhat kind to myself I must report there was more whiskey and beer on those trains than there were in some of the barrooms I had visited. In every car there were clusters of boisterous soldiers, both men and women, drinking openly together and offering drinks to anyone nearby. As usual, I said "No thanks" the first few times a drink was offered, but I was fascinated by, and attracted to the laughter and the camaraderie that was flowing so freely among them. My loneliness seemed to become heavier as our train sped southward. By the time Boston was a hundred miles behind us I had ingratiated myself into a group of soldiers who occupied the three seats in front of me. In less time than it takes to tell, I felt as though I had known those people for a long time, and I liked them all, even if I did have to pay for a bottle to join them.

CHICAGO

One of the soldiers in the group, an eighteen year old named Stanley, lived in Chicago, Illinois, and when he heard my route to Kansas was to take me through Chicago, he invited me to be his guest. He said his parents had a big house there, and they would be glad to put me up for a few days. That seemed to be an exciting idea, and so we became inseparable companions the rest of the trip. When we had to wait for three hours in New York to make our Chicago connection, we spent that time in a bar near the station.

It was two o'clock on a Saturday morning when our train finally pulled into the station in Chicago. It had taken almost twenty-four hours to get there from New York. Many of those hours had been spent waiting on a siding for other troop trains to pass, just as we had done before. By then, both Stanley and I were pretty drunk, and I was afraid his parents would be annoyed with us. I needn't have worried though, because they had been drinking themselves, and were in no condition to judge how high we were. Aside from that, I was fascinated by the number of people who had come to greet us. I not only met Stanley's parents that morning --- I met a crowd! There was an aunt and uncle, and three cousins in the group. Then there were Ralph and Herby, Stanley's two older brothers. Three older married couples, all friends of Stanley's mom and dad, brought the number in the party to fifteen. I could see all of the adults had been drinking, and by the looks of them they had been at it for some time. It was a noisy gang that headed for the parking lot a few minutes after our arrival, and a noisier one still that piled into four different cars and headed for Stanley's house.

During that ride, a ride that took almost two hours, we learned that Ralph, Stanley's oldest brother, was getting married at three o'clock that afternoon. The marriage was to take place in the living room of their home. Friends and relatives had already begun to arrive and the house was alive with people when we got there at four A.M.. It seemed everybody was drinking, and every time I turned around someone would put a full glass in my hand.

Stanley told me he suspected Ralph and Jane would marry some day; they had been going steady for the past two years. However, he said, he was shocked to hear it was going to happen so soon. Knowing his brother was in the army for the duration of the war, like himself, Stanley said he really thought they would wait. Stanley's mother told him it had all happened so fast she had no opportunity to let him know. She said Ralph had received his orders on Monday of that week; his outfit was going overseas. Jane had wanted to get married before Ralph left, his mother said.

A few hours sleep and we were ready for the big event. The wedding lasted only about twenty minutes, but the party afterwards lasted for days! It seemed to me nobody went home. People ate and drank until they were exhausted, then they fell asleep on the nearest bed or sofa. As soon as they woke up they would join the party again, and someone else would fall into the bed that had just been vacated. I had never seen anything like it. The few people who had jobs to go to would be right back the minute they got out of work.

I lost the better part of four days in that house --- it was the most horrible experience I ever had. Even when I tried to stop drinking to get myself under control I wasn't allowed to. There was always someone present to shove another drink in my hand and insist that I down it. At first I was glad there was so much booze available. But after two days of constant drinking, eating almost nothing, and getting very little sleep, I was a nervous wreck. And I wanted out. However, I became so physically weak I could not fend off the well-meaning people who kept insisting that all I needed was another drink to fix me up. As a result of their good intentions I was in a blackout most of the time, and I passed out often.

During those four days I never knew what time of the day or night it was, and I was too sick to give a damn. On top of that, I had lost track of Stanley, and no one knew where he had gone. Without his company I felt like a total stranger in that house and I had an eerie sensation I was living in a bad dream. I had drunk myself into an alcoholic trance that I could not seem to break out of. I don't know how long that nightmare would have continued if Stanley's father hadn't tossed me out on my ear.

I hadn't been told to leave without just cause though. In fact, if I had been Stanley's father, I would have thrown a guy like me out sooner. Several times I had gotten into heated arguments with some of the other houseguests, and because I was saturated with alcohol, I had been loud, vulgar, and at times, vicious. The arguments came close to becoming fights more than once, and only the intervention of others saved the day. Some of those "discussions" I could vaguely remember, but many of them were complete blanks. I only knew about them because someone would tell me what an ass I had made of myself afterward.

Then, there was the time that Stanley's mother had taken me aside and dressed me down for making passes at some of the girls at the party. It seemed I wanted someone to go to bed with me, and I wasn't very tactful, nor private, about the way I made my wishes known. Those episodes were also blanks in my memory, and they were certainly out of character. Usually, under normal circumstances, I was too shy around women to even drum up a friendly conversation. However, none of those incidents bothered Stanley's father too much; there had been others who had done something similar, or worse, and he didn't get very excited about any of them. It appeared to me he expected behavior of that kind in a drinking party, and I didn't think it was unreasonable for him to have that attitude. Nevertheless, when I stole a twenty-dollar bill out of his wife's pocketbook, he'd had enough!

They couldn't prove it was me who had taken the money; no one had seen me with my hand in her purse. But I was the only one who had the opportunity. Gloria's pocketbook was in the room they had allowed me to sleep in that afternoon. She had left it in there just minutes before I had gone in, and she picked it up again as soon as she heard me moving about in the bathroom a couple of hours later. Oh! I had taken it all right, but when Gloria asked me if I had seen her money, I pretended I hadn't known her purse had been in the room. Then, when she actually accused me of being a thief, I acted as if I had been insulted, and feigned indignation. Gloria became furious over my act, and began to scream obscenities at me. When she saw I wasn't effected by her outburst she spun on her heels and went storming through the door. I heard her going down the stairs, muttering under her breath about what a bastard I was. I had been left quite shaken by her tirade, but I tried not to let anyone see it, especially her.

When I was fairly sure Gloria had gone, I went to join the party still going on in the kitchen. Just a few minutes of being there though, and I could feel I wasn't welcome. Next I sauntered into the living room, only to find three couples necking passionately.

I was sober enough at the moment to be embarrassed by their lack of modesty, and it was obvious they were interested in no one but themselves. I left as quietly as I had come in and I don't believe any of them knew I had been there.

Having nowhere else to go, and still feeling a little sick to my stomach, I decided to slip into an empty bedroom and lie down for a while. The bride and groom were in the first bedroom I checked, and I didn't want to ruin their privacy. Quietly I eased the door closed and headed for the next bedroom to see if it was empty. Halfway down the hall I came face-to-face with Paul, Stanley's father. He told me he had been looking for me, and by the expression on his face, I knew he was angry.

"Freeman, let's go out on the front porch where we can talk in private," he said.

His gruff manner, his set jaw, and his clenched fists told me I was in trouble. The short walk down the stairs, and out the front door, only took a couple of minutes. During that brief period I thought of giving the money back one second, and of not admitting my guilt, even if he killed me, the next. I was angry at myself for getting into that mess, but I was also afraid of what Stanley's father was going to do about it.

The cool air on my face as we stepped out the door was most refreshing. It made me conscious of the fact I hadn't been outdoors for almost four whole days. However, Paul didn't give me any time to enjoy it. As soon as we were through the door he pushed me hard against the wall and held me there with one hand planted firmly on my chest. I thought for a moment he was going to hit me because his other hand was still balled into a fist. Instead, he thrust his face inches from mine, and through clenched teeth he said,

"Don't you say one goddamed word if you know what's good for you!"

He was so angry his face was beet red, and I could see he was trembling all over. As frightened as I was of him at that moment he didn't have to worry about me saying anything. I knew better than to aggravate him any more than he already was.

"We know you stole the twenty dollars, Freeman," he said, "we can't prove it because we don't know how much money you had on you when you first got here, but we know you got it just the same."

I made a feeble attempt to deny my guilt once more, but Paul must have anticipated that, because he shut me up quickly, and he wasn't gentle about it either. Forcefully he pulled me away from the wall by the front of my shirt, tearing off a button as he did so. Then, in the same smooth motion, he slammed me back against the wall so hard the back of my head developed a large knot on it. I felt it growing as we stood there, and I wondered if it was bleeding. Again Paul stuck his face close to mine, so close our noses were almost touching. I was really frightened then and wished for the ordeal to be ended.

"I told you to keep your mouth shut," Paul said, "I'm doing the talking today. We don't want you here any longer. You're not welcome. Even without the question of the money," he continued, "you have been a troublemaker since the day you arrived. I'm fed up with hearing about you and your antics every day. If Stanley was just half a man he would have told you to leave two days ago when I asked him to."

Gloria came to the door just then, and although I hadn't wanted anyone to be a witness to my embarrassing situation, I was grateful for the diversion her presence created. For just a minute Paul's attention was taken off me. Ignoring me as if I wasn't there, Gloria looked at Paul and said,

"I made the call, Paul, and he said he would be here in twenty minutes."

"Good," Paul said, "maybe we can put an end to

this bullshit!"

I thought they had called the police and I might go to jail. I could feel panic welling up inside of me then, and I couldn't think clearly. My brain stopped working and I seemed to be suspended right where I was. Paul didn't keep me guessing long though. Turning his attention back to me he said,

"Freeman, we have called a taxi for you. We are sending you back to the railroad station where we picked you up. The fare will be about eight bucks but we feel you won't have any trouble paying it, you've got lots of money. You heard Gloria say the cab will be here in twenty minutes," he went on, "that's exactly the amount of time you have to get your things together. I want you out front when the cab shows up."

Paul didn't waste any more time on me after he delivered his ultimatum. Dropping his hand from my chest, he took Gloria by the elbow and they disappeared inside.

The moment Paul left I experienced a feeling of relief. I was thrilled that Paul hadn't insisted I return the twenty dollars, and that he hadn't hurt me very much. I was also relieved that my visit to Stanley's house was over. I was finally leaving a party that didn't seem to have an end. At that point I forgot all about being weak and sick. All of the confusion vanished, and I felt alive again for the first time in days.

Frantically I went looking for my things. I wanted to get away from that place as badly as Paul wanted me gone. Within fifteen minutes I had located and stuffed my two duffel bags and my one suitcase. However, I could not find my small carrying bag. That bag was important because it had all my toiletries in it. I had a half dozen packages of cigarettes, some underwear and a couple of pairs of socks in it as well. I was still roaming the house, searching for the bag when the cab pulled up out front. When the driver didn't find me waiting for him he began blowing his horn impatiently. That alerted Paul and he came looking for me with fire in his eyes. I was coming down the stairs when I bumped into him. Without saying a word, he grabbed me by one arm and the back of my neck, and rushed me right through the front door.

"Now get in that cab, and get the hell out of here!" he said. I knew then it was best to keep my mouth shut and go.

As the taxi wended its way through traffic my emotions were tumbling all over themselves. I felt humiliated, angry, ashamed, guilty, and hurt. But I also felt as though I had gotten away with something. I reasoned that if the cab cost me eight dollars, I was still twelve dollars ahead of the game. Then I realized I would have to spend some of that to replace my shaving gear and the other things that were in my lost bag. I was even conscious of the fact that that kind of thinking was in itself a little crazy, and so with a great deal of difficulty I wrenched my mind away from the events of the last few days. I began to concentrate on what I would do next.

I CONTINUED TO DRINK

At the station it cost me nine dollars to satisfy the cab driver, but I still had over forty dollars left. I was too sick to want another drink just then, and as it was six-thirty in the evening I went into a restaurant to see if I could get some food into my stomach. I was able to eat over half of a large bowl of beef stew and two dinner rolls. Then, in a service men's lounge, I slept for over ten uninterrupted hours.

According to my army papers, the next leg of my journey would take me to Kansas City, Kansas. With tickets in hand I went looking for a train to take me there. A ticket agent told me there would be a train

heading west in three hours. What better way to kill
a little time, I thought, than with a nice cold glass
of beer or two. I reasoned that having just eaten a
good breakfast, I would be able to handle my liquor
better. Besides, I told myself, I always kept out of
trouble when I drank by myself, and being in a sullen
mood that day I had no desire for company. With a
determination to take it easy I went looking for a
bar.

The first place that was open was only two
blocks from the station. Quietly I entered and slid
onto a stool just inside the door. I was always self-
conscious, and a little embarrassed, whenever I found
myself drinking early in the morning. However, I
didn't feel quite so bad that day, because I was not
the only customer in the place. Although the bar had
been opened less than a half hour there were five
other people there, each with his favorite "eye
opener" in hand. I ordered a beer, and gave every
indication that I wanted to be left alone. For the
next hour I sat there and nursed one beer after
another. During that time not one person said a word
to me. Even the bartender kept his distance. At
different times each one of the men had glanced in my
direction a time or two. However, the expression on
my face told them I wanted no part of their company,
and wanting no trouble they were only to glad to let
me be.

The train ride to Kansas City was the same as
any other train trip during the war. The cars were
always crowded, and most of the passengers were in
uniform, both men and women. Every fifty miles or so
we were shunted off to a siding to wait for a troop
train that had been given priority of the tracks.
When a few people would get off at any given station,
usually twice as many would get on. We had come to
expect that kind of cramping whenever we had to
travel. Because of that I was pleasantly surprised
when, at the station in Saint Louis, Missouri, three-
quarters of the passengers got off and only a handful
of new riders got on. Then, for the next three hours,
until we pulled into Columbia, Missouri, the train was

only sparsely occupied. The seat next to me remained empty for some time, and I was able to enjoy my dark mood to the limit. I felt like a zombie. I hadn't gotten out of my seat but once, to use the bathroom, since we left Chicago. I remained in that trance-like state until late that evening when a good-looking woman, in her late twenties, plunked herself in the seat alongside of me. Within five minutes she began complaining to me about her drunken husband. Her gripe was that every time they were together he would get drunk.

"Right now," she said angrily, "just three hours into his first furlough, and he is out like a light in the next car there. I'm fed up with him," she concluded.

Not knowing what to say, but wanting to be polite, I stammered,

"How long have you been married?"

"Six lousy years," she blurted, "but I am damn sure it won't be seven."

She didn't stay more than twenty minutes, and I'm sure she had no other interest in me except that I was someone who would listen when she needed to talk. That was fine with me. I didn't want to get into a family feud should her husband come looking for her. However, her intrusion into my private world served to snap me out of my doldrums.

For the first time since I had sat down I became aware of the beautiful countryside gliding past my window. Then, just a short time later, I realized I was hungry, so I went looking for the dining car. Of course a stop in the club car had to be made first, but I was able to eat a large meal after drinking only one bottle of beer.

Back in my seat after dinner I watched the train slowly fill to capacity. By ten o'clock that night there was standing room only again and soon even that room was used up. For self-preservation I stayed in my seat and fell asleep. About ten minutes to four the next morning the conductor came through the car shouting,

"Next stop, Kansas City, Kansas. We will be coming into the station in a half hour."

Soon there was the usual flurry of activity as everyone tried to get their things together under those packed conditions. Just as we could see the lights of the station about a mile away, the train came to a dead stop in the middle of nowhere. We waited, and we waited. After thirty minutes or so of that, we tried to get the conductor to open the doors, telling him we would walk to the station, but he refused in the name of safety. Everyone's nerves were frayed by the time we got the signal to move. It was then five o'clock in the morning. We had been held up for an hour. For about three or four minutes we moved in a straight line at a good speed, then we slowed to about five miles an hour, and amid the hissing of escaping steam, and the screeching of protesting rails, we went around a big curve in the tracks, and chugged our way into the terminal. As we were covering the last hundred yards or so the conductor was back.

"End of the line, everybody off," he was calling over and over again as he fought his way from car to car.

Just as it was breaking day, after a serious jostling from hundreds of rushing people, I was standing in the railroad station in Kansas City, Kansas. In the center of the terminal I spotted an information booth that had been set up especially for service personnel. From the corporal behind the counter, I learned where I could check my bags, and where I could get a free meal. Again the U.S.O. was there. They had a building just two blocks from the station. There you could get a meal, a lounge to rest in, and even a room for the night if needed. All that was free just by showing your army papers.

I spent two quiet days in that U.S.O. reading, resting and getting myself in shape.

At four o'clock in the morning of the third day I was on a train to Great Bend, Kansas.

We arrived at our destination at two-thirty the next day and I was in the orderly room by four. A private gave me a few general instructions, assigned me to a bunk, and then let me go to the mess hall for dinner. I had made it to my new assignment with twenty-four hours to spare!

Alone after dinner, as I was putting my clothes away, I suddenly thought about my wife, Irene. She had been in the back of my mind right along, but only as a vague shadow. But at that moment she stood out sharp and clear. It dawned on me that I hadn't sent her even a postcard. I had some tall explaining to do and there was no time to waste. The next hour was spent feverishly writing.

COOKS AND BAKERS SCHOOL

The next morning I reported to the first sergeant as I had been instructed.

"Freeman," he said, as I stood at attention in front of his desk, "we are sending you to Cooks and Bakers school for six weeks training. The school is only thirty miles from here so we will send you by jeep tomorrow. Keep your gear packed and be ready to leave at ten-hundred hours."

When I walked out of the sergeant's office I swore I was going to stay away from alcohol and make something out of myself. If they were going to send me to school I was going to do my best and take advantage of the break.

The very next day I had lunch at Walker Army Air Base in Victoria, Kansas. The day after that I was in class.

Meanwhile I had been writing to Irene twice a day to make up for lost time. As soon as she heard I would be in one place for six weeks, she borrowed two hundred dollars from her father and came out to join me. She didn't ask me if she could come, she told me she was coming. I only had three days notice to get us a furnished room off base, but I did.

A PERIOD OF SANITY

During that time, the latter part of 1943, the war news was changing for the better. Until then the headlines had been reporting Hitler's conquests and brutality. Now they were reporting events much more to our liking. For example, Germany had taken a terrible beating at the hands of the Russians at Stalingrad. Although the Russians had lost a million people, civilian and military, they defeated the Germans by killing 110,500 and capturing 49,000 more. The R.A.F. was conducting daily air-raids on Berlin. Those raids wrecked havoc on the morale of the German people.

Then the Germans suffered a decisive blow when, at Kursk, they lost 20 Panzer divisions. That battle became known as "The Death Ride of the Panzers". It was also the time when the Allies began to drive the Germans out of Sicily. Benito Mussolini was assassinated and Italy was no longer an Axis partner.

General Eisenhower was appointed Supreme Commander for the invasion of Europe, and with Air Chief Marshal Tedder, R.A.F., as his deputy, the outcome was inevitable. The next ten months, with Irene as my constant companion during my off duty hours, I faired well. When the six weeks of cooking school were over I was sent back to the base at Great Bend. Irene was allowed to come right along with me and we again settled into a furnished room off base. I got mildly drunk on that weekend, but the only trouble I had was a big head the next morning.

Christmas of 1943 was the best Christmas of my life until then. Irene was working in a bar as a waitress and she was making good tips. I drank a lot of free beer at her place, but I seemed to be able to hold myself in check. I got mildly drunk several times but never as out of control as I had in the past.

MY FAMILY'S PROGRESS

It was during that time I was able to make contact with Erma again. Through her I was brought up-to-date with the members of my family. Erma told me that mother had learned somehow that dad had gone back to Halifax, Nova Scotia. With Lisa the baby still with her, she quit her job and went back to Canada chasing dad. In a way I was not surprised.

My older sister, Ericka, was involved with a divorced, ex-sailor who was always drunk and out of work. He didn't believe in marriage and he let everyone know that. However, regardless of how much Johnny belittled or embarrassed Ericka, she could not leave him. She claimed she loved him and she said she was sure that he loved her in his own way. I was disgusted.

Erma and Ed were still just making ends meet so there was nothing new in her circumstances.

However, it was the news about Jake and Eileen that shocked me the most. Erma had written that Jake had been drafted six months before. He had taken Veronica with him. "Yes," Erma wrote back, "he was still wetting the bed every night." Even being married had not stopped that. I couldn't understand why Veronica was still with him. I wondered what the army was going to be able to do with him when everyone else had failed. I knew we would hear more about him as time went by.

And last, Erma wrote about my sister Eileen. It seemed she had gotten herself in trouble with the family who had taken her in when mother had closed her house. Mr. Smith, the man of the house, was having an affair with Eileen, right in his own home. There was hell to pay when his wife found out about it and she kicked them both out. Eileen then married a school chum of mine whom she had been dating off and on. According to Erma, Eileen and Frank were happy and doing just fine. However, knowing Eileen as I did, I was concerned for my friend Frank. I couldn't help but think that my family was still as crazy as when I saw them last. I found myself being a bit curious and slightly interested in their doings but I couldn't get too excited about them. I was having a hard enough time just getting by myself.

While all of that was going on with my family, I was having a spell of good fortune as I mentioned earlier. I had been promoted to Private First Class and I was pleased with my accomplishments. However, that ugly ghost, doubt, was lingering in the back of my mind. It would not let me rest easy. It kept reminding me of the messes I had created in the past. The ghost kept whispering to me that this newfound stability would not last. It very effectively reminded me I didn't deserve the good life. That was for others, not me.

D-DAY

Nevertheless, my good fortune continued well into June and beyond. June was an important month for many reasons. Many people believed that the events of June that year decided the outcome of World War II. The invasion of Italy was moving forward with the fall of Rome on June 5th. The allies could now pursue the enemy north of Rome, thus ever bringing the war closer to Germany.

On 6 June 1944 --- D-Day --- the Allies landed on five different beaches along the Normandy coastline. Although every inch of gain had to be wrenched from a well-prepared and efficient German army, at a terrible loss of men, our beachheads were established and the invasion of Europe became a certainty.

In the Pacific also the news was getting better. We had unleashed offensives in the central and southwest areas, broken Japanese air power in the Marianas and landed on Siapan. It was exciting news, and with each passing day our morale climbed higher.

Of course June was also my first wedding anniversary. I had some time-off coming and was able to get a ten-day furlough. We used the time to go back to Irene's home and visit with her folks. By that time we were sure that Irene was pregnant and we would soon be parents! I couldn't figure out if I was glad or mad. I think I was scared. A baby would mean more responsibility.

We had no sooner gotten back from my furlough when rumors of our outfit going overseas began to circulate. If that did happen our base would be placed on alert, all soldiers would be confined to base, and all wives and children would be sent home. We were apprehensive to say the least.

However, life does go on and I had to think about getting Irene back home before our outfit got its shipping orders. Our money was low, as we had spent a lot while on furlough. Her dad came through again with a gift large enough for her ticket with some to spare. But I didn't want to let her go until after the holiday unless I was forced to.

The fourth of July that year fell on a Tuesday, so our base commander planned a celebration for Saturday, July the first. That day, all the wives were invited to dinner in our mess hall. And that evening there was to be a big party in one of our hangars. We would have live music from an air force band and local talent was going to be brought in for entertainment. There would be lots of free beer.

287

Irene and I had planned to attend the affair, spend Sunday together, then get her on a train bound for home on Monday July 3rd. It was to be our last few days together until --- only God knew when. I was highly nervous all that week, I was going to be alone again. To make things worse, that Friday morning my mess sergeant put me in charge of the refreshments for the party.

"What a responsibility, what an opportunity, what a temptation!" I thought. Nevertheless, I was both angry and scared. Angry because I didn't want the responsibility. Scared because I might be tempted to drink. Scared also because I might fail my responsibility in some unforeseen way and again prove myself a fool.

"What the hell is wrong with me", I wondered, "some men can willingly pilot a fighter-bomber, others can be responsible bombardiers and perform heroically under fire. Still others enjoy positions of leadership. I can't even be put in charge of a few cases of beer without developing a strong case of the jitters". In spite of that, I didn't tell the sergeant what I was thinking. Instead, I just went about the business of carrying out my instructions. By noon on Saturday everything was ready.

Until then, I had kept myself busy and had not even thought about taking a drink. However, when my two helpers asked if they could have a beer before they left I was tempted to join them; but I didn't. Nevertheless, standing alone in the midst of all that iced beer, on a hot day, with a party coming on, what was one to do? I had a few hours to kill and no one to report to. "Besides", I thought, "what good is there in being in charge of anything if a person can't get something extra out of it for himself". --- I took a cold beer. --- I had another. Boy! they were good. --- During the rest of the afternoon I nursed a few more. I was moderately high before dinner.

Irene and I had a fight that night. A fight over how much I drank and about my rude behavior. I began to wish her departure time would come. I am not proud of it, but I really wanted her out of my hair. I wanted to be free of her watchful eye and her sharp tongue. All day Sunday and all Sunday evening I was irritable and nasty. Even the few drinks I had brought home from the party didn't help my mood. However, I did not want to send her away hurt and angry, so from the time we got up on Monday morning until her train left at ten o'clock I was able to hide my true feelings and we parted lovingly. But before her train was five miles down the track I had a fifth of whiskey tucked under my arm as I headed back to base. By nursing that bottle carefully I was able to get completely sober again by Wednesday morning.

During the next three months I seldom drank. That was only because I was afraid of getting into trouble if I did. Even with that fear hanging over me though, I still lost control a couple of times. By that I mean I drank much more than I wanted to and went into a blackout. However, I got away with it only because my mess sergeant was drinking with me and we were bosom buddies.

JAKE WAS THROWN OUT OF THE ARMY

On October 10th, 1944 I got another jolt from out of the blue. Early that morning my company commander called me into his office. When the military formalities were out of the way he showed me a letter he had received from a Major Brown at Fort Leonard Wood, in Missouri. The letter was addressed to my commander, but it was about my brother Jake. Jake was in the stockade there waiting to be court-martialed. Although the major didn't say what the charges were, he did say he wanted to talk to me, Jake's only brother, before the court-martial. My commander was willing to give me the necessary time-off and all my expenses would be paid for by the military.

On the one hand I didn't want to go. I was still hurt and angry over Jake marrying my girlfriend. However, I was married to Irene and had almost forgotten Veronica. Besides, I wanted to know what my stupid brother had done to get in so much trouble. I'm ashamed to admit it but I was excited and wanted the adventure. I wasn't too concerned about Jake's welfare.

It was only a two hour flight for the B-17 I was allowed to board. Although Major Brown was out when I reported to his office his clerk had been expecting me. He wrote me a pass so I could visit Jake in the stockade, told me where I could stay for the night and made a nine o'clock appointment for me for the next morning.

Jake seemed to be glad to see me, but with him I never could be sure about anything. The moment he came into the room my heart went out to him. He was overweight as usual. His uniform was too big for him and he looked as though he had slept in his clothes for days. I felt both compassion and shame for him.

Jake told me he was being thrown out of the army with a dishonorable discharge because he had gone A.W.O.L., that is, Absent Without Leave. I could hardly believe that. A court-martial and a dishonorable discharge seemed to be severe punishment for such a minor offense. Especially as I considered the many breaks I had been given for actions that were much worse.

We didn't talk about his betrayal, but I did ask him where Veronica was and how she was doing. To my astonishment Jake knew nothing about her. He said he guessed she had gone home after his arrest ten days ago but she had not contacted him as yet. For some unknown reason I did not tell Jake I had come to see him in answer to Major Brown's request. I told him I had heard he was in the guardhouse, and, as I wasn't far away I came to see him. He accepted that explanation without question and we spent another half hour together before I began to get uncomfortable. I

290

really never felt at ease around Jake. It was most difficult to keep a conversation going with him, it always had been.

In bed that evening, old nightmares returned. Black empty houses with Jake huddled under dirty blankets in the corner. People chasing us while we ran for our lives. Needless to say my night was hell. I looked better than I felt when I presented myself to Major Brown the next morning.

Major Brown invited me to sit down and immediately asked me to tell him about my brother, Jake. I felt very uneasy, almost like a Benedict Arnold, and wanted to keep family secrets. I did not want to hurt Jake in spite of the pain he had caused me. When the major recognized my discomfort he said;

"Private Carpenter, I am trying to help your brother not hurt him. Did you know he has been in the army fourteen months and he has been A.W.O.L. twelve times?" I was stunned; Jake, as usual, had told me nothing about the trouble he was in. The major continued,

"Even when I had an MP assigned to him, and had him confined to the company area he escaped."

The major went on and on citing incident after incident of Jake's dereliction of duty. Then he added,

"Soldier, a dishonorable discharge is a disgrace to heap on a man, especially a man like your brother who did not ask to be drafted in the first place. If I can find enough evidence to suggest Jake is not responsible for his behavior, I can recommend a discharge without honor for the convenience of the government, rather than a court-martial." Then he asked, "Can you help me? What was your brother like as a child? What kind of a family did you boys come from?"

I was still suspicious of anyone in authority

but I felt the sincerity in Major Brown and decided to risk trusting him. "After all, what does Jake have to lose at this point?" I asked myself.

I modified the conditions of our childhood while telling them to the major. Not because I wanted to deceive him, but because I sensed that my family was "way out", if you will. I was ashamed of my childhood. Evidently I had told him enough though, because he stopped me with a wave of his hand.

"I had suspected something like that," he said. "I want to thank you for your honesty. Your brother will not be court-martialed. We will let him go."

I thanked the major and left to go back to my own outfit. On the way back I felt good. I had a feeling of power, someone had really listened to me, I really did make a difference, especially in Jake's case.

I don't think Jake knew I had a hand in his discharge and I didn't want him to. My brother and I didn't see each other again until after the war when we were both back in civilian clothes. Nevertheless, it was over a month before the bad dreams about him faded away.

THE WAR CONTINUES

Meanwhile, the tide of the war in Europe was changing in our favor. In May the Soviets had retaken Leningrad and Ukraine. In June the allied forces had begun the liberation of Paris and Northern France. And in July of that year a serious attempt had been made to assassinate Hitler.

In the Pacific the news was also getting better each month. Some of us skeptical soldiers began to believe we were going to win the war on both fronts after all. I often wonder if my many different commanders would have been so lenient over my erratic shenanigans had we not been such a powerful nation with so many healthy, heroic people. I rather think not.

OUR SON IS BORN

During that time Irene and I had been constant in our letter writing. When I missed a day or two, as I often did, I would back-date a few letters so I could blame the delay on the post office, not on my negligence. Through those letters I was kept up-to-date on Irene's pregnancy. The doctor predicted the birth would be on November 15th. He missed by only one day. Our son was born on the 16th.

However, I was not allowed to be there. Our commander was sympathetic but adamant. He told me our base had been on Red Alert for the past ten days, he could not let anyone go anywhere.

I got drunk and went A.W.O.L. I began to hitchhike to Bangor Maine. Five days later I was standing in my wife's room in the hospital holding our son.

To me the baby seemed awfully small, but he was beautiful. As I looked down on him asleep in my arms I was glad I had made the trip. As for Irene, she said I was the best medicine anyone could have given her. Until I had showed up, she said, she had felt alone even though her family was close by.

IRENE'S FAMILY

The Monroes, Irene's parents, lived just three miles from the hospital and were back and forth constantly. Irene was able to call her mother at six o'clock that morning to let her know I was there. In less than twenty minutes her mother and one of her sisters were there to take me home. Needless to say,

293

I was most welcome and they treated me royally. After a hearty breakfast I fell into bed and slept deeply for over twelve hours.

Briefly I must say a bit about the Monroe family. Irene was the oldest daughter in a family of eight children. There was one brother older than she and four younger. She had two younger sisters. For the sake of accuracy in my historical account, I must say the Monroe family would certainly have been classified dysfunctional by today's standards. In kindness to everyone involved though, I can not be more specific. Every member of that family tried to love me in their own way, and every one of them were willing to accept me as I was. I am grateful to them for much and I am glad I had the opportunity to have been a part of their life. However, I had to deal with each member of that family for years. It was not too difficult a task when I was into my own dysfunctional behavior, but later on, when I began to make changes in my own life, they threw up a zillion roadblocks for me to jump over. But for now, let's get back to November 21, 1944.

Two days after I got there Irene was released from the hospital. For the next few days I was able to bask in the arms of Irene and the bosom of her family. I felt safe there, as though the army and the war were relics from a dimly remembered nightmare --- not real. I was able to stop all my drinking by then and the alcohol slowly left my system.

Reality began to creep back into my consciousness that Sunday. I realized then I had been gone from my base for nine days and I hadn't heard a word from anyone. Although my wife's name, address and telephone number were listed in my files back on base, we hadn't even gotten a phone call. By Tuesday afternoon the enormity of my predicament hit home with the impact of a sledgehammer. During wartime a soldier could be court-martialed, jailed, and even shot for deserting his post. As I had gone A.W.O.L. when my outfit was on alert, I could be charged with desertion. The more I pondered what to do next, the more paralyzed my thinking apparatus became. Any time alone would find me staring off into space like a zombie. And because I hadn't told Irene about our Red Alert I couldn't share my worries with her either. I probably hadn't told her in the first place because I didn't want her to know how stupid I could be at times.

I GOT ARRESTED

Thursday, the last day of November, was a bleak day to say the least. It was cloudy and cold with winds gusting to twenty miles an hour. Besides that, it looked and felt like it was going to snow. Looking out the window I noticed there was hardly anyone on the street. Even the usual weekday traffic was absent. It really was a good day to stay indoors by the fire, and I had planned on doing just that.

By ten-thirty that morning Sarah had the kitchen stove going full blast. They were burning wood and coal back then, and I was drawn to the stove as steel is drawn to a magnet. The fire was hypnotic. The warmth of the fire and the aroma of baking bread was all through the house and I wished I could stay there forever. I had never felt so connected before. I was deep in that pleasant reverie when there came such a forceful pounding on the front door --- I nearly jumped out of my shoes! I became frightened, and without knowing how I knew, I did know that my freedom was over.

When Sarah answered the door, I heard a deep, masculine voice say, "Good morning madame, are you Mrs. Monroe?"

"Yes I am," Sarah answered.

"Well! I'm Mr. Carson from the Provost Marshall's office in Boston," the voice said sternly. "Do you happen to be Freeman Carpenter's mother-in-law?"

"Yes I am," Sarah answered again.

"Does Freeman happen to be home today?" Mr. Carson asked.

That time Sarah's "yes" was almost a whisper, and I could sense her intimidation.

Mr. Carson's voice rose an octave then as he said,

"Tell him to come out here, now."

In a meek and tremulous voice Sarah called me from my cozy spot at the fireside, and just as meekly I came.

As I came up to the front door Sarah stepped back out of the way, and I came face to face with Mr. Carson. I was both surprised and relieved. I had expected an MP in full uniform with a gun strapped to his side and a billy-club hooked to his belt. Instead I was looking at a short, stout man in his mid-fifties. He was wearing an old, dark-brown, rumpled suit and a topcoat just as wrinkled. His soft hat was all crumpled and his shoes were a bit shabby. There was a half-smoked cigar in the corner of his mouth that was not lit. His appearance was unimpressive, belying the importance of his mission.

"Are you Private Freeman Carpenter?" Mr. Carson asked the minute he saw me.

Meekly I answered, "Yes sir."

"You are under arrest, soldier. I have been instructed to bring you in."

"Can I say goodbye to my wife and get my bag?" I asked.

"Only if I can come in and stay at your side," he said.

I invited him in, and as he stepped past me, he said quietly in my ear,

"Don't give me any reason to put handcuffs on you and I won't."

"Thank you, sir, I won't give you any trouble," I said.

There were no tears as I said goodbye to Irene. I wasn't holding them in; it was just that I was numb. As though some switch had been thrown and all my emotions were shut down. I wasn't feeling anything. Irene's eyes were brimming over but my stoic posture encouraged her to keep her tears in check. Less than fifteen minutes after Mr. Carson had knocked on our door we were walking down the driveway headed for his car, with him holding my upper arm in a firm grip. I didn't believe anyone would realize I was being arrested if they saw us and I was thankful for that. I didn't like being under arrest but I was glad the ordeal was over and I didn't have to hide anymore.

Then I saw his car parked at the curb, some fifty yards up the street. The car matched Mr. Carson's personality perfectly. It was an eight-year-old, black Pontiac. It must have been a beautiful car at one time, but now it showed years of abuse and neglect. It was badly in need of a paint job but anyone could see it would cost more than the car was worth just to clean it up. I wondered if the heater was working, and if the car could get us all the way to Boston!

As we got near the car I noticed there was a man at the wheel and two passengers in the backseat. Without a word of introduction, Mr. Carson opened the backdoor and told me to sit between the two men. I learned the two men were A.W.O.L. soldiers, now prisoners, like myself. However, I was still in uniform while they both were in civilian clothes. The man sitting on my right was a tall, slim man in his mid- or late-twenties. He was dressed neatly in dungarees and a fresh, blue work shirt. His heavy winter jacket with its big zippers and lined hood looked almost new, as did his work boots.

The man on my left was tall and thin too, but there the similarities ended. I guessed him to be forty-five or fifty. "Quite old to be an A.W.O.L. soldier", I thought. Although he wore dungarees also, they were threadbare and torn at both knees. His woolen, red-and-black checkered shirt was filthy and his worn work boots had farm dirt all over them. His thin jacket was torn at the collar and on one sleeve. It too was dirty and it was too small for him to zip up. When he smiled one could see that his teeth were all black and a few were broken off at the gums.

Then I noticed that there were no handles for the doors or windows on the inside of the car. For just a minute I felt claustrophobic and scared. Next I felt humiliated and angry. Nevertheless, I was able to crush those feelings and accept my lot.

Meanwhile, I had learned the driver's name was Mr. Jones. He was a tall, thin man, in his late thirties, with small beady eyes, sharp facial features, and a set jaw. His silence, and his deadpan manner generated an air of authority about him. Without any tangible reason, I had the impression he was the man in charge. I also felt that even though I hadn't seen a gun on either Mr. Carson or Mr. Jones, these men would be capable of handling us if we gave them any trouble.

Nevertheless, even they were not going to take unnecessary chances. When we stopped to eat they put the handcuffs on us. The other two prisoners were handcuffed together while I was cuffed to Mr. Carson. Those two stops were extremely embarrassing for me, and it was most difficult to eat with my left hand only.

However, there was one small consolation that made me smile. I had the amusing idea anyone looking at us might be inclined to think Mr. Carson, in his rumpled civilian clothes, was my prisoner rather than me his! That fantasy helped just a little to get me through both lunch and dinner.

At seven-thirty that evening our trip came to an abrupt end. Unexpectedly Mr. Jones drove the car into the basement garage of an eight-storied building in downtown Boston. The building looked like an old courthouse or something just as ominous. All five of us crowded into a small elevator and took it right to the top floor.

We were soon to learn that the entire top floor had been turned into a jail for the military and we were locked up.

As we were being shown to our bunks I asked the MP how long I would be kept there.

"I can't answer that, soldier," he said. "The captain will explain all that when you see him in the morning."

A moment later the MP went through the door and I heard the key turn in the lock. My attention was drawn to the other men, the men I would be spending some time with.

I scanned the room and counted nineteen men including myself and the two who had come in with me. Adding the five who were lying on their bunks, the total count was twenty-four. Out of that number only four were over twenty-two, most of them were under twenty.

I quickly learned we were not allowed to have a radio, and of course television had not been perfected yet. We could write two letters a week but even they were censored. Nevertheless, aside from that, except for the locked doors and the constant presence of the MPs, it was just like being in a barracks.

I slept very good that night as strange as that may seem. Although I knew I was in serious trouble with the authorities I felt safe just the same. I could not explain that, not even to myself. In spite of that, I was rested and polished, even though very nervous, when I was brought before the captain at ten o'clock the next morning.

Just after breakfast, an MP, one I hadn't seen before, came into the rec room with a clipboard in his hand.

"If I call your name," he said, "I want you to line up by the door."

Jake, the older man, who had come with me from Maine, was the first to be called. Next was an alleged rapist, and then me. Two others, men I didn't know anything about, made us a group of five.

"Follow me, men," the MP said, as he unlocked the big door and stepped through.

As the last man came through the door we were joined by another MP, and the two of them took us into the elevator and down one floor.

Getting off the elevator we found ourselves in a room similar to the one above but there were no desks there. In fact, the room was bare except for three long benches along the walls. I noticed at once the stairs were wide-open. There were no locked doors on that floor. The MPs motioned us to sit on the benches and I fantasized myself walking, nonchalantly down the stairs by myself. Although I knew I wouldn't dare try it, it was a nice fantasy just the same.

From where we sat on the benches we could see four big oak doors. They must have been office doors because each one had a nameplate on it. While one MP stood at the top of the stairs the other fellow disappeared behind a door marked Provost Marshall. Five minutes later he came out and escorted Jake inside. I never saw him again.

Then it was my turn. I was led through the

door, down a narrow hallway and right into the Provost Marshall's office. As I stood at attention the MP read the charges against me,

"Sir," the MP said, "this soldier is accused of deserting his post when his unit was on alert."

It must have been the way he worded his report that made me realize clearly, and probably for the first time, just how serious my predicament was. I had heard, a long time before, any desertion from any post during a war could lead to execution. I was terrified, and for good reason. However, I had no time to dwell on that at the moment because the MP was still giving his report. He told the captain how long I had been gone, and where I had been found and arrested. When he finished reading his report, he placed the papers on the captain's desk and stepped to one side, there to stand like a marble statue. The captain looked the papers over for a few minutes then looked up at me and said,

"Soldier, give me any passes or identification papers you have on you."

With hands that were trembling so noticeably I was embarrassed, I searched through my wallet. I found an old, dog-eared, invalid weekend pass. Nothing more. This I placed in front of the captain and waited.

"Is this the only identification you have, soldier?" the captain asked, incredulously.

"Yes sir," I answered.

"Do you mean to tell me you traveled all the way from Great Bend, Kansas to Bangor, Maine without any official papers?" he asked.

Again I answered, "Yes sir."

"If I was your commander," he said, "I would give you a medal instead of a court-martial! You are

301

either crazy or you have a lot of guts."

I liked this captain immediately. I took his words as a compliment even though I knew he would have to do with me what he would.

"Soldier," the captain said, "this is only a holding area for prisoners until we can get them back to their outfits. We will notify your commander in Kansas telling him we have you, and we will ask him for further instructions. Your commander may send two MPs after you. In that case we will keep you here until they pick you up."

"Incidentally," he said, "if he does send for you, you will be charged with all expenses the MPs accrue, their train fares, their meals, and even their hotel bills if they stay overnight anywhere."

The captain paused then to let me digest the implications of such an event. That was a hard piece of news to swallow.

"On the other hand," the captain continued, "your commander may give me instructions to send you back on your own recognizance. In that case I would give you a train ticket, some meal vouchers, and your identification papers. Then it would be up to you to get back to Great Bend, Kansas as fast as you could."

I didn't know what to say at that point so I kept still. There were a dozen questions I wanted to ask but I felt, as a prisoner, I had no right to ask any. I was embarrassed, scared and angry. I was furious at myself for being so stupid and getting myself into this horrible mess. However, the captain's words began to penetrate my thoughts again so I forced myself to pay attention.

"You should be with us for a week to ten days, no longer," he was saying. "While you are here we expect you to behave yourself. If you do, your stay won't be too uncomfortable."

After another long pause, during which he looked me over from head to foot very intently, he nodded to the MP and we swiftly marched out of there. I felt like a bug under a microscope in the captain's office and was glad to leave when the MP motioned me out. I breathed a sigh of relief when that ordeal was over.

I played cards with some of the boys, and I read a lot. The weekend, including Monday went flying by. Then on Tuesday morning I was again ushered in to see the captain. As soon as I was brought into his office he looked up from his papers and said,

"Well, soldier, we have heard from your company commander. He wants you to write him a letter telling him what you would do if he allowed you to come back on your own. I want you to have that letter written before four o'clock this afternoon because I want to include it with my own comments to your commander."

Even before the captain had finished speaking, a wave of relief swept over me. I thought if my commander would let me come back by myself, it meant he wasn't too mad at me. There would be a good chance he wouldn't have me shot!

Back in our rec room a few minutes later, I wasted no time in getting that letter started. I explained I was so excited about being a father, and so frustrated about not being there I wasn't thinking straight. I told him how my father-in-law had thrown my wife out of his house when she had her first child, and I wanted to show Irene she had a man that would stand by her. I then told him how much I would respect his trust in me by letting me come back on my own. I told him I would honor that trust by reporting to him as soon as the train could get me there.

I never mentioned my drinking. I thought if I told him I was a drinker it would go against me. Fortunately for me, the letter, perhaps helped by a recommendation from the provost marshall, worked. Early on Monday morning December 11th 1944, I was given my papers as promised and I walked out a free man, even if only for a short time. Technically I was still a prisoner but at least I was being given a chance to redeem myself a bit. What a marvelous feeling to walk down the street unescorted. After ten days of being locked up like a criminal, the freedom was intoxicating. I was walking on air!

Although I had been given the train tickets and meal vouchers I wasn't given any money, nor did they escort me to the train station which was twenty miles away. In order to save what little money I did have, I decided to hitchhike to the station. It took me much longer than I thought it would but I eventually got there. Then, just as I got out of a pick-up truck at the station, I was stopped by an MP asking me for my identification. I felt a little smug as I handed him my papers even though they had the provost marshall's seal on them. At least this MP couldn't detain me and that made me feel good.

At eight o'clock that evening I was on a train heading west again, to face only God knew what. With several delays because of troop movements taking priority, it was Friday morning before I got back to my own base. Immediately I went straight to the orderly room to report. The company commander was not in but the first sergeant was at his desk. He took my papers and sent me back to my barracks to wait until I was sent for.

It was two o'clock that afternoon before the first sergeant sent for me. When I reported to him he told me to go right into the commander's office just behind his desk. The office door was wide-open, so I tapped on the doorjamb and stepped briskly in front of the major. I offered him a smart salute, came to stiff attention and waited. My whole nervous system was in revolt, even the flesh on my stomach was vibrating. On top of that, I had begun to sweat profusely, and I felt nauseous.

"At ease, soldier," the major said, and I relaxed just a little.

"Well, I see you made it back," he said.

"Yes sir," I responded.

"You realize that you will be court-martialed don't you?" he asked.

"Yes sir," I said.

"You are very fortunate this outfit didn't get it's shipping orders while you were gone," he said. "The charges against you would be much more serious if it had."

"I understand that now, sir," I said, feeling the fear grow in the pit of my stomach.

"I am going to confine you to the guardhouse until we can set up the court-martial," he said.

Again I said, "Yes sir."

"I am very disappointed in you, Freeman. You were given good grades in the cooking school we sent you to and your mess sergeant had many good things to say about your work. I had expected much more from you," the major said. "That's all I have to say to you for now."

When he was silent for a few minutes I thought he had finished with me, so I offered him a salute and turned to leave.

"Where do you think you're going, soldier?" he asked.

"I was going to report to the guardhouse, sir," I answered.

"I didn't tell you to leave; you're not going anywhere until I tell you to," he shot back. He was angry. I was surprised and nervous over the change.

"I have sent for two MPs," the major said.

"They will escort you to the guardhouse."

Again I was taken aback. I thought, "My God, I came all the way from Boston by myself, surely I can walk the six blocks to the guardhouse". I could not make sense out of it but I didn't dare talk back to the major at that point. Sure enough, five minutes later, two big MPs in full regalia, came into the major's office and saluted him.

"Take this prisoner over to Captain Ames at the guardhouse," the major instructed.

And so there I was, between those two, walking down my own company street where all my buddies could see. I felt like crawling under a rock and staying there.

The first three days in that guardhouse were horrible. Not that I was treated badly; I wasn't. In fact some of the guards were very pleasant. However, the policy in that particular place was isolation for the new prisoners until they earned their way into the group. It was no more than keeping you locked up in your cell, letting you out only at meal times. Even then I had to eat alone at a table in a corner reserved for that purpose. In other words, I had plenty of time to think. Thinking had always been a bad thing for me. I could only focus on my failures, never on my achievements. The more I thought the deeper the depression. I had come to expect it and it surely was with me in that guardhouse.

"Here I am, almost twenty-five years old and I'm locked-up again," I thought. "Christmas is only a few days away and I haven't even thought of a gift for Irene, never mind buying her one. A hell of a husband I am. I don't belong in jail and yet I don't fit in society; there is no place for me". The depression was deep and black. I didn't want to eat, and I slept only two hours at a time.

Sometime during the third day in isolation, I made a decision to take my

own life if things got any worse for me.
I had no idea I was an alcoholic and it
was the effects of alcohol on my behavior
that was causing my problems. I thought
I was crazy, and if I couldn't find a
way to live decently I wanted out. The
decision I made that day was different
than all the other times I had thought
of suicide. Before it had been only a
halfhearted wish, but that time it was
a deep determination. I knew I would
do it given the right circumstances.
That decision took a lot of stress out
of the situation for me. My headache
disappeared, a degree of peace settled
over me, and my depression lifted. From
then on it was like having an ace in the
hole I could use, and win, if the cards
were stacked against me.

I spent only six days in that guardhouse. It
should have been much longer but my mess sergeant
pleaded with the major, telling him he needed me
desperately. Although it was true the sergeant could
use me in his kitchen, I think there was a little more
to it than that. There had been a certain amount of
comradery between us before I had gone A.W.O.L. and I
believe he wanted to see me get a break.
Nevertheless, whatever prompted him, he did help to
get me out of the guardhouse.

Early in the morning of what would have been my
seventh day of incarceration, I was told to get into
my class A uniform because my company commander wanted
to see me. I thought I was going for my court-martial
and a blanket of fear settled over me. However, when
I was escorted into the major's office, I saw my mess
sergeant there and wondered what was going to happen.

"Private Carpenter," the commander said, as soon
as I walked in, "I am going to turn you over to
Sergeant Jones here until your court-martial comes up.
He says he needs you in the kitchen and you are no
good to me in the guardhouse."

As he spoke I didn't miss his emphasis on the words "Private Carpenter", in his address. "There goes my stripe", I thought, and with it my hopes of adding others to it.

"Can you conduct yourself as a soldier if I release you from the guardhouse and let you go back to work?" he asked.

"I can and I will sir," I answered. A surge of excitement shot through me like a bolt of lightning. I was going to go back to work! Work had always been a source of pleasure for me. It made my self-esteem go up immensely. I had found out years before when my hands were busy my mind was at peace.

The mess hall I worked in fed twenty-two hundred men three meals a day. Besides that, we were open all night, every night, feeding paratroopers and air-force personnel who were either coming from or going on missions abroad. It was not unusual to find out later we fed an outfit that went right into battle from our base. We often fed paratroopers who had just come back from the war zone to regroup. The stories they told were hair-raising. It was exciting just to be close to them. They were a different breed of men, or at least I thought they were. We had standing orders to feed them anything they wanted, day or night, with no questions asked. And we were proud to do so.

With Christmas only four days away, everyone seemed to be caught up in the excitement of the season.

The meal that day was a huge success. From eleven-thirty until three o'clock in the afternoon there were two chow lines steadily feeding anyone who came along. There was lots of food left over so we didn't cook dinner that evening. We just left the food on the line and anyone could serve himself as they straggled in.

All during the few days before Christmas and Christmas day itself, I had kept myself so busy I didn't think of my troubles. In fact, even when my crew was off-duty I volunteered to help the other cooks because I needed to be busy. The conditions of my release from the guardhouse were that I was confined to the area. Being busy insured me against doing something foolish I may have to pay dearly for later. However, the day after Christmas the whole base was quiet as though three-quarters of the personnel were on furlough. The stillness of the anticlimax really got to me. I became very anxious and afraid. The old feeling of impending disaster was with me again, only that time it was strengthened by the knowledge of my upcoming court-martial.

Our company commander said nothing to me the few times I saw him in the mess hall. He acted as though there were nothing unusual between us and I didn't know whether to be glad or anxious over that. I took the attitude --- no news was good news --- and that helped a little. Then, when another week went by I began to hope that my case may have been lost and I would never come to trial. However, that was not to be.

On Thursday January 4, 1945, the mess sergeant told me I was to report to the commanding officer on Monday morning at nine o'clock. He told me to be in class A uniform because I was going to my court-martial.

"Don't worry," my sergeant said, "I will be there for you as a character reference. The major may not go so hard on you if I put in a good word."

I was grateful to have someone on my side for a change. From the moment the sergeant told me it would happen on Monday, my fears returned in full force. I developed a bad case of diarrhea that stayed with me even after my trial was over. It was hard to fall asleep at night and even then I would only sleep a few hours. Nightmares and restlessness kept me as tired as when I went to bed.

Nevertheless, I was in the orderly room

reporting to the first sergeant at eight-thirty that morning. I wanted to get the ordeal over with. Besides, I thought it would help if I showed the major I was sorry and was willing to pay for my misconduct. The room was very quiet. Even the first sergeant and his clerk, the only two on duty, were not making a sound. It was eerie, almost as if I was watching a silent dream. At eight-fifty my mess sergeant came in and sat alongside me. We nodded, and I gave him a weak smile but we didn't talk. The tension was mounting.

At nine o'clock on the dot the company commander came in. I was almost paralyzed with fear by then, but with a lot of effort I kept it hidden.

I opted for a summary court-martial again and hoped for the best.

The commander called in my mess sergeant and the trial was in progress. The major read the charges:

1) Being absent without leave
2) Desertion of post while on alert, and
3) Conduct unbecoming a soldier

I pleaded guilty to all three charges. Then I asked the major to consider that it was my first experience at being a father. I told him I thought it was the concern I had for my wife and child that had clouded my thinking and made me react in such an irresponsible manner. The mess sergeant spoke highly of my work and asked the major to consider how desperately he needed me in the mess hall.

There followed five solid minutes of dead silence. I could even hear the first sergeant moving papers at his desk even though the door was closed. The major would look up from his papers, look me over for a minute or two without saying a word, and then look down again. I could hear soldiers talking as they walked by the building and I thought how good it was to be free like them. The waiting was agonizing.

Finally the major stood up and said,

"Private First Class Carpenter, it is the sentence of this court that you forfeit your Private First Class status. You are reduced to the rank of private. Furthermore, you will forfeit two-thirds of your base pay for the next three months. It is also the desire of this court," the major continued, "that you serve six months in the guardhouse in order to teach you the value of responsibility."

My heart sank on that last one. I didn't mind losing the stripe; I had expected it. I didn't like losing the money, but as long as they didn't touch the money that was going to Irene I was willing to put up with being broke for a few months. But taking my freedom was a bit much, especially as I had worked so hard to keep from going back. Again it was the mess sergeant who saved the day. He even offered to be personally responsible for me if the major would turn me over to him. I was surprised that someone would go that far-out on a limb for me. Another period of silence followed while the major looked as though he was going to refuse the sergeant's request.

All at once he turned to the sergeant and said, "Done, sergeant, you can have him."

Then he turned to face me as he said, "Private Carpenter, if I hear one word of complaint about you, it will be the last. Let me tell you, soldier," he continued sternly, "if I have to put you in the guardhouse it will be for a lot longer than six months. Do you understand me?" he asked.

"Yes, sir," I answered stiffly as I slowly exhaled the breath I had been holding for the past two or three minutes.

"This court-martial is over," the major said. "You are dismissed."

When the sergeant and I stepped out of the orderly room and the cold air hit me in the face, I

311

realized I had been sweating profusely. My shirt and waistband were soaked clear through. The cool breeze made me shiver and I longed for the comfort of the warm mess hall. Still smarting from the humiliating tongue-lashing I had just received from the major, I was resentful and angry. The walk back to the mess hall was somber and silent. Except for thanking the sergeant for his help I had nothing to say.

After waiting so long for my day of reckoning I could not fully comprehend it was finally over. It had happened so fast it left me feeling kind of numb. I was so angry at myself and so frustrated over my behavior that for just a few minutes I wished the commander had thrown me in the guardhouse. "At least I would have been safe from myself in there", I thought.

Looking back, I wonder if the many good people who had given me break after break along the way had actually done me more harm than good. For some reason, unknown even to myself, I was not able to maintain the degree of self-discipline necessary to stay away from alcohol. Whenever the compulsion to drink came over me, it was all-encompassing. If I didn't give in to it immediately it would get stronger by the day. As soon as I had gotten out of a mess I had created I would think, "Thank God, I got out of that one". Then, within a few weeks, I would forget how serious the situation had been. I would even forget how desperate I had felt and the vows I had made to my superior, to myself, and even to God.

I wasn't lying nor being deceitful when I made those vows; I was as sincere as any man could be. I meant every word I said at the moment I said them. However, after a period of sobriety, say four or five weeks, I would become anxious, restless, and fearful again. My self-esteem would take a sharp nosedive and a deep depression would engulf me. I knew a drink or two would relieve those feelings. That's when the compulsion would present itself. Once given into, a cycle would be repeated, sometimes with disastrous results.

As all this self-examination was running through my head, we arrived at the mess hall. The sergeant opened the door for me as he said,

"Let's get a cup of coffee and we can talk a bit."

Sitting in his office a few minutes later he said,

"Freeman, all you have to do for me is what you have been doing since you came back. There is nothing wrong with your work. You're not only a good cook, but you organize the KPs very efficiently on our shift. I had even put you in for corporal three days before you took off on us."

At that announcement I had another reason to feel stupid and guilty, and I wished the sergeant had not told me of my loss. However, the sergeant was still talking so I listened.

"You have the run of the whole base," he said, "but for God's sake, don't pull a fast one and go in town. If you treat me right I'll see you get a break," he continued. "You can even earn a bit of cash by working for one of the other cooks when they want an extra day off."

The only thing I could do was thank the sergeant and promise him I would live up to his expectations.

"Now go back to your barracks," the sergeant said, "change your clothes and come back to work."

WAR NEWS GOT BETTER

Meanwhile, the war in Europe was raging at fever pitch. Newspapers were grabbed as fast as they hit the streets, broadcasters had millions of ears glued to radios morning, noon, and night. Every magazine article about the war was passed around until everyone in the barracks had read it.

By late 1944, with his armed forces in retreat on all fronts, and the Allied armies ready to strike into the heart of Germany, Hitler was becoming desperate. In an effort to turn the tables on his enemies, Hitler ordered his generals to launch a massive counterattack on the Western Front. What has become known as The Battle of the Bulge erupted on December 16, 1944. In a horrible, bloody battle that lasted just four to five weeks the losses on both sides were staggering. 8497 Americans killed, 46,000 wounded, and another 21,000 missing or in German POW camps. According to available records the German losses were nearly 120,000 (12,652 killed, 57,000 wounded and 50,000 captured). Although the Germans were able to delay the Allied advances somewhat, they paid a steep price. They not only lost the battle, but later on when they desperately needed reserves on other fronts they had none.

My emotions were constantly in a turmoil all during the war. Whenever I heard news of the beating our troops were taking, I wanted to volunteer for overseas duty I was so mad. But then, I couldn't muster up the courage to do that and I would feel ashamed. "What will I do if they ship us over?" I thought. There was talk almost every day about our going. I was terrified that in battle my cowardice would be exposed.

I had good reason to be worried though; our unit had been on alert since the first week in November. No one was allowed off base for any reason. The waiting was getting on everyone's nerves. Because of the tension, drinking, gambling and fighting steadily increased. Even the officers knew something would have to be done soon if we didn't ship out.

However, I did what I had done so often before in order to keep myself out of trouble. I worked long hours even though I didn't have to. On my days off I worked for a cook on another shift and earned a five-dollar bill. When there were no cooks to work for, I could always find a K.P. who wanted to get out of his unpleasant duty. I could earn as much as ten dollars and a fifth of whiskey for those jobs. I would save the money and sell the whiskey. I didn't dare keep a bottle even overnight least the very possession would become a temptation. With that routine I was able to earn enough money to send for Irene and the baby if they ever lifted the alert.

Then there was the question of my citizenship. I had thought volunteering for duty would automatically give me citizenship status. "No," they told me. Becoming an American soldier just declared my intentions. I still needed to get my final papers. In order to do that I had to make a request and fill out forms. If accepted I would go to court and be sworn in. However, I was not allowed to do that until I had been assigned to a permanent unit.

I had turned in my request, just after I finished cooking school, and waited. In the excitement of my son's birth and everything that had taken place since then, I had almost forgotten about my papers. In fact, for what I had done I considered myself fortunate to be alive, never mind being a citizen!

Nevertheless, just two weeks after my court-martial, I was sent notice my request would be granted. I was to be in civilian court at ten o'clock on Saturday morning, February 5th at Hays, Kansas. I would need two character witnesses and my company commander's signature. The witnesses were no problem but the major refused to sign. He further humiliated me by saying,

"We have enough misfits in this country already without making you a citizen too."

I might have accepted the major's refusal to sign my papers because I still felt guilty over my recent behavior. Besides, I hardly ever stuck up for myself on anything. People could push me around and usually I would do nothing about it. However, my citizenship was important. I had been sober just long enough by then to have regained a little spunk. And so when the major spoke to me that way, I got so damned mad I threw caution to the winds and said,

"I want to see the base commander about this, sir."

Under military law he could not refuse and so I was given an audience two days later. I told the commander all about my behavior over the past few months and why. I told him how rash and stupid I had been and how badly I wanted to be an American. Of course, I didn't tell him I had been in and out of trouble since I was sixteen, and I surely wouldn't tell him I was a drinker. I was afraid he would look at my record and see some of the messes I had been in just since I had become a soldier, but I guess he didn't take the time to do so.

Evidently the commander accepted my explanation and believed me when I told him I would make a good citizen and a fine soldier. Because, three days later I was again standing in front of my company commander. After the major had returned my salute he said,

"At ease, soldier."

And I wondered if he ever forgot to say that to a soldier, as I relaxed into a more comfortable stance.

"I'll tell you what I'm going to do," the major said, "I'm going to give you a break and sign those papers for you."

"I'm going to let you have a command car and a driver to take you to court come next Saturday," he was saying, "and I will give you meal vouchers and a special pass so you can get off base for the day."

I was ecstatic. I don't know whether I was excited because I was going to be naturalized or because I had won a point over my superior. Nevertheless, I kept my wits and thanked the major profusely as though he alone was responsible for his change of attitude.

The three of us, with our driver, left the base at seven o'clock that Saturday morning. Although Hays, Kansas was only about forty-five miles away, I didn't know where the courthouse was and we wanted to be on time for that special occasion. There were two other soldiers and seven civilians waiting to be sworn in when we got there. The civilians told us they had been given an oral and written test the day before and had passed. They were as excited as little children about to be taken to a circus. We soldiers did not have to take those tests because we had pledged our allegiance to the United States of America when we became soldiers.

We were ushered into the courtroom about nine-thirty by a court clerk. Two long wooden benches had been reserved for us right up front near the judge's bench. We filled those benches with no room to spare. There were about forty spectators in the courtroom as well. We found out later the spectators were family members of those being sworn in.

At exactly ten o'clock the judge entered the courtroom and we all stood at the command,

"All rise. The court is now is session."

The judge was a huge man; he could have made two of me, and I was impressed. The robe he had on looked too big for him but it added to his ominous figure. When the judge sat down everyone else followed suit.

The ceremony, although solemn, was brief. The clerk of the court called our names alphabetically and one by one we lined up facing the judge. When we were all standing, the judge asked us to raise our right hand and repeat after him the words he needed to hear from us. The litany lasted all of two minutes with much of the time being spent on waiting for our responses. Then the judge himself stood up and said,

"By the power invested in me, I now pronounce

you citizens of the United States of America," or
words to that effect. It was very impressive and a
cold shiver went up my spine.

The judge left the courtroom right after wishing
us all good fortune in our new land. The clerk then
gave each one of us our official naturalization papers
with our names and our pictures on them. It was all
over. I was an American citizen at last!

With the meal vouchers I had, I took our driver
and my two witnesses into an exclusive restaurant for
a steak dinner. My two buddies bought themselves a
few beers but the driver was a teetotaler and I was
afraid to drink. But God! how I wanted to. I wanted
to celebrate that special day in a big way but I
didn't know how to do that without alcohol. Although
I didn't know I was an alcoholic, I did know my
reaction to alcohol, at any given time, was so
unpredictable I didn't dare risk it. After all, I was
still on restriction and after reporting my major to
the base commander, I was afraid he might welcome the
chance to get back at me.

Although we could have stayed away from the base
the rest of the day, I insisted that we go back right
after dinner. My buddies didn't like that one bit and
they were angry because they said they could not
understand me. However, I was able to appease them
somewhat when I gave each one of them, including our
driver, a five-dollar bill. That gesture was my way
of relieving my guilt for spoiling their day. By
three o'clock that afternoon we were back at the base
and I felt safe again. Once back home the desire for
a drink began to fade and by the next morning it was
completely gone --- another crisis was over.

I BECAME ANXIOUS AND DEPRESSED

I slipped easily back into my routine and tried
to make some sense out of my emotions. I had felt a
certain amount of pride in being an American, but it

318

was not what I had expected. I honestly didn't know what I did expect, but I didn't feel much different. In fact, it was just another event in my life that left me asking myself, "Is this all there is to it?" I felt somewhat disappointed but I couldn't tell why. Nevertheless, I made my usual vows to exert more willpower and make something of myself.

By working long hours, and writing letters to Irene, the days began to slowly slide by. One day, near the end of February, our company commander was transferred out of our unit and a young lieutenant took his place. Although I was apprehensive about the new commander, I was glad the major was gone. I hadn't felt comfortable in his presence for a long time. That switch in commanders proved to be another lifesaver for me later on.

While these changes were taking place in the office the men in our barracks were becoming restless and unruly. The more restless they became the more uncomfortable I felt being around them. Day by day it got worse and more than once the first sergeant had to break up a fight. The old desire to run away came over me again. I tried to stay out of the barracks as much as possible and I began to experience that terrible feeling of moroseness that comes just before the depression. I even lost the desire to write to Irene, so letters to her stopped. I had no idea a person could go to a doctor with those complaints and get relief. My childhood experience had only taught me doctors were not to be trusted.

Just three days before my twenty-fifth birthday the base was taken off alert. The gates were flung wide-open and everyone was allowed off base for the first time in almost five months. Even the soldiers like myself who were on restriction were given a short reprieve. The level of excitement that swept over us was astronomical and it carried me along with it. My depression vanished almost instantly. For the next few days the soldiers swarmed all over the town. They smashed windows while drunk and they tore up more than one barroom. The MPs were kept busy and had to put on extra men. There were hundreds of arrests every night for over a week before the fire had burned itself out and things got back to normal.

Meantime, I was doing fairly well. That first night I had been invited to go in town with the other cooks to have some fun. The excitement I felt was high enough to give me a false sense of potency and I drank again. However, I experienced one of those rare times when I didn't go into a blackout and I didn't do anything foolish. We cooks stuck together all evening and had one hell of a good time. My spirits felt free as though I could do anything. Once again I felt sure my problem-drinking days were over; I thought I had conquered the problem --- I had drank like everyone else. The next morning my hangover was almost nonexistent and I took that as another sign I had the problem licked. I never once thought of the mess I had gotten into just a few months before nor the vows I had made! There was still that little voice in the back of my head that tried to caution me though, but he was very weak that night so I shut him up quickly. I didn't want to hear from him just then; too bad I didn't. I didn't drink again for two whole days just to prove to myself that I could stop whenever I wanted to.

Then on my birthday, Monday, March the twelfth, I had the day off and I took it. My restriction didn't allow me off base but I could drink beer in the P.X.. Once again I had a good time without any repercussions. In spite of that my small voice was regaining his strength and he began to haunt me.

"Stop fooling yourself you stupid jerk", it said. "Send for Irene. She will be good for you and she will keep you out of trouble".

I knew my little voice was right. I did want Irene to be with me, and I had enough money to send for her, but I wanted some fun first. I had learned being married had its own restrictions. However, in honor of my little voice, I didn't drink all the rest of that week and again I felt in complete control.

320

That is I did until Friday.

Late Friday afternoon our mess lieutenant sent for me. When I knocked on his office door he hollered,

"Come in." I entered, saluted, and stood at attention waiting.

"At ease, soldier," the lieutenant said. "I want you to do me a favor tonight."

I had only a slight acquaintance with Lieutenant Jones, and even that only as his subordinate, so I was surprised when he asked me to do him a favor. Still I answered as expected by saying,

"I'd be glad to sir."

"Good," the lieutenant responded, as he took two fifths of whiskey from a desk drawer.

"I have a date tonight with Sam the butcher and three nice women," the lieutenant said, "I'm supposed to bring the liquor and be there by six o'clock. Sam tells me you can be trusted to take the liquor to the girl's apartment and keep quiet about it," the lieutenant continued. "Tell them I can't get there until about seven-thirty."

My heart sank as I said,

"I can't leave the base, sir; if I could I'd be glad to run the errand for you."

"That's no problem Freeman," the lieutenant said, as he leaned over his desk and scribbled me a weekend pass. As he handed me the pass and the two bottles of whiskey he said,

"You can join the party, Freeman --- you would be good company for the odd girl."

He gave me the girl's address and a small map to

321

help me find it. Then he added,

"You'd better leave now if you want to get there by six o'clock." I didn't have to be told twice!

I arrived at the address at exactly six o'clock and found it was a two-car garage that had been converted into an apartment. It wasn't very big, but it was cozy and neat. Sam opened the door in response to my knock and I could see by his relaxed appearance he had been there for some time. He was glad to see me and practically pulled me through the door. The three girls were beautiful.

It was obvious they weren't waiting for my liquor --- they had plenty of their own. And it was just as obvious they had a lot to drink already. I started immediately to try to catch up and one of the girls seemed to be willing to help me. We were all pretty high and in a party mood by the time the lieutenant showed up around eight o'clock. The landlord, who lived only a few yards away, had already knocked on the door once and told us to keep the noise down but we ignored him.

The lieutenant had been with us for just a short while when we discovered that we both came from Cambridge, Massachusetts. That fact made us feel closer and we became buddies, at least for that night anyway. The landlord knocked on the door again and threatened to call the police. That quieted us for a short time, but not for long.

Then the lieutenant, of course it was Eugene by then, became maudlin. He began to pat me on the back and tell me what a great guy I was. Even being drunk I found that kind of behavior embarrassing. Eugene said anybody from Cambridge, Massachusetts was a good man. Then he told me I deserved to be a commissioned officer more than he did. Under his directions and with Sam and the girls as witnesses, Eugene created a mock ceremony. Taking his lieutenant bars off his jacket and shirt he pinned them on me and declared me a commissioned officer. That's the last thing I remember until I came out of the fog and found myself in a police station at four o'clock in the morning. Sam, the three girls, and I were all sitting on the same long bench waiting for something.

"What the hell are we doing here?" I whispered to Sam, who was sitting next to me.

"Keep quiet," Sam said, "we were arrested for disturbing the peace and resisting arrest."

"Where's the lieutenant?" I asked as I looked at his bars on my shirt.

"He's inside with the policeman who arrested us," Sam said, "they are waiting for the MPs to take him back to the base."

I looked across the room at the policeman behind the desk and I whispered to Sam, "Let's jump this s.o.b. and get the hell out of here."

Sam said, "Shut up you damn fool, we're not going to jump anybody."

"But Sam," I whispered again, "once they lock us up we won't have a chance of getting away."

Sam paid no attention to me so I fell asleep on the hard bench.

The MPs were called to claim us and we were brought back to the base under arrest.

Eugene was waiting for us in the provost marshall's office when we were brought in that afternoon. After a brief report was developed and filed on each of us, we were turned over to our mess lieutenant rather than being put in the guardhouse.

By that time I had taken the lieutenant's bars off and had wrapped them in paper. I didn't want to be charged with the serious crime of impersonating an officer. As soon as I had an opportunity I discreetly

323

slipped them to the lieutenant. I was also sensible enough to know it was no longer "Eugene;" it was back to Lieutenant Jones.

"Let's go in my office and talk," the lieutenant said to us as soon as we got out of the provost marshall's office. The first thing the lieutenant asked us as we took our seats was, "Did you boys have a good time last night?"

"Yes sir," Sam said, "it was a damn good party until those cops showed up."

"We really got smashed didn't we?" the lieutenant said with a big grin on his face. "We would have been OK if the girls hadn't made the cops mad."

The lieutenant assured us that he would make sure we didn't get into any trouble over our night out and sent us back to work.

On Tuesday when the company commander came into the mess hall for lunch he asked me to come to his table.

"Sit down for a few minutes," the commander said.

As I slid into the bench in front of him he asked,

"Private Carpenter, do you realize you almost got yourself thrown in the guardhouse again?"

Even before I could answer he went on. "Good God, Freeman," he said, "your restriction is almost half over and you were doing fine. If it wasn't for your mess lieutenant you'd be in the guardhouse right now." I didn't know what to say so I said nothing, but I was feeling plenty. I felt stupid, embarrassed and ashamed.

"You are not to go in town or anywhere else

unless I tell you you can go," the commander said. "I don't care who signs a pass for you I will not accept that as an excuse. Is that clear?" he asked.
The only thing I could say was, "Yes sir."

Then the commander asked me a question that made me bristle.

"Freeman," he asked, "do you have a drinking problem?"

"No sir, not me," I shot back, as a flash of fear hit me in the pit of my stomach. "I can take it or leave it," I said.

"Well," the commander said, ignoring my sharp reply, "I have noticed by your records every time you get into some kind of a mess there seems to be drinking involved."

Still I denied there was anything wrong with the way I drank and the commander didn't push. However, I felt extremely uncomfortable; it was one thing for me to be concerned about my drinking, but I felt no one else had the right to pry into my private affairs. I thought it was none of his business.

"Why don't you send for your wife now that the unit is no longer on alert?" the commander asked. "She would be good for you."

"I can't go off base sir," I said, "you just told me so yourself."

"If you had your wife here I would extend the boundaries of your restriction to include your address in town," the commander said. "I would even give you a special pass so you could look for an apartment in town if you promise to stay out of mischief."

I was elated; I hadn't expected to see Irene again until after my restriction was over.

That evening I wrote a letter to Irene, the first one in almost two weeks. I told her to get her things together because I would be sending for her as soon as I found a place. In the letter I had included a money order for two hundred dollars, money I had earned by working in someone else's place on my days off.

It took me a full week to find the right place for Irene and the baby, then it took another five days before she could get there. But on Sunday, April 1st, 1945 we were a family again. We had cooking privileges where we were and it was nice not to have to fight the restaurant crowds. The landlady even found a crib for our son, Keith, and for a while things went smoothly.

VE-DAY

My sobriety lasted until May 8, 1945. That was one day I can honestly say I couldn't help myself. I didn't drink because I was in one of my depressed moods. I wasn't angry at anyone. I had no axe to grind. But that day Germany finally surrendered --- the war in Europe was over! There was plenty of free beer at the P.X. and even the soldiers on duty were getting drunk. In order to reduce damage to private property in town only married men whose wives were living with them could go off base that night. I could have gone, but once I had a taste of that free beer I wanted to be in on the party. And so I called Irene and told her our entire unit had been put on restriction for forty-eight hours because the base commander was afraid the soldiers would wreck the town. She didn't like it, but accepted it as part of being a soldier's wife.

That binge lasted just one evening, but it was the most destructive drunk I had ever been on. Had I been forced to pay for the damages we caused that night I would still be working for the government!

There had been talk of the war in Europe coming to an end for a longtime, but I couldn't take something as serious as that on rumor. Like many others I was skeptical, I had to be shown. And so when it did finally happen we were caught by surprise. That helped to make the day more memorable. Let me tell you about that historical day as I saw it from where we were.

May 8, 1945 started out like any other workday for us. My shift was starting at noon that day so we helped to serve lunch and began preparing dinner. About three-thirty we could see the roast beef was coming along fine, it would be out of the ovens on time. The vegetables were cooking on top of the stoves, and the desserts were all ready and in the walk-in refrigerator. We cooks were just beginning to relax a little. Suddenly we heard a loud cheering coming from the headquarters building about five hundred yards away. It sounded to me like someone had hit a homer in an important ball game and the fans were cheering wildly. A few minutes later hundreds of soldiers came streaming out of the building screaming something at the top of their voices. I couldn't make out what they were hollering and I became frightened. I thought the building was on fire or something. However, their cry was taken up by everyone in a matter of minutes! Finally I could make out the words --- "Germany has surrendered! Germany has surrendered! Germany has surrendered!" they were screaming. Then the loud speakers throughout the base began to repeat the news over and over again --- "Germany has surrendered! Germany has surrendered!"

A chill went up and down my spine. Large goose pimples appeared on my arms, and the hair on the back of my neck stood on end. It was an eerie feeling.

Cooks everywhere enjoy a certain amount of popularity in the service and we had our share of friends. About an hour after we received the exciting news, a couple of friends from the supply room came in the back door with three cases of beer. They told us

there was to be free beer in the P.X. all evening.
They said it was the base commander's way of keeping
the soldiers away from town and out of harms way.

The public-address system confirmed the fact the
gates were closed. That's when I found out married
men could go home to their wives if they were in town.
However, as I have said, I didn't want to go anywhere
but to the party at the P.X..

The usual crowd for dinner that night was
nonexistent. Of course there were some chow-hounds
who would eat even if they had to miss a visit from
the good Lord Himself! But that night --- most of us
were too excited to eat. Much of the food we cooked
had to be cooled and stored for another day.

When I got off duty around seven o'clock I made
a bee-line for the P.X.. By that time there were so
many soldiers looking for the free beer the P.X. was
packed, and still they kept coming. They started to
pass cases of beer through the windows and extended
the party to the outdoors. Although we were not
allowed to take any beer away from the P.X. we could
have all we wanted. The bartenders were serving the
beer by the case, it was the only way they could keep
up with the demand. A couple of soldiers tried to
take a case of beer to their barracks but they were
brought back by two MPs.

There were several MPs scattered throughout the
crowd in the early part of the evening, but as the
party progressed and got rowdier they began to
disappear one by one.

Everybody was in a euphoric mood that day even
before they had any beer. Knowing the war in Europe
was over did that for us. In the early stages of the
party there was plenty of laughter and good
fellowship. However, that wasn't exciting enough for
many of us. This was an historical day and we felt it
called for a celebration --- we wanted some action.

I believe that the craziness began when one of the soldiers got the bright idea to bomb passing cars. For ammunition he took a condom out of his pocket, stretched it over the neck of a bottle of beer, then shook the bottle to create as much foam as possible. When the condom was about half-full of this foam he tied a knot in it like you do a balloon. Then swinging this "bomb" over his head he let it fly over the fence to pelt the next car that came along. We all thought it was a brilliant idea and quickly followed suit. Pretty soon the street outside our fence was littered with busted condoms and spilled beer. Many cars drove through the gauntlet, and not a few left with a condom plastered to their hood or windshield. I often wondered if the beer damaged the paint. Nevertheless, as much fun as that was, it still wasn't enough. We started to pelt each other. Soon we were not wasting time with the condoms but started shaking the bottles and spraying anyone who happened to be close enough.

It got out of hand when others began throwing balloons filled with water. They were throwing them so hard that when they hit --- they hurt. More than one soldier had a black eye the next morning from that game. The P.X. closed at eleven P.M. and they drove us out. Many of us had hidden three or four bottles of beer in our clothes, but I guess by that time no one cared. I was pretty drunk by then and I don't think I was the only one.

I had nowhere to go but back to the kitchen. That was all right with me because I was due back on duty at four in the morning. I knew if I went to sleep as drunk as I was I would oversleep. I think things wouldn't have turned out so bad if the party had died out there, but that was not to be. We were still too excited to let that happen. One of the cooks invited us over to his barracks. He said he had two-fifths of whiskey stashed in his footlocker that he had been keeping just for this day, so over we went.

There were four of us sitting on the edge of the

bunks speculating on how long it would take to beat
the Japanese and then how much longer it would be
before we could go home. We were on our third whiskey
and coke when all hell broke loose. Three guys from
our barracks came bursting through the door screaming
their heads off. They were being chased by a half
dozen men from the barracks next door. I could see
they were all soaking wet. They were still having a
water fight, but this time the guys from the other
barracks had pulled the fire extinguishers off the
wall in their barracks and were spraying our buddies
with the white foamy stuff. Without wasting a second
we pulled the fire extinguishers off our walls and put
the intruders to rout! For hours after that we
sneaked around the buildings carrying our fire
extinguishers "looking for the enemy". Whenever we
saw someone, anyone by that time, we let loose with
our ammunition. Sometime during that fight I went
into another blackout and didn't come out of it until
I was serving breakfast on schedule. Evidently I had
gotten to work on time even if I was drunk and in a
blackout.

The other cooks were not treating me as though I
had the plague so I assumed I hadn't done anything
spectacular, at least not in the kitchen. However,
after daylight, remembering some of the antics in the
barracks, I slipped out to take a look. I was
appalled at the sight that greeted my eyes. The
chemicals from the fire extinguishers had left a white
stain all over the walls, the windows, the beds, and
even the floors. The inside of two barracks were like
that as well as the outside walls of the buildings. I
became afraid that we may have blinded or hurt someone
because I didn't know what chemicals they were. My
own uniform was beyond saving and I could only guess
how many others would have to bury theirs. I thought
I was done for that time. The damages were staggering.
And even though every nerve in my body was screaming
for more alcohol I was scared enough to deny myself
the relief a drink would have brought.

When I got off duty I borrowed a uniform from

one of the other cooks and went home to Irene. I told
her the restriction had been lifted for us married men
just that morning. It's a good thing for me she
didn't mingle with the other soldier's wives or I
couldn't have played so many tricks on her.

Every day for the next three or four weeks I had
expected to be called on the carpet, but nothing ever
happened. I had kept my ears open to hear if anybody
had reported being injured, but again nothing. I had
the feeling that the fear I had felt was shared by
others and they wouldn't report anything even if they
had been hurt. I had a hundred unanswered questions
but I dared not ask one of them.

Meantime though, there began a massive movement
of troops. Thousands of soldiers from the European
theater were being brought back for discharge or for
reassignment. Many of them were shipped right into
the conflict in the Pacific while others were assigned
to our unit until they could be sent home. As a
result we had so many cooks in our kitchen we didn't
know what to do with them! I was beginning to get a
little restless then and so I asked if I could be
reassigned to some other job.

To my pleasant surprise I was promoted to
private first class and transferred to Fort Meade,
Maryland. I was able to take Irene and the baby right
along with me.

VJ-DAY

Then on August 6, 1945 just before lunch, news
was flashed around the world about the atomic bomb
being dropped on the Japanese city of Hiroshima. None
of us had any idea that such a bomb existed. It was
estimated that some 130,000 residents of Hiroshima
were killed that day or would eventually die from the
effects of the bomb. One bomb laid waste an entire
city of 350,000 people.

Still the Japanese refused to surrender. Most of us soldiers couldn't believe an entire nation would be willing to face annihilation, but it was in keeping with all we had heard of the Japanese till then. As a result of their obstinacy, three days later, a second bomb was dropped on Nagasaki with a loss of 25,000 more Japanese lives. On that same day Russia declared war on Japan, something we Americans and our allies had wanted for a longtime.

Most of my buddies and I believed we would have to invade Japan at a terrible loss of American lives before they would admit defeat and quit. And so it came as a thrilling surprise when, six days after the second bomb was dropped, they surrendered unconditionally.

It slowly dawned on me that the war was really over and soon we would be discharged. My greatest fear of going into battle only to have my cowardice exposed was no longer a threat! Then too, my fear of being court-martialed again if I got in trouble would disappear with my discharge. If ever a man had a reason to celebrate his good fortune, I did.

Beer and whiskey began to appear out of nowhere. Any soldier who had a bottle passed it around willingly. Free beer was again offered at the P.X., and I didn't even think to refuse.

I didn't bother to call Irene that time because I got drunk too fast. I was drinking anything that was offered --- wine, vodka, beer, whiskey, and a sweet liqueur called Southern Comfort. By ten-thirty or so I was in my customary blackout and before midnight I had passed out.

I didn't wake up, or come to, until eleven o'clock the next morning. My buddies had put me to bed in an empty barracks to let me sleep it off. I was so sick that I wanted to die but was afraid I was going to. I needed a drink desperately if I was to live. Fortunately someone had left almost a full bottle of whiskey on the bed with me and I didn't hesitate to get some into my stomach. The first three drinks went right down the toilet along with everything I had eaten in the last twenty-four hours. My stomach felt as though it had been kicked by a horse. Nevertheless, the fourth drink did stay down and I began to feel that I just might live after all. I was really frightened that time because I had gotten drunk so fast and I was so sick the next morning.

Then too, I didn't want to lose my stripe again. I always thought of those things after I had gotten drunk. Too bad I couldn't think of them beforehand. My luck had been with me so far but I knew I couldn't afford to take any more risks like that, especially since my army life was almost over. My uniform looked terrible. I had slept in it and evidently I hadn't made it to the bathroom when I should have. That was most embarrassing because I had all my clothes in town with Irene.

After nursing my bottle for a half hour or so I was able to get up and about. I borrowed a pair of pants from one of my buddies and changed clothes. However, it took another hour and about four more drinks before I could get up the courage to go home to Irene. Of course I took my bottle with me even though I didn't know who owned it.

It took me two full days to nurse myself off that binge and I had to buy another fifth of whiskey to do it. I was as irritable as hell all through the ordeal and Irene even threatened to go home when she caught me with the second bottle. However, she didn't leave and when Monday came around I was out of the woods and ready for work. That was the last time I got drunk while I was in uniform. It was not because I didn't want to drink --- it was because I was afraid to.

On September 2, 1945, the formal Japanese

surrender papers were signed as members of the nations involved met on the battleship USS Missouri. World War II was over.

Fort Meade was turned into a discharge facility and I was appointed as a guide to help discharge thousands of soldiers. I kept that job until my own discharge came through.

Meantime I had earned two more stripes and was a sergeant when I finally got my discharge on March 16 1946.

I BECAME A CIVILIAN AGAIN

The morning after my discharge we headed for my sister Ericka's place in Cambridge, Massachusetts and I had high hopes of living a decent normal life. My enthusiasm was short-lived though because I could not find work; nor could I find a place to live. Thousands of men were coming home from the army, and factories were laying people off. My sister, Ericka, took us in temporarily, but I felt uncomfortable causing her the inconvenience. The real estate people were putting pressure on us to buy a house under the G.I. Bill which guaranteed a veteran's mortgage to the bank. We were able to buy a two-and-a-half-story house, with a paying tenant on the first floor. We were going to live on the second floor and everything should have been fine. The trouble was though, we couldn't take possession and move in until the last of June. Ericka was staying at her boyfriend's house and she said she would stay there until we could move into our own place. That solved one problem but I still hadn't found a job, and the mortgage payment of eighty-six dollars a month terrified me. Even when we were signing papers at the bank I had the uncomfortable feeling I wasn't going to be able to keep the place.

Looking for work every day allowed me to be free from the watchful eye of Irene and so I began to drink

334

again. At first it was just a beer here and there along the way because I was not quite sure if I could control my drinking or not, but I had to try. Fortunately, I was able to walk out of a bar after a beer or two when I first started and so my guard was down. Nevertheless, I kept looking for work and after four solid weeks of searching I was hired as a short-order cook in a busy diner in Boston. By that time my drinking had escalated to a dangerous degree and in less than six weeks I was fired.

I told Irene I had been let go because the man who had the job before me had just been discharged from the army and he wanted his job back. I had four days pay coming from that restaurant but I never went back to collect, I was too ashamed of being fired.

Then, the government created a plan in order to help the veterans adjust to civilian life. If a veteran was out of work he could draw twenty dollars a week from the government for as long as a full year. We called it the 52-20 club and it was managed by the state employment office. At first I was too proud to sign up for it, but after losing the job that had taken me a month to find I figured I better take all the help I could get.

Day after day I went looking for work without finding any. My drinking escalated to the point where I didn't even leave the barroom some days to look for work. I was drinking then in order not to get sick. I was afraid of the terror of withdraw.

Meantime, my money was almost gone and Irene needed to see a doctor. I didn't like this responsibility game one bit, so I kept on drinking. However, my conscience wouldn't let me rest. My inner voice was berating me constantly. The only way I could shut him up was to drink more. The vicious cycle that I knew so well was in full-swing and I didn't know how to put on the brakes.

I was eating very little and sleeping lightly for only a few hours. Finally, the day came when I was too sick to keep on drinking. That day turned out to be the most important day of my life. So important in fact that I want to record it here exactly as it happened.

Then there was John, a neighbor, who died at the age of 37. He had died from sclerosis of the liver, the result of years of heavy drinking. During the viewing an acquaintance asked John's widow if John had ever tried Alcoholics Anonymous. "Good God man," she exclaimed, "John was never that bad.

Ralph was a man in his late fifties but he looked eighty. This particular morning he found himself in front of a judge for being drunk in public.

"Ralph," the judge said, "this is the fourth time you have been in front of me in less than three months. You drink a lot don't you?" he asked.

"No sir, I don't," said Ralph who by then was shaking from head to foot. Holding out his trembling hands he said, "I spill most of it don't you see!"

PART THREE

THE BIRTH OF A MIRACLE

THE MAN EMERGES

THE DAY I TOOK MY --- LAST DRINK

Although it had been sometime after midnight when I fell into bed, it was four A.M. when I woke in the morning. I was as rum-sick as only a man could be who had been on a drinking spree for the past several days. God, did I need a drink to stop the shakes and settle my stomach! Frantically, my throbbing brain tried to remember if I had any booze hidden in the house. I vaguely recalled hiding a fifth of whiskey up among the springs of the old sofa in the front room, but I couldn't remember when I had done that or even if it would still be there. My wife, Irene, was getting good at finding my stash and dumping it down the sink.

I lay there for what seemed like hours. Every nerve in my body was silently screaming; every sound was magnified a hundred-fold. I could hear the big clock in the hall ticking away the minutes. Off in the distance a police car wailed as it raced to some troubled spot. Suddenly, two tomcats, fighting over the territory outside our ground floor window, scared the devil out of me with their unexpected, inhuman cries. I knew I had to get up or go crazy, but still I lay there. I was terrified I might wake Irene by moving about; God forbid that should happen. I couldn't handle another of her lectures. As I listened, Irene's breathing was deep and steady. I decided to make my move. Slowly, I slipped out of bed, actually holding my breath, hoping I wouldn't wake her ..... I made it.

There was plenty of light in our small apartment
--- it was coming from a streetlight right outside our
front room window. It allowed me to move about
freely. My head was pounding as if it had been hit by
a sledgehammer. Gingerly I eased myself onto the
floor in front of the sofa. For a moment my heart
sank, as I fumbled among the springs and found
nothing. I kept searching though, and sure enough it
was there, jammed between the springs, right where I
had hidden it. Although the bottle was only a quarter
full, I was elated; I felt safe. I knew I had enough
alcohol to keep me alive until the liquor stores
opened at eight o'clock. Just holding the whiskey in
my hand calmed my nerves somewhat. As strange as that
may seem, it always worked that way for me.

Holding the bottle close to my leg, (the leg
farthest from the bedroom door, just in case Irene
should wake up), I headed for the kitchen. Quietly, I
eased open the refrigerator door, looking for some
ginger ale. There was nothing on the shelves but a
quart of milk. I had never used milk as a mixer
before, but I knew I could not drink the whiskey
straight without gagging. I was willing to take my
chances. It tasted rather odd, and I wouldn't
recommend it to anyone, but at least I kept the drink
down. Within fifteen or twenty minutes my nerves were
settled and my thinking became clearer. Alone in that
dark kitchen, with plenty of time on my hands, I began
to take stock of my life once more. I was especially
worried, because now I was a married man. It was no
longer just myself I had to be concerned with.

Reflecting back, I realized that ever since I
had been introduced to alcohol it had been both a joy
and a curse to me. Drinking gave me a feeling of
well-being that I found irresistible. Alcohol had
always given me a degree of courage I could not muster
on my own. It had allowed me to mingle socially and
had filled many an hour with a fellowship I didn't
know how to get in any other way. It had even given
me the guts to ask Irene to marry me, just three weeks

after I met her.

However, it was now interfering with my life to such a degree that I knew I had to do something about it. I promised myself to stop drinking that day.

It had been daylight for sometime, when rustling from the bedroom shook me from my reverie and warned me Irene was up. I glanced at the clock on the wall. It was ten after seven, and I realized I had been musing there for over two hours. My liquor was all gone, but my nerves were fairly calm and my hands were steady. Nevertheless, I knew I would need a few more drinks to get me through the morning.

I could see my hangovers were getting worse. After years of heavy drinking they were lasting longer, and they were demanding more alcohol to get me through them. However, I dared not share that knowledge with anyone. I was afraid they would say "Stop your drinking," and I knew I couldn't do that. I had tried over and over again and had failed each time.

While Irene was in the bathroom tending to her morning chores, I hid the empty bottle under the sink and began to make the morning coffee. The aroma of the fresh-brewed coffee brought Irene into the kitchen. She poured herself a cup and joined me at the table.

"How long have you been up, Freeman," she asked.

I had been afraid she would ask me that. When she did, a pang of guilt shot through me; but, as usual, I hid it well. Nonchalantly I answered,

"Oh, only about a half hour."

By the look on her face I don't think she believed me; but she didn't press the point, and I was only too willing to drop the subject.

Although Irene served a wholesome breakfast of

bacon, eggs, home-fried potatoes, orange juice, toast and coffee, I couldn't eat a thing. Just the smell of the food threatened to propel me into the bathroom to greet the toilet.

By eight-thirty, I couldn't stand it any longer. I just had to get another drink. On the pretext of going for a pack of cigarettes, I headed for the nearest liquor store with high expectations. Less than thirty minutes later I was standing in an alley with a fifth of whiskey and a bottle of coca-cola.

As I was pouring some of the coke onto the ground to make room for the booze, a feeling of disgust swept over me like a blast from a hot-air furnace. I began to talk aloud to myself, as I was apt to do when my emotions were especially high --- "You really are a rummy", I said, "only rummies hide in alleys sneaking their drinks. A normal drinker would take their bottle home. You are right where you belong, in a filthy alley along with the rest of the trash".

As soon as I got a good strong drink into my belly however, those thoughts vanished and I felt all right again. Just the same though, those feelings of guilt and shame never completely left me. They only went way down inside somewhere, where I could almost ignore them most of the time; but I was always vaguely aware of their presence. And every once in a while, they would overpower me for a few moments. There were nights when I would feel so ashamed of the way I was living and so afraid of my future, that I would silently cry myself to sleep.

Back home, while Irene was tending to our son in the bedroom, I was able to hide my new bottle in the hamper before she knew I had returned. With the whiskey well-hidden I felt relieved, because I had been worried Irene would catch me with it and begin preaching again. Over the next hour I made several trips into the bathroom for a quick drink. It wasn't long, though, before I realized I was in trouble.

342

Not long after my introduction to alcohol, I had learned that the cure for a hangover was a couple of strong drinks the next morning. Those drinks would set me on my feet and get me going again. Although they would not take the pain away completely, they would reduce the shakes enough so I could stand the rest of the torture and get through the withdrawal. In other words, I could get sober. And when I did, I could usually stay sober for some time. Lately, however, the morning drinks would often become a detonator for the overpowering compulsion to drink more. When that happened, my drunk would continue and I would lose another day. To make matters worse, I always knew I would have to repeat the ritual over again the next morning, without being sure of the outcome.

That was the trouble I found myself in that day. I can still remember when that detonator went off and I felt the compulsion kick in. I knew at that moment I was going to get drunk again, and I would be powerless to keep it from happening.

When I was single and the morning drink triggered the compulsion I wouldn't get too upset. Oh, I would feel a degree of fear over the loss of control. And yes, I did become angry over the hold alcohol had on me. Nevertheless, those negative feelings wouldn't last; a drink or two and they would fade. Then I would accept my fate, resign myself to the inevitable, and enjoy as much of the day as possible. My attitude during those days had been, "To hell with everyone --- I want what I want when I want it and I will have it regardless of the consequences to myself or others". But things were much different that day. I had a pregnant wife and a child to think of. I couldn't let this drinking continue. It was at that moment I felt fear as I had never felt it before. Then, in my terror, I became enraged at my inability to break the chains that enslaved me to alcohol.

I was in the bedroom with my bottle by that time, having shifted my hiding place to safer ground. With the bedroom door closed, I was engaged in taking a good stiff drink, (about my tenth since I had gotten out of bed), when the compulsion announced it's unwelcome presence. As tears of fear and rage literally poured down my face, I held the bottle of whiskey high in the air in my left hand. And, while shaking my right fist violently at the bottle, I hissed passionately, so Irene wouldn't hear, "You son-of-a-bitch --- you've got me again!" Then in complete desperation I added, "If there is a God in this damned world, please help me." The moment passed, and I was able to regain my composure. Feeling tired and emotionally drained, I put my bottle away in it's hiding place and rather humbly slinked into the kitchen.

Irene was standing at the sink washing dishes. Keith, the baby, was playing on the floor nearby where she could keep a mother's eye on him. Looking at that family scene from the doorway, I felt out of place; as though I was not a part of it at all. It was like being in a dream, looking at two strangers who were indifferent to my presence. The feelings of guilt and shame I had experienced in the alley came over me again. They were stronger than I had ever felt them. Watching Irene being a wife and mother --- doing her duty to both offices without complaint --- only deepened my sense of unworthiness. I felt guilty, because I thought I had tricked Irene into the marriage by not telling her I had a drinking problem. I began to think about how I had married her, taken her away from her home, from her loved ones, and even from her friends. I thought about how I had moved her into my hometown where she knew no one, and of how often I had left her alone for hours at a time while I was out drinking with my friends. I thought about how she was still a child herself at twenty-one, and yet she had one child already with another well on the way. I also thought about the many jobs I had lost and the number of times I had been arrested because of my drinking. Suddenly, as clearly as if someone had turned a light on in my brain, I saw that I could not have a family and my alcohol, too.

I knew from experience I couldn't give up my drinking. At that moment, I made a sad but critical decision. I would give up my family, abandon the dream of ever becoming a decent responsible person, and resign myself to being a drunk. The prospect of giving up the struggle and living on skid-row began to look very attractive.

But how could I get Irene to leave? We had been married three years, we had a family started, and we had just bought a house together. I was pretty sure Irene would not want to go, regardless of what I said, at least not just then. To soften the blow, I conceived the idea of talking her into going home on a visit. I thought that if I could get her back to her loved ones, where she and Keith would be cared for, then I could disappear. That way, she would be rid of me and I would no longer be responsible for her.

However, before I could talk Irene into anything, I needed another drink. The scene in the kitchen had sobered me completely. Back I went to my precious bottle in the bedroom, but much to my surprise, that drink had no effect on me. I felt kind of numb, but that was all. The second drink did nothing for me either; it was like drinking a glass of flat coca-cola. Knowing I couldn't hide in the bedroom any longer without arousing suspicion, I went back to the kitchen to talk to Irene.

"Irene dear," I said "you know your mother has been ill and our money won't last much longer. Why don't you take a few dollars and go home for a visit? By the time you come back we can move into our new home and chances are good that I will have a job by then."

Nevertheless, Irene wouldn't budge. She refused to listen to anything I said. I think she was afraid I would quickly go to hell without her. What she didn't know was that I was going to hell anyway. With or without her, it wouldn't make much difference.

345

Except that if she stayed, she would go down with me.

I really didn't want that to happen to Irene. I knew only too well the pain and the misery that comes to a woman who is married to a drunkard. There had been several of them in the neighborhood I was brought up in. I felt a compassion for Irene that was stronger than any I had ever felt for anyone, including myself. I realized then that I loved her enough to let her go rather than ruin her life, regardless of how much it hurt.

Once again my mind became crystal clear; I knew what I had to do. I had to tell Irene the truth about myself. The idea frightened me and I wasn't sure I could do it. However, I knew, for everyone's sake, I had to try.

Walking across the kitchen, sidestepping Keith as I went, I took the dishcloth out of Irene's hands and laid it on the edge of the sink. As I guided her to a chair near the table, I said,

"Please Irene, I have to talk to you and I want you to listen."

"What's there to talk about?" she snapped, with fire in her eyes, "I'm not going anywhere, no matter what you say. If you'd stop your bull-shit and get a job we'd all be better off."

"But Irene there are hundreds of men out there looking for every available job," I said, not wanting to say what I really needed to say.

Irene turned red in the face, she was so angry.

"If you'd spend less time drinking and more time looking for a job," she screamed, "you'd be working right now. Do you think for a minute I don't know you went out and bought a bottle this morning? You're half drunk right now," she said. "I can smell it on your breath and see it in your eyes."

346

At first her words shocked me, I had no idea she was aware of what I had been up to. But then I felt a sense of relief as I realized she knew more than I thought she did. I hadn't completely fooled her. Two minutes later, though, I became indignant at her accusations. "Who the hell does she think she is?" I thought, "I'm the man of the house, I pay all the bills around here, how dare she infringe on my privacy and confront me like that."

Still I knew she had a right to stand up to me. I also knew she was right in most of the things she said. For the next few minutes my emotions were in a turmoil. They were changing so rapidly, all I could do was keep my mouth shut and wait for them to settle down. Finally, remorse settled over me like a smothering fog. Irene's accusing look cut me to the quick; I felt shame to the very depths of my soul. I knew the charade was over.

"Irene," I said very calmly, "I want you to take Keith and go home to your mother. You don't know it, but you're married to a drunk. I've been a damned drunk since I was sixteen and I can't stop drinking, not even for you."

When the reality of what I had just said hit me, I started to cry. I felt lost and alone, really alone and hopeless.

Irene looked at me, dumbfounded, and I could see the confusion in her eyes. However, I was as confused as she was; I couldn't understand what was happening to me either. I had never let anyone see me cry real tears before, and yet that day I was not ashamed of them. I had no desire to swallow them as I usually did. It seemed as though a dam had burst and everything was being washed away.

Irene's continued silence unnerved me. I could see she was regaining her composure and I was afraid she would not believe how serious I was. Without thinking, I threw myself on my knees in front of her. Taking both of her hands in mine I said, through my

347

tears,

"I'm no good for you, Irene, I can't keep a job,
I can't stop drinking, and I am not dependable. If
you don't leave me now, you will have to leave sooner
or later. And if you stay with me much longer, you
may have more kids to worry about. I didn't tell you
how bad it really was before this because I honestly
thought that marrying you would help me to change. I
know now nothing can make me give up my drinking, not
even my family."

I was amazed at how open I had been with Irene -
-- it made me feel strangely calm. My tears were over
--- not because I had suppressed them, but because
there were none left. I felt as though a great weight
had been lifted from my shoulders.

Irene said nothing, she just stared at me. I
began to feel awkward kneeling there on the floor.
Sheepishly, I got up and sat on the chair at the
opposite end of the table. Even Keith was
exceptionally quiet for the next few minutes as though
he sensed something profound was going on. Just as I
began to think I might have to be the first one to
break the silence, Irene spoke.

"Freeman, I think you are making a big thing out
of nothing," she said. "All you need is a job, and
you'll get your feet on solid ground again. I read an
article the other day that said you veterans were
going to have a difficult time adjusting to civilian
life. They called it Post-War Stress, or something
like that. They said it would pass, but it would take
some time."

It was my turn to be dumbfounded. I realized
Irene hadn't believed a word I had said about my
drinking problem. At first I was hurt and angry. I
had bared my soul to this woman. She had been allowed
to see a side of me no other person in the world had
seen. And I felt she had brushed it off as something
unimportant. Then, slowly, it dawned on me that as
long as Irene knew I was a drinker and she didn't see

anything wrong with that, I could drink whenever I felt like it. And if later on she didn't like it, what could she say? I had thought that I had to give up my wife and family in order to keep on drinking. Evidently I had been wrong. I began to toy with the idea of getting my bottle out of hiding and plunking it right in the middle of the kitchen table. My thoughts were interrupted, though, when Irene said,

"Freeman I'm told that sometimes things look much different if they are left alone for a while. I don't want to talk about this any more today. I want time to think, OK?"

I was so angry I couldn't speak right at the moment. I was thinking, "Goddam it, the first time in my life I am ready to talk honestly about my drinking and she won't listen". Taking my silence to mean I agreed with her, Irene changed the subject.

"You do remember that you promised your sister, Erma, we would go visit her today, don't you?", she asked.

I really had forgotten that promise. Nevertheless, I didn't want to see Erma with her filthy house, her two noisy kids, and her drunken husband --- that day or any other day! Besides, she lived about fifty miles outside of Boston. "That's a long bus ride with nothing to drink", I thought.

"I really don't want to go," I told Irene. "Can't you call and tell Erma we'll make it some other time?"

"No, I won't, Freeman," Irene said. "We really must go. You know we won't be able to go once you start working. Remember, Erma hasn't seen you in your uniform yet, and she won't give us any peace until she does. Besides, Freeman, you haven't seen your sister in almost four years, and I haven't met her yet," she added.

I finally agreed to go, only because Irene was

so persistent. She told me later she thought a change of scenery would snap me out of my morbid frame of mind.

I often look back on that day and think of how the meeting with my brother-in-law, Ed, changed my whole life. And I shudder inwardly when I think of how hard I had tried to avoid the trip.

After one more drink, out in the open that time, I was able to make a phone call to Erma. She was excited to hear we were heading her way, and she promised us a nice dinner. When I told her I didn't know how to get to her house, she said she would have Ed meet us at the bus stop.

While Irene was getting our things together, I was sitting at the kitchen table trying to think of a way to take some whiskey with me. Irene, however, spoiled any ideas I may have come up with when she said,

"And I don't want you drinking any more today either; you've had enough."

She had spoken so firmly, I knew I had better not cross her. Especially after what I had just told her about my drinking. For the next few minutes I mentally kicked myself for being such a weak, sentimental fool. On the other hand though, I was glad I had told her. I decided I would not be so secretive about my drinking any longer; there would be no reason to.

One hour later we were in the Greyhound Bus Terminal in Boston with tickets to our destination. I was so exhausted I fell asleep as soon as we boarded the bus. However, it wasn't a restful sleep. It was one of those where one is half-asleep and half-awake. I would snap alert when the bus stopped abruptly, or swerved a bit too sharply, but then I would immediately drop back into my stupor. The hour and a half slipped hazily by and soon Irene was shaking me awake. We were there.

My first thought was "I need a drink badly". My hands were beginning to tremble noticeably and my mouth felt like a dry woolen mitten. As I got unsteadily to my feet to leave the bus, I wondered if Ed would really be waiting for us. In the past I had learned he was as unpredictable as any drunk. He would promise anything but never keep a promise. Much of the time he was nowhere to be found.

I had no respect for Ed at all. In fact I found him to be a disgusting individual. He was forty-five years old, twelve years older than my sister Erma. He would not work, or when he occasionally did he wouldn't stay at the job long enough to earn more than one or two paychecks. He had been a drunk for more than thirty years, and he was a panhandler. That's how he got his drinking money. The only food brought into his house was the food my sister brought in --- bought with her meager earnings as a waitress in a local coffee shop. To make matters worse, Ed's clothes always looked as though he slept in them, and there was never a time when he didn't need a bath. I hadn't liked him from the beginning. In fact I had stayed away from my sister as much as I could even before the war because of him. However, that day I was hoping he would be there to meet us, because then I would have a drinking companion, and Irene wouldn't be able to say much in front of him if she didn't like it.

Ed was there all right. I spotted him even before we got off the bus. Immediately I noticed a difference. He was clean-shaven and neatly dressed. In fact, he was wearing a suit and tie. His face was bright, and he wore a nice warm smile. What surprised me most though, was the fact that he was sober. He was not the Ed I remembered. Although I was taken aback by his appearance, my real concern was for my own immediate needs .... I needed a drink.

With the introductions to my wife and child out of the way, I turned to Ed and said,

"Ed, I was drunk last night and I'm rum-sick. If you take us to the nearest bar, I will buy the drinks."

As much as I didn't like Ed, I knew he would understand, and at that moment I was glad he was a comrade in my misery.

"I'll take you into the bar, Freeman," Ed answered, "but I don't want anything. I'm not drinking today."

I was speechless. I felt as though I was in the company of a stranger. I felt embarrassed in front of him because of my need for a drink. I was still mute ten minutes later when the four of us filed into a bar two blocks away. However, as we slid into a booth facing each other, I couldn't hide the sarcasm in my voice as I asked,

"How long on the wagon this time, Ed?"

"Nine months," he answered quickly, and I didn't miss the sparkle in his eyes.

I was stunned; I couldn't believe it. Ed, my drunken brother-in-law --- sober for nine months! "That really could be called a miracle", I thought. I sat there, silent, as the waitress brought us our drinks.

There was a rum and coke for me, a Tom Collins for Irene and a ginger ale for Ed. Before the waitress had set the last drink down, mine was gone, and I ordered another. I could see the anger in Irene's eyes, but I knew she wouldn't say anything in front of Ed. When the waitress set my second drink in front of me, she spilled some on the table and left it there.

As soon as the waitress was out of hearing, Irene turned to face me. Quietly, but with deliberate control, she said,

352

"Freeman, after that drink, I don't want you to have anymore. Do you understand me?"

Just as I was about to make a sarcastic reply, Ed took the attention onto himself and saved us from an awkward moment. He laid both of his hands flat on the table --- in the pool of spilt liquor. Then he rubbed his hands all over his face as he said,

"See, Freeman, I can be near it, even smell it, and it doesn't bother me. I don't need it anymore."

I became envious over Ed's apparent freedom from alcohol, and I was impressed by his self-confidence. I became deadly serious as I leaned over the table and asked,

"My God, Ed, how are you doing it?"

"I joined Alcoholics Anonymous," he said.

"What in hell is Alcoholics Anonymous?" I asked.

"They're a good bunch of fellows and gals who are staying sober by helping each other," he answered. "If anyone is having a problem with their drinking, they would do themselves a favor by looking into Alcoholics Anonymous. They may find they belong there."

Then, for the second time that day I was able to tell another human being I had a problem with my drinking. I leaned across the table to get closer, and in a low voice I said,

"Ed, I have had a problem with my drinking ever since I took my first drink ten years ago. I have tried many times to stop but I can't. I don't know what to do. I am terrified when I think of where my life is going. There are times when I think I'm going crazy."

Ed tried to assure me that he didn't think I was insane. He suggested I might be an alcoholic, like himself. I listened intensely to his every word. We talked about drinking in general, and about alcoholism in particular, for a long time. Meanwhile, Irene never said a word. She just sat there with Keith in her lap, twirling her untouched drink, and looking very troubled.

I didn't know it then, but I had bought my last drink of alcohol that afternoon. That was Thursday, June 20th, 1946.

MY SOBRIETY BEGINS

It was almost four o'clock when we left the bar and walked the three blocks to Erma's house. Erma was setting the table when we walked in, and Irene jumped right in to help. After a delicious dinner, my first full meal in about five days, Ed and I retired to the front room. While Irene helped Erma clean up, Ed and I continued the conversation we had started in the bar. The visit that I had insisted would last only one hour lasted six.

Ed did most of the talking that evening while I listened, spellbound. He told me about his life as a drunk --- how he had started drinking innocently with some friends at an early age, and of how he had soon lost those friends because he drank differently than they did. In a way, he was telling my life story. However, he had a thirty-two year drinking history to my ten.

He told me about Alcoholics Anonymous, and about how the members had helped him, especially during his first three weeks of sobriety. Through his story, I could see what was in store for me if I kept on drinking. But I saw a lot more too. For the first time in my life, I realized I was not alone. Ed told me there were many people like myself in this world --- people who drank the way I did, who had the same kinds of problems I had when they drank. And he told me they drank even when they didn't want to, just as I had. He told me they understood what it was like to be a drunk and to be scorned by everyone, including themselves. But most importantly, he told me they had found a way to stop their drinking. They had found what I had been looking for for ten years.

Later that evening, as we got on the bus to go home, Ed gave me two things to take with me. One was a piece of paper with a number on it, the phone number to the club room of Alcoholics Anonymous in Boston. The other was a card to ponder over. It read, "It's not your drinking that makes you stinking, it's your stinking thinking that keeps you drinking".

I loved that immediately because it answered a question I had been asking myself again and again for years --- "How come I can stop drinking when things get bad enough, but I can't seem to stay stopped for long even though I want to with all my heart?"

It was too late to call A.A. when we got home that night, but I made the call the first thing the next morning. I knew if I didn't call then, the chances were I wouldn't call at all.

"Hello," a pleasant voice said, "this is A.A... How can I help you?"

"My name is Freeman Carpenter," I answered, "my brother-in-law suggested I call you people and talk to you."

"OK" the voice said, "are you sober now?"

That question struck me as being pretty damned personal and for just a few seconds I resented this stranger asking it of me. However, I had to admit I was the one who called and I did want to know more about A.A. so I bit my tongue and answered,

"Yes sir, I had my last drink about three-thirty yesterday afternoon."

"Do you want to stay sober?" the voice asked. Again I felt funny talking to a stranger about this, but I answered,

"Yes I do."

But the minute I said that I began to tremble and I felt sick to my stomach.

"What the hell are you doing?" I asked myself, "you don't need to go this far do you?"

However, the fellow on the phone interrupted my thoughts by saying,

"Where are you calling from, Freeman?"

"I'm in Central Square, Cambridge," I answered.

"You are only three miles away," he said, "why don't you jump on a streetcar and come on over."

I didn't want to go, for some reason I was very afraid, but I couldn't tell why. However, I knew if I didn't go then I would probably not go at all, so I said,

"OK I'll come right over."

He gave me the address on Boyleston St., told me his name was Ray and said he would be waiting for me.

Forty minutes later I was standing outside the club room looking at a small sign in the door. It said "A.A." --- that was all. The next forty-five minutes were pure hell. I was afraid to go in and afraid not to. I knew I needed to stop drinking and I was afraid that A.A. had the answer as to how I could stop. But I really didn't want to quit. I was afraid of what my life would be like without drinking. "Besides", I said to myself, "what will people think if they see me going into an A.A. club room? God forbid they should think I am an alcoholic". Finally,

although I didn't know what my life would be like
without alcohol, I did know what it was like with it,
so up the stairs I went.

When I stepped through the door I thought I was
in an old man's club with all the overstuffed chairs
and dark heavy tables. The room was huge. Ray was
the only person there that morning. He said he had
been waiting for me. I was flattered and impressed.

I MET RAY

Ray was a man in his late fifties or early
sixties. He was about six feet tall and weighed about
one hundred-ninety pounds. His full head of hair was
completely white and made him look distinguished. He
wore a white suit, white shirt and white shoes. There
was a Panama hat on the table that I knew was his. He
had a big black cigar stuck in his mouth and he looked
the picture of success. As soon as he saw me he came
forward with outstretched hand and said,

"Hello, my name is Ray, and I am an alcoholic."

I was speechless as I shook his hand, I don't
think I told him my name I was so stunned. "An
alcoholic is not supposed to look like Ray", I
thought.

"Are you the fellow who called me from Central
Square, Cambridge?" Ray asked.

"Yes, I am," I answered timidly.

"Let's sit down," Ray said, as he led me to a
big sofa along the wall. He sat across from me in a
big easy chair and started to talk.

"Two and a half years ago," Ray said, "I was
sleeping in Boston Common, I didn't have a dime to my
name, my family had kicked me out years before because
I was a drunk. The soles were out of my shoes, I had

357

no underwear and the seat was out of the ass of my pants. What's more," he said, "I didn't want to stop drinking. I only came in here to get warm and to get a cup of coffee."

Ray went on for the next two hours telling me, a stranger, all about his life as a drunk. He never once asked me about my drinking. He didn't seem to be interested in what I had done or anything. I tried to figure out what his game was, what he wanted from me. I really couldn't believe anyone would spend that much time with me without wanting something in return. Finally, Ray unexpectedly asked,

"Can you stay sober until tomorrow night?"

"Oh sure," I said, "I'll be OK now for a week or so."

"OK," Ray said, as he wrote an address on a piece of paper.

"Here is where the meeting will be held," he said, "I don't believe in taking people to meetings, I believe they have to come because they want to. However, I will be waiting for you just inside the door at eight o'clock."

I took my leave then and all the way home my head was spinning. "What did this all mean? Why did Ray spend so much time with me? How come he didn't want to know anything about me?" I really was confused.

I didn't think of a drink all that day but I did think of Ray. In fact, I couldn't get him out of my mind. I slept soundly that night and woke up refreshed Saturday morning. What's more, I didn't want a drink....

I felt guilty when I told Irene I was going to a meeting that night because every time I had left her alone before it was to go out and drink. I was sure she would be suspicious of me and I knew I deserved the suspicion. Nevertheless, I went to the meeting anyway and true to his promise, Ray was there at the door to shake my hand.

There were about thirty people in the room that night, mostly men but about three or four women. I was not paying attention to numbers, I was only interested in what they looked like and what they had to say.

It was all so new to me that I didn't get much out of the meeting. I did hear several people say they were alcoholics and I could see they were sober. They talked about twelve steps and I thought they were referring to the steps we used to get up to the meeting room. I promised myself I would count them when I went out. There were eighteen steps so I was more confused than before!

Most of the people at the meeting were neatly dressed and many of them had a smile on their face. They looked and acted as though they were happy. I was shocked at how openly they had talked about their drinking days. The stories I heard were incredible. What struck me too, was the fact that there was a lot of laughter among people who, by their own admission, had done some terrible things, and had suffered the consequences deeply. However, I felt a warmth and a genuineness about those people that was so comforting I didn't want to leave their company even when the meeting was over. To me it was like finding a nice warm stove in the middle of a blizzard. I had a sense that these people really did understand and they seemed willing to accept me just as I was. Like Ray, they didn't ask me about my drinking either, they told me about theirs. I knew I would be back.

Ray shook my hand again as I was leaving that night as he said,

"Will you stay sober and come to the meeting next Saturday, Freeman?"

"Yes, Ray," I answered. "I'm pretty sure I can

359

do that."

"Remember," Ray said, "if it gets tough for you, call the club room. There is always someone there."

"Thanks Ray," I hollered over my shoulder as I headed for the bus.

I could hardly go to sleep that night I was so excited. I had found out that just maybe I was not crazy, there was a good chance now I wouldn't have to kill myself after all. There was a strong possibility I might be an alcoholic, and if so all I needed to do was to stop my drinking. I had learned no longer would I be alone, I would have friends who would show me the way if I really wanted to go with them. I wasn't quite sure if I could or wanted to.

One fellow gave me hope when he said,

"Freeman, if you don't know whether Alcoholics Anonymous is for you or not, why don't you stick around for three or four months to see for yourself. If at that time you decide A.A. is not for you, you will find all the barrooms still open."

That seemed to me to be a reasonable idea, but still I couldn't verbally commit myself. We didn't have sponsorship as it is known today so I could be pretty secretive without much difficulty.

Things started to fall in place quite rapidly for me then. Five days after my first A.A. meeting I got a job as a cook-manager in a small local diner. The following Saturday I was sober and at the meeting. I felt a little proud of myself as I shook Ray's hand and said,

"Hello Ray, I haven't had a drink all week."

I guess I expected him to give me a pat on the back for a job well done. Instead he said,

"I knew you wouldn't Freeman."

I was disappointed that he didn't acknowledge my accomplishment, but flattered by his trust. Then I was confused, "How did he know that I wouldn't take a drink when I didn't know it myself?" I thought.

That evening before the meeting, I talked to a couple of men who were sitting together off to one side. First I told them just a little about my drinking and then I asked them if they thought I was an alcoholic. I really wanted them to say I wasn't so I could leave with a clear conscience. Then I became afraid that if they did say I wasn't an alcoholic where could I go with my problems? Fortunately for me the men were wise fellows. One of them looked hard at me for a full minute before he said,

"Son, we don't tell people whether they are alcoholics or not, we tell them what we think an alcoholic is and if they feel the description fits them, and if they want to use the program of Alcoholics Anonymous to overcome their alcoholism, then they are welcome."

I went away from that second meeting still confused and frightened. For one thing I didn't want anything to do with the God business in A.A. and yet I couldn't duck it. I knew by that time I did have a drinking problem and probably I was an alcoholic, but I had abandoned the idea of God a long time ago and thought that anyone who prayed was a fool. It was at that time I began to experience severe migraine headaches. I never had them before. The only headaches I ever had were hangover headaches that would go away after the withdrawal period was over. These headaches were different. They were so severe that I felt like banging my head against a wall. Then, because I was afraid of my addictive personality, something I was just learning about in A.A., I wouldn't even take an aspirin to relieve my distress.

Then on June 30th 1946 we moved into our new home. The distraction was good for me and my headaches quieted down a bit but they did not subside completely.

Then, at my third A.A. meeting, I began to hear about the twelve steps of recovery. I didn't like a lot of things I was hearing, especially the advice I was given about honesty. When I first started living away from home I had learned how to steal just to survive. Then later, when I began to drink heavily, I needed to steal to keep on drinking. I got good at stealing and thought I was clever. And so when I went to work at my new job I carried my dishonesty with me. I would go in to work alone at five o'clock in the morning and open the diner for breakfast. Then, every hour the cost of three or four meals went into my pocket instead of the cash register. I had always done that wherever I worked. So I didn't like it when I heard someone in A.A. speak of the need for honesty in order to overcome their drinking. "After all", I thought, "I'm sober now and doing OK, what more do I need? Those guys may need to become honest in order to stay sober, but not me. Besides", I reasoned, "every manager knows that all short-order cooks steal. And in order to get a good cook, one that is fast and reliable, most managers were willing to put up with a certain amount of stealing. Then, to offset those losses the managers would offer a prospective employee twenty per cent less than he was willing to pay for the job".

With that kind of reasoning it was obvious to me I was being underpaid, so I had to steal at least twenty percent of my salary to break even. In other words I didn't think of it as actually stealing I thought of it as just drawing part of my salary in advance.

I was to learn later that my devious mind could rationalize away many of my defects of character in much the same way. This then, is the stinking thinking that kept me drinking.

It so happened, that on my fourth Saturday evening meeting, still sober, still having migraine headaches, still confused about how much I was willing

362

to give myself to this A.A. program, we had two
dynamic speakers. One spoke of the gift of sobriety,
the joy he had found and how God had changed his life.
The other fellow spoke of honesty, gratitude, and
peace of mind. I guess I was touched deeper than I
realized.

My sleep that night was restless and I was
forced to get up earlier than necessary. At work that
Sunday morning I went through my usual routine. The
breakfast crowd was heavy and loud, I didn't have time
to think. However, I did find the time to steal. A
dollar for the boss and then a dollar for me. It went
that way all through breakfast until my counterman
came in at ten-thirty. Then as usual, I turned the
counter over to him and went into the kitchen to
prepare lunch and dinner. As soon as the big doors
closed behind me and the noise from the counter was
faint, I began to think again about the meeting of the
night before. My first thought was, "I wonder if
there really is a God".

The next thought was, "If there is a God I
wonder if He would touch me as I had seen that He had
touched those two speakers from last night".

Then it happened! I had a sensation
that someone had placed their hand firmly
on my shoulder as a voice said clearly,

"Freeman, you damned fool, you were
told you have an incurable disease called
alcoholism, you were told the alcoholism
could be arrested if you had the capacity
to be honest, and yet you have twelve
dollars of your boss' money in your pocket."

The hairs on the back of my neck were standing
straight up. My knees were weak, and I was glad that
I was alone --- I am sure I must have turned white for
a few minutes. Even though I knew the voice was in my
own head, it was audible enough so that I looked over
my shoulder just to see if there was someone standing
there. I knew then what I had to do. I had to put

those twelve dollars back in the cash register. Many times later I have thought how ironic it was, twelve steps and twelve dollars. Just a dollar a step for recovery. It was the best bargain of my life!

During lunch, serving behind the counter with my counterman, I carefully put the money back a little at a time. I had to work fast though, because my shift would be over at three o'clock and I had to have all the money returned by then.

When the last quarter went into the cash register, something in the pit of my stomach literally clicked into place. I immediately felt different.

I couldn't reason it out at the time but I now believe God touched me in the kitchen that morning. I also believe now that I became an A.A. member the moment the last quarter went back into the cash drawer. A miracle had taken place that day, an untrustworthy young man became trustworthy. What a wonderful feeling it gave me!

When I walked down the street that afternoon, on my way to catch the bus, I was walking on air. The sun was brighter then I had ever seen it, the grass was greener, and the smell of fresh spring flowers was sharper than ever. Every sense of my being seemed to be alive as never before. That day I began to pay attention to the twelve suggested steps of the A.A. program. I began to take my fourth step inventory that same evening.

At my next A.A. meeting I told a couple of the men what had happened to me in the diner. Instead of laughing at me as I thought they might, they told me about a few of their own spiritual awakenings. That was the best meeting of them all for me because I really did feel a part of the whole thing. I began to understand just what the program was trying to do for us.

FAMILY TIES

Meantime I was reconnecting with my family. I had always been close to Ericka and it was she who made it possible for Irene and me to get our start after my discharge. I was pleased when she and her ex-sailor boyfriend, Johnny, broke up in June of 1944. Then, just a year after that Ericka married Leon, one of her childhood sweethearts. Leon was a non-drinker and a non-smoker. He was a soft-spoken, gentle man and I thought that he and Ericka would be married for life. However, much to everyone's surprise, they were divorced in January of 1946. Ericka told me one day years later that life with Leon was too boring. When I came home in March of that same year, Ericka was making plans to marry her current boyfriend, Charlie.

My sister Erma was three months into her pregnancy and she was growing so large we were afraid for her. The doctor said she was going to have twins and he was worried about her coming delivery. Even though her husband Ed had stopped his drinking, her house was no cleaner than it had been before. I hated going there and avoided doing so as often as possible. That was difficult for me because I believed Ed had saved my life by directing me to Alcoholics Anonymous. I felt guilty whenever I refused their invitation. However, they never pressured me and for that I was grateful.

My brother Jake was working as a maintenance man in an apartment building in Boston. He was earning a decent salary and his rent was free. He and Veronica had a six month old baby boy and at the moment they seemed to be doing all right. He never mentioned his army discharge and I wouldn't ask him about it even though I wanted to. I considered that another embarrassment to the Carpenter family, and it would be better to leave it alone.

My sister Eileen and her husband Frank had two daughters by then, Cathy who was four years old and

Nancy who was two. Frank had worked in the Boston Navy Yard all during the war and was still there when I came home. He was a radio and television technician and his knowledge kept him from being drafted. I was a little jealous of Frank. His skills allowed him to earn big money all the time I was drawing a soldier's pay. They lived in a nice big home in an exclusive neighborhood in the suburbs of Boston. However, even then his marriage to my sister was hell. Eileen was the domineering character in that relationship and Frank was as passive as my father used to be. I was astonished as I watched the interaction between those two --- it was like watching my mother and father all over again. I asked Frank bluntly, more than once, why he took her verbal abuse. However, he always avoided answering by ignoring my question.

About a month after we had moved into our new home, Eileen asked me if I would take my mother in for a short time. It turned out that Eileen had kept in touch with mother over the years. Through her letters Eileen had found out that mother had divorced dad and had recently remarried. Now mother wanted to come back to the United States with her new husband and Eileen didn't have enough room for them. Without thinking twice I said, "Sure". I had forgotten that my mother was a troublemaker. I had forgotten how she had thrown me out of her home not too many years before. I had even forgotten that she had deserted Eileen just when Eileen needed her so badly. Nevertheless, I considered this an opportunity to make amends to mother because I had caused her plenty of grief over the years due to my drinking. However, mother was capable of destroying the best of intentions and she wasted no time undermining our efforts to help her.

When mother did come back, in the middle of August, she not only brought her husband, Larry, she brought one of their friends too. Norman was a twenty year old Canadian who lived near mother in Halifax, Nova Scotia. It seems that he had always wanted to come to the United States so mother and Larry just brought him along! I wasn't expecting three people

366

but I couldn't refuse. Besides, he was a likable fellow and he paid his own way all the while he lived with us.

My baby sister, Lisa, was working in Canada at the time, and she didn't want to give up her job when mother decided to leave, so mother left her with some neighbors for the time being. With everyone accounted for I settled into a routine familiar to all family men. I went to work every day and to my A.A. meeting on Saturday nights.

WORKING WITH OTHERS

Not long after I joined Alcoholics Anonymous, while we were milling around the room one night waiting for the meeting to begin, one of the men said to me,

"Freeman, have you carried the message to another alcoholic yet?" I can still remember the flash of fear that shot through me.

"My God, Jim," I answered, "I don't know if I'm going to make it. What can I say to another man?"

"Look," Jim said, "if you have been sober for a few weeks and the person calling for help is still drinking, you have good sobriety to share with him. And because you know where the meetings are, you know more than he does. Besides, if you have a different idea about how to stay sober than you ever had before --- you have a spiritual message to carry to him --- the message of Alcoholics Anonymous."

Then another fellow chimed in and said, "You've got to give it away in order to keep it, son." And Jim added,

"Remember, if you don't become the doctor as soon as you can, if you remain the patient too long, you will not stay sober."

367

I was frightened by his words, but as usual I said nothing.

There were no detoxification units, no rehabilitation facilities, and no halfway houses back then. In fact, you could not get a hospital in my area to accept a patient with a diagnosis of alcoholism. Nevertheless, I took Jim's words seriously because I really wanted to stay sober. I began to look around to see what I could do to get involved.

Not long after that I met a forty year old man at our meeting who had no place to live. I took him home with me that night and gave him a room in my house. The only stipulation was that he stay sober. Of course I only allowed him in the house while I was there --- he had to leave whenever I did. However, he knew he had a roof over his head until he got on his feet.

Next, I started answering calls for help that were coming in on the Boston Hot-line. Then I was asked to be the coffee maker for our Saturday evening group. I kept that job faithfully for over two years without missing a meeting.

Although we were advised to never go on a Twelve Step call alone, there were a few times we had to or the call would have gone unanswered. Regardless of how tactful we were, there were times when we would find ourselves in the middle of a domestic squabble. And once I had the frightful duty of taking a loaded gun away from an intoxicated man before someone got hurt. When I would complain about the dangers involved, I was always reminded that this was a program of action.

In September of 1946 my brother, Jake, lost his job. I found out much later it was because he was collecting rent money from the tenants and not turning it over to his employer. When he lost his job he had no place to live, so I took him in. Of course that meant Veronica and the baby too. After all I was his brother and I had the room. I didn't think about his bed-wetting or anything else, just that he was in need and I could help. After all, isn't that what any good co-dependent would have done? Then, as if that wasn't enough, I found another homeless alcoholic and brought him home. My house was full!

Irene was going crazy. There she was with Keith the baby; she was six months into her pregnancy and getting bigger each week. She was cooking for a house-full of people with no one helping her. I didn't know about that part of it until much later. And there's more. No one was offering her any money for groceries even when they had it.

To keep peace in the family I gave my brother and my step-father each a ten-dollar bill one day. I told them to give it to Irene for groceries without telling her where they got it. I wanted her to think they had given it to her out of the goodness of their hearts. Instead of giving the money to Irene they went out drinking together that evening. To make matters worse mother and Irene were at each other's throats and both of them were coming to me with their complaints. One of my alcoholic friends would not stop drinking and the other fellow couldn't seem to find a job.

I didn't know what to do. My migraine headaches returned and I was an emotional wreck.

Finally I was desperate enough to tell a couple of the older men in my group what was going on at home. They gave me some sound advice that night. I came away from the meeting with a new sense of direction. I knew what I had to do. I had to clean house.

It took me three weeks to get everybody out of my house, but as hard as it was for me to do --- I did it! I was most afraid of my brother Jake. I was terrified that he might come back undercover of night and set my house on fire. I knew he was capable of doing just that but I felt I had no choice. I was willing to rely on the serenity prayer, a prayer I have said many times since I first saw it on the wall in our meeting room. I can't help but write it out for you on just the odd chance you have not seen it yourself. It goes:

God grant me the serenity to accept the things I can not change, the courage to change the things I can, and the wisdom to know the difference.

I did have a few nights where every noise would wake me and every nerve would be on edge, but nothing ever happened and I eventually felt safe again, but it was a rough time.

Since then I have watched good men and women lose their loved ones in an automobile accident, or a fire, and stay sober through it all. I have watched others lose their jobs and get drunk. I knew who I wanted to follow.

As soon as I cleared my house of so many undesirables I began to refocus on my recovery program. My headaches disappeared never to return.

By late November, my sister Erma was so large with her pregnancy I was afraid for her. The doctor insisted she go into the hospital, but Erma refused even when we offered to pay for it. Even though the twins were born without complications, Erma never regained her strength. Within the year she developed cancer of the uterus. Regardless of what the doctors did for her, nothing helped. The cancer ate at her for three years before she died. It was horrible for us to stand by and watch as she slowly wasted away. From a woman who weighed one hundred eighty-seven pounds she went down to a mere eighty-five pounds at her death. We had a closed casket at her funeral. The four boys were taken in by one of Ed's brothers to raise as his own. Over the years we lost contact with them because Ed's brother wanted no interference from any of us and we were satisfied with that. I had enough to deal with then anyway.

Surprisingly, after four years of sobriety, Ed got drunk even before we buried Erma. After all he had gone through during her illness, I was stunned. Then I became afraid for myself. I wondered if I would drink again some day regardless of how long I stayed sober. In the next three years Ed actually drank himself to death and I was at a loss for an explanation. I had done all I could to get him back on track but to no avail. I was finally able to set that puzzle aside and go on with my own life.

Meantime, Irene went into the hospital, and on December 7, 1946, she gave birth to a beautiful baby girl. We called her Regina Marie and I loved her immediately. I was proud of myself for being sober and able to attend to my husbandly duties.

Then, on Christmas eve of that same year, a Tuesday, I started an A.A. meeting closer to my home. Only one man showed up to keep me company that night but I felt good to have been there for him. It only takes two people to have an A.A. meeting anyway. That group became stable and was still going strong when I moved away in 1950.

I MET BILL W.

One of the most important events that happened to me in 1947, when my emotions were so unpredictable, was the day I met Bill W. for the first time. Bill W. as you may know was one of the co-founders of Alcoholics Anonymous. One evening the chairman of our Saturday night meeting announced that Bill was coming to Boston for a weekend. He said Bill would be staying at one of the larger hotels and would have his suite open for visitors during certain hours. I made sure I was there.

That Saturday afternoon there were over two hundred people waiting to see Bill when I arrived. To accommodate the number of visitors, the leaders

371

created groups of fifteen people and gave each group a twenty minute time period to visit with Bill. I was in the fourth group and it proved to be worth the two hour wait.

We were ushered into a lounge that was large enough to accommodate the fifteen of us comfortably. There were four medium-sized sofas and six overstuffed chairs to sit in. Bill was sitting in one of the chairs facing the door when I first saw him. He was dressed in a modest brown suit, white shirt, and brown striped tie. Even his shoes and socks were brown. He stood up to shake our hands as we walked in and to me he looked to be about six feet tall. I could see that he was slender and well-built. His handshake was firm and warm.

However, it wasn't his physical appearance that impressed me as much as it was the spiritual aura that seemed to permeate the whole room. Bill seemed to be unaware of the phenomenon and even of his part in it, but to me it was real yet unnatural. I was so awed by his presence that to this day I can't tell you what we talked about, but I will never forget the feeling. I wasn't alone in that either. It was not just my youthful impressionability; other men older than I had felt it too.

When I walked away from Bill that day I knew I had been in the presence of some spiritual force. The strange warm feeling I took away from that encounter lasted for several days. I had the privilege of repeating that experience once again a year later and I had exactly the same reaction to him then as I did the first time. I would have moved to New York just to be near him if I could have.

FAMILY DYNAMICS CONTINUE

Sometime during 1947 my brother Jake deserted his wife and child. Over the years he looked me up several times, always to ask for a handout. In the summer of 1954 I saw him for the last time. To this day I don't know what happened to him, but I feel that he is dead. I am sure if he was alive he would still be asking for my help.

During the latter part of 1947 Lisa came back from Canada and stayed with Irene and me for a few weeks until she got a job and went out on her own. She was seventeen then and very pretty. I was pleased with her appearance and her sophistication. It wasn't long before she met and fell in love with Mike. Mike had served valiantly during World War II and was a survivor of the Battle of the Bulge in Europe. As soon as I met Mike, I liked him and knew my sister would be in good hands. They were married in 1948.

As soon as my mother moved in with us my sister Eileen began to be a constant visitor. She proved to be as skilled a troublemaker as mother was. Although Eileen never drank she acted like a drunkard. She would leave home whenever she felt like it and she'd be gone for a week or more. Nobody knew where she went and Frank never confronted her. Cathy, her oldest daughter was full of her mother's strength; but Nancy, the youngest, was timid and shy throughout her life and in her teens became extremely depressed. She was a beautiful young woman but never could see herself that way. In the summer of 1969, when Nancy was twenty five, she took her own life by overdosing on tranquilizers.

Cathy had left home and married three years before Nancy's suicide. Then, less than a year after the tragedy Frank and Eileen were finally divorced. About two years later Frank married a divorced woman who had two grown sons. The three of them took Frank for everything he had when the woman divorced him a year after the marriage. He was such an emotional wreck by then I didn't want to have anything more to do with him and so I deliberately broke off our relationship. I have no idea what became of him, but I suspect if he is still alive he is in a destructive relationship of some kind.

Right after her divorce, Eileen started to drink and instantly found herself to be an uncontrollable, compulsive drinker. Her reaction to alcohol was exactly as mine had been when I took my first drink years before. It was ironic --- she was the only one who would confront me about my drinking and yet she turned out to be the only other alcoholic in our family. Even though Eileen didn't pick up a drink until she was in her late fifties, she quickly made up for lost time. The last time I heard anything about her she had been in several automobile accidents while driving drunk. I am told that in one of those accidents she went right through the windshield and had scarred her pretty face horribly. Even her daughter hasn't heard from her in the past ten years and so I must conclude that she is also dead by now.

Meanwhile, Ericka and Charlie got a divorce. It seemed that Ericka was true to her vows, but Charlie could not keep his. In the six years they had been married, he had several affairs. When he began to bring his women into their home, Ericka called it quits! There had been no children in that marriage so it wasn't as bad as it might have been. Ericka is living comfortably now in an apartment in Cambridge, Massachusetts, not far from where she spent most of her life. We communicate by phone about once a week and I visit her at least once a year.

LOOKING FOR ANSWERS

During all that time my sobriety was still intact, but I was on an emotional roller-coaster. After my experience in the diner that morning, the experience that had forced me to look at my honesty, I no longer doubted that there were unseen forces at work in this world. I just didn't know how they related to me. "If God was going to take care of me if I took care of others, how come I'm having so much trouble with the ones I'm trying to help?" I thought. Then, I began to believe all I needed to do was to try harder. When that didn't work I became more confused. One day I wanted to save all the alcoholics in the world, then the next day I didn't care if I saved even myself. I would be spiritually high for several days, then I would experience days of deep depression.

My confusion and despair were due to a great degree to the things that were happening to me at the time. I not only had problems at home to contend with, unexpectedly I lost my job through no fault of my own. One Saturday evening about a hundred neighborhood boys, out on a wild rampage, wrecked the diner I worked in so badly they put my employer out of business, and of course, me out of work. It took me three months to find another job and by then we were becoming financially desperate.

Meantime, the bank that held the mortgage on our house was after me to replace the roof. The old water pipes in the cellar burst and a whole new system had to be installed. Then, to make matters worse, Irene went into the hospital and gave birth to Arline, our third child. The baby was beautiful and healthy, she weighed six and three-quarters pounds and was eighteen inches long. Irene didn't have an ounce of trouble with the birth and for that we were grateful. However, the bills were coming in from all directions and Christmas was only a month away. Then too, I was becoming concerned for Irene about that time.

She had been a pretty woman when we married. She had a beautiful full figure and long wavy hair that fell down her back to her waist. Just a month after we married, without saying a word to me, she had her hair cut short and never let it grow long again. I was saddened and angry about that, but I wouldn't let Irene know how deeply I had been hurt.

There were times when I would wake up at night and hear her crying in the dark. I would turn on the light and ask her what was wrong. Then she would complain about the way her mother and father had treated her as she was growing up. No amount of assurance from me that the past was over, and that I loved her, was of any help. After the birth of our second child, Irene began to put on weight and didn't seem to care what she looked like. She was often sick and we spent many hours in doctor's offices for one complaint or another. The doctors were at a loss as to what was wrong. When I had found Alcoholics Anonymous and stopped my drinking, we had been married for three years. I was sure that because I was sober our marriage would be so much better, but it wasn't. In fact, it got worse.

If I went to a meeting alone I would be greeted with two or three days of ugly silence. If I took her to an open meeting with me she would count all the women she was sure I was "trying to make." Whenever I tried to talk to her about these concerns she would deny everything and accuse me of imagining the whole thing. However, I wanted the marriage to work --- I was still in love with her. Besides, I wasn't going to be like my father --- I was determined to stick by my marriage vows through thick and thin. Whenever Irene and I came up against a disagreement I would think it was my fault because I was the alcoholic. I had learned I had a grave mental, emotional and spiritual disorder, and I must work hard at getting better. Many times I had heard that if an alcoholic's wife or husband was emotionally ill, it was because of the behavior of the alcoholic. I felt guilty about that for a long time. However, watching my own efforts at being a peacemaker fail, and working with other married alcoholics, I have come to the conclusion that a goodly number of their mates were emotionally ill long before they met and married the alcoholic.

In March of 1948 Irene was rushed into the hospital for an operation. They said they had to remove a gallstone. While she was away I had the roof replaced, but then the bank wanted me to paint the outside of the house. They claimed they had to protect their investment. I began to feel like a glorified janitor rather than a "home owner"! I was never able to pay all of my bills on time and I was constantly broke. More than once I caught myself reverting back to my old habit of stealing. However, I could no longer justify my actions and always ended by making restitution. It took about eight years to get rid of that defect of character for good.

On June 5, 1949, on our sixth anniversary, Irene gave birth to Freeman, our fourth child. He was a beautiful healthy boy and I was proud of him. He had an outgoing personality and took to everyone. I was told by Ericka and others that he was the perfect image of myself when I was born. No father could have been more proud of his son than I was that day!

Nevertheless, I was going crazy with mounting responsibilities. During those financially difficult times my involvement in A.A. was a blessing. Unlike a few of the old-timers of the day, I did believe in taking people to meetings. I learned that whenever I found myself working with another alcoholic I could get away from myself and my own problems for a while. Regardless of how tired or depressed I was when I started out to help another person, I always came home refreshed. My anniversary dates kept coming without me being aware of them. Whenever someone recognized my anniversary I would be pleased but also surprised. In spite of everything I was going through, my A.A. meetings were like an oasis to me. The fellowship I enjoyed kept my spirits high even in the toughest of times.

During those years just after the war there was a fear of an atomic bomb being dropped on Boston or New York should we be attacked. If a person could not afford to build their own air-raid shelter, we were advised to learn where the public buildings were that had one. Daily one could read articles in the papers about the things needed in a shelter if you were to survive an attack. Some of the lists were ridiculously long and expensive. Many of us believed it was a real threat and I was uncomfortable having my family live so close to where a bomb might be dropped.

Everything considered, it was a welcome relief when, in 1950, my father-in-law offered me a job in

the paper mill where he worked. It meant that we had
to leave Cambridge, Massachusetts and move to a small
town in Maine, but I was only too glad to go by then.

We didn't have any trouble selling our house,
but by the time the bank and the contractors got
theirs we were lucky to break even. I had less than
five-hundred dollars in my pocket for being the
caretaker of that property for four years. I was glad
to see it go.

MAINE

Now let's take a look at our activities in
Maine. For one thing, Irene and I hadn't planned to
have four children in six years. Oh! we both wanted
kids all right, we just didn't expect them quite so
fast. We even practiced birth control sporadically in
an attempt to gain some time between births. However,
we were sexually active in our earlier years and
evidently very fertile. We were married seventeen
months before Keith came along but after that the
slightest neglect of precautionary measures would find
Irene pregnant. We both loved each child dearly as
they came into our lives but the additional
responsibilities that came with them were devastating.
Raising four children on a laborer's wages was
difficult for everyone involved. Besides the meager
earnings there were the periods of unemployment most
general laborers are familiar with.

Nevertheless, although there were some slim
times, the children had plenty of warm clothes and no
one ever went hungry. There was always enough fuel to
keep us warm regardless of how cold the winters were.
Fortunately, due to my continued sobriety, the
physical needs of my children were adequately provided
throughout their childhood.

Meanwhile, even though I was only a general
laborer in the mill, I became interested in the union
and soon was elected shop steward for my department.

378

I also began to sign up for different jobs as they became available in an effort to get out of the labor pool. It took over a year, but I was finally given a position inside the mill and my income slowly increased. Things were beginning to look better for us.

Then, the day after Christmas of 1951 Irene gave birth to Andrea our fifth and last child. She was a beautiful baby and her birth made us a family of seven. Even though my father-in-law had plenty of room and wanted us to live with him I wanted a place of our own. I soon found that very few landlords wanted to rent to a man with a large family. I could not afford to buy a place at the time so I built my own home from scratch. That was a project. In order to get the lumber to build with I tore down an old house that had twenty-two rooms in it. I was able to save almost everything. The house had been given to me with the understanding I would remove it from the center of town without causing any damage to the surrounding buildings. It was a dangerous and tedious job, but after ten weeks in my off duty hours from the mill, I had it down. I bought two acres of land for six hundred dollars and then paid a trucker to haul the lumber onto my land. Fortunately I found and rented a large house near where we were building and I set to work. Two years later we moved into our own house, a house that had no mortgage.

Meantime I was attending our weekly meeting in Bangor twelve miles from my home. That group had twenty-two members with varying lengths of sobriety from six months to five years. With the exception of seven members who were as excited about their sobriety as I was about mine, the majority of the men came to their Wednesday night meeting, played cards with each other, sat through the meeting and went home. They seemed to be able to maintain their sobriety that way. Any attempt on my part to get them involved in public information or twelve step work outside of the four walls of the meeting room was met with open hostility. The only twelve step work that could be done was when a newcomer dropped in on our Wednesday meeting. And every other month or so a minister, a police officer, or a disgruntled wife would get in touch with us asking for help or information. However, the zealots among us, including myself, were so excited about our sobriety and our spiritual awakening we could not be held back.

The first thing we did was to start a Saturday evening meeting in Old Town, just a mile from my father-in-law's house. Then we found several opportunities to share the good news of A.A. with the general public. With the help of my new friends we began an open A.A. meeting and invited local doctors, nurses and ministers to be our guests. To our delight we had many accept our invitation and the word spread. Then we were invited to speak at the University of Maine at Orono. There we addressed student social workers and future psychologists about alcoholism as we understood it and told them what the program of Alcoholics Anonymous had done for us individually.

Because of those activities I became an active member of a local committee on alcoholism and for a short time served as their president. Through their efforts many professionals were introduced to individuals who were working the program of Alcoholics Anonymous. The committee was also responsible for getting some of us on local TV talk shows. There the camera showed us from the neck down and we used our first names only.

Through all those activities, even though I abided by our eleventh tradition and presented myself to the public anonymously, I began to have a serious problem with my ego. I believe it is called big-shot-ism!

It came to a head for me when the committee offered to pay my way to the Summer School of Alcohol Studies held at Yale University. The paper mill where I worked would give me the time off, but they would not pay me while I was gone. My family needed the income so I could not go. I began to resent my family then, blaming them for holding me back. I never let them know that though; as usual I kept my thoughts to myself. They had no idea what I was going through.

I became depressed, sullen and angry. I stayed that way for two full months. However, my program, in step ten, asks me to continue to take a personal inventory and when wrong to promptly admit it. I know that two months is not very prompt, but I finally did get around to it. Through that inventory I realized I had forgotten I was an alcoholic in recovery. Somewhere along the way I had lost my gratitude for my sobriety. I knew from watching others going through similar circumstances that the next step might be the loss of that sobriety. My ego collapsed and I surrendered my will.

That day I resigned as the president of the committee and I cancelled some speaking engagements. My resentment toward my family evaporated and I believe I became an A.A. member in good standing once again.

While I was having my own personal war with my ego, the Saturday evening meeting in Old Town was creeping along. It took about a year to get a dozen members who could stay sober and begin to carry the message. The interesting part of that group was that several of the members were related to each other. That fact set the stage for some unique twelve step work, much of which did not work!

The rapid growth of Alcoholics Anonymous, first in this country and later in several other countries throughout the world has spoken loudly of it's effectiveness. I have had the privilege of sharing in a number of successes myself, aside from my own.

During the years I lived in Maine I was faithful to my Wednesday evening group in Bangor and my Saturday evening group in Old Town. One of the highlights of that time was our trips to the Thomaston State Prison at Thomaston, Maine. At least once a month we would pile into two or three cars and drive the ninety miles to bring the inmates an A.A. meeting. Those trips were very special to me. The camaraderie generated in those few hours was delightful. One evening we would discuss the twelve steps of the program in great detail. Another night would find us telling jokes all the way out and back. Every trip was refreshing and enjoyable. Then, once we were there the sharing was uplifting. Hearing some of the stories from the prisoners helped me to keep my gratitude and my humility. There was no question in my mind but for the grace of God I could have been one of those inmates.

Then there were the hours I spent with the Indians. Less than a quarter mile off shore, on the northern end of Old Town, in the Penobscot river, sits Indian Island. It's not a big island. A person could drive completely around it in fifteen or twenty minutes. It is the homeland of the Penobscot Indians. I don't know how many Indians live on that island but I would guess less than a thousand.

Many of those Indians work in the mills on the mainland and just as many suffer from alcoholism like the rest of us. It was only natural for some of them to drift into our meeting and just as natural for us to accept them as our equals and to offer them our help. In doing so there were the usual joys and disappointments. However, over time, I was privileged to meet several Indians who were deeply spiritual. Several of those Indians had no problem with alcohol themselves but had a loved one who was afflicted.

Sometimes one of my A.A. buddies and I would ride over the one-lane bridge onto the island to see a man who had attended our meeting. A few times we missed the man we had come to see but ended up spending over an hour with his uncle or grandfather. One particular older man was especially good for me. Whenever I spent time with him I could feel that I was in the presence of an extraordinarily spiritual man. My spiritual life was enriched by those men every time I visited with them. It wasn't long before I began looking for excuses to go over the bridge just to chat with them. When we had to move out of the state of Maine I missed the visits to Indian Island very much.

WE ALMOST LOST OUR HOUSE

By the time we had our house built and were able to move into it my concern for Irene, keen enough already, deepened considerably. At that time my uneasiness was over the way she would leave the children alone while I was at work.

When we had moved to Maine in 1950 Irene had been able to reestablish contact with several of her childhood friends. Many of them were married by then and had a home of their own. In fact, the reason we purchased the particular parcel of land to build on was because several of Irene's friends lived in that general area. At least five of them lived within a mile of our house. I thought it would be good for Irene to be near them.

I had no idea that she was leaving the children unattended until I came home sick one day about three hours ahead of my usual time. The four children were playing in the street but Irene and the baby were nowhere around. Keith told me she might be at Jane's house a block away but Regina thought she might be at Gloria's way down the street. She was at neither. When Keith realized how angry I was he volunteered the information that his mother always leaves them alone, sometimes for hours at a time. I was incensed.

Irene didn't come home until a quarter-to-six, just about a half hour before I was due home. I was so angry by that time I was afraid to talk to her. I was afraid I would lose my temper and say things I really didn't mean. I had done that a few times already. Still I had to let her know how fearful and upset I was. Somehow I had to get her to see how dangerous it was to leave the children that way. I ranted at her for a long time that evening and she just sat there and listened. Taking her silence as an admission of guilt, and reasoning she had gotten the message, I foolishly thought the issue was resolved. However, that was not the case. It wasn't long before her continued neglect of the children almost cost us our home.

It was a very hot day in the middle of July 1954. I had been working on the installation of a couple of three-way switches in our bedroom. Due to my limited knowledge of wiring I couldn't get the switches to work, so I called the electrician for help. He promised to come the next day. Meantime, I had no electricity in the house but I didn't want to disturb the work I had already done just for that. My father-in-law helped to solve the lighting problem by giving me two kerosene lamps. Having done as much as I could for that day I went to work on the evening shift.

When I came out of the mill just after eleven P.M. the night was warm but very dark. The sky was banked with heavy black clouds and it looked as though we were in for a bad thunderstorm. As I quietly got out of the car in front of my house twenty minutes later, a man's voice came out of the darkness,

"Freeman, is that you?" the voice called.

I was startled because I couldn't see anyone even looking across the street in the direction of the voice. But I answered,

"Yes, it's me. Who's calling?"

"It's me --- Mr. Jones, your neighbor. Come over for a minute, I want to talk to you," the voice said.

I was concerned then because Mr. Jones was a neighbor who had always kept to himself. Although we had lived across the street from each other for over a year we just barely said "Hello" when we met. As I neared his porch-steps I could just make out his silhouette sitting there.

"Come sit a minute," he said as he made room for me on the bench.

"What's wrong, Mr. Jones?" I asked as I slid onto the seat next to him.

"Your house almost burned down tonight," he said. "Your wife had put the kids to bed about nine o'clock and had gone to the corner store for something. She had left the two lamps lit, one upstairs and one down. Of course the kids were out of bed the minute she was gone. Keith went to move the upstairs lamp and he dropped it. The oil went into the cracks of the floor and immediately caught fire. Mr. Jordan, my next door neighbor, and I had a hell of a time putting the fire out. You almost didn't have a house tonight," he said.

I thanked him profusely for his quick action but I felt awkward too. I didn't know what to say to this man who had prevented a disaster for me. A disaster that my wife should not have let happen in the first place. However, Mr. Jones had more to say. I could see that he was concerned.

"Freeman, I don't want to be a troublemaker," he said, "but you should know that your wife leaves those kids alone often. Sometimes she is gone for a couple of hours. I think you should do something about that before something happens. If Victor and I had not been here this evening you would not have a house right now, and who knows what might have happened to your kids."

There was a moment of awkward silence as I couldn't think of anything to say. I sensed that Mr. Jones had said all he wanted to say and I wanted to end that uncomfortable conversation as soon as possible. I broke the silence by thanking him again and I promised I would discuss the issue with Irene.

When I quietly opened the back door a few

385

minutes later I could smell the mixture of burnt wood, smoke and kerosene. I was thankful that Mr. Jones had talked to me first because I know I would have panicked if he hadn't. Everyone in the house was asleep or so I thought they were. I knew I couldn't talk to Irene that night because I wanted to kill her and I was having a great deal of difficulty keeping the rage in check. Quietly I undressed and gently slid into the bed. To my surprise Irene spoke to me in the dark.

"Freeman, I want to talk to you about something that happened tonight," she said.

"Mr. Jones has told me all about it already," I answered sullenly, "and I don't want to talk about it just now."

For about ten minutes the house was deadly quiet and I was slowly beginning to relax. Suddenly I was startled when Irene got out of bed and started to get dressed. When she saw I was awake she said,

"Freeman, do you have any money I can have? I'm leaving."

"There's about thirty-five dollars in my wallet," I said. "Take it all and get the hell out of here. I will consider myself lucky to have gotten off so cheap." I felt guilty the minute I said it but I didn't care, I was so mad and frustrated over the whole thing.

Strangely I was able to do some breathing exercises I had learned and soon I fell asleep. When I woke up the next morning Irene was sleeping alongside of me as though nothing had happened between us.

In fairness to Irene, I believe the scare was enough to get her to see the danger I had tried to make her see for a long time. We never did sit down to talk about that near-tragedy but I could sense a difference in Irene and as far as I knew she never left the children alone like that again.

One of the reasons Irene and I didn't get to talk about that problem was because she went into the hospital again just three days after she had threatened to leave her family. There had not been enough time for me to get my anger sufficiently under control before she was gone.

That particular hospitalization started as so many others had. First there had been two days of silence with neither of us saying any more to each other than we needed to. Then all during the second night Irene was moaning and tossing about restlessly. I pretended to be asleep in order to avoid dealing with her. The next morning she could hardly straighten up she was in so much pain. Feeling guilty but frightened and angry I took her to the emergency room of the Eastern Maine General Hospital and they called our family doctor.

When the doctor couldn't determine what was wrong with Irene he decided to admit her and do a D. and C.. According to the doctor she would be in the hospital for only three days or less.

We had to hire a baby-sitter we couldn't afford and once again I felt defeated. For a long time I had suspected that Irene would feign a physical problem and go to a doctor whenever there was an issue between us. But then, if she was admitted into a hospital, as she often was, I would feel guilty for being selfish and suspicious. Usually they would release her in a day or two and my suspicions would return. Evidently she was really sick that time because her doctor let me know he was concerned. That made me feel all the worse for my suspicions.

Nevertheless, the D. and C. proved to be routine and nothing serious had been discovered. We could breathe easy again.

I LOST INTEREST IN MY HOUSE

After Irene's hospitalization I settled into my familiar routine. I would work in the mill for eight hours, come home, eat and then work on the house for four or six hours. On Wednesday evenings I would attend the A.A. meeting in Bangor and on Saturday evenings our meeting in Old Town. For a long time everything ran smoothly. Irene was feeling well and the house was slowly becoming a comfortable place to live in. It wasn't finished by any means but I was beginning to see the results of my work and I was proud of my accomplishment. Then, something happened that hurt me so deeply I never did recover from it.

We were sitting around the kitchen table having dinner one beautiful cool evening in July of 1955. I was very tired that evening having worked an extra shift in the mill. I was mentally congratulating myself because my overtime pay would allow me to buy a washstand making my bathroom complete. A friend of ours had promised to help me install the washstand that weekend. Irene had cooked a delicious meal of baked stuffed pork chops with plenty of mashed potatoes and vegetables. I ate a little too much and did not want to move when the meal was over. Our two boys had asked to be excused so they could go out to play and they bolted out the door the minute permission was given.

Irene was sitting at one end of the table and I was at the other. The three girls were flitting around the kitchen making a pretence out of cleaning the dirty dishes. At that point I was feeling so relaxed my mind began to drift. In that semiconscious state I glanced over at Irene. She was looking directly at me and she had such a strange expression on her face I was prompted to ask,

"What's wrong, hon?"

"Let's sell this goddamed place," she blurted,

388

"and buy a good house."

I don't believe I have ever fainted in my life so I don't know what it feels like to faint. But, if ever I came close to doing so I believe it was then. Irene's words had cut me as if a knife had been savagely thrust into my heart. The physical pain was real and it was intense. I couldn't speak. Then, about ten seconds later, I felt all my energy leave my body through my legs and feet. It was just as if someone had pulled a plug and everything ran out and was gone. I was left feeling as weak as a dishrag. My interest in that house vanished on the spot and it never returned.

I bought the washstand only because I had ordered it but it never got installed. And even though we lived in that house for almost two more years I never drove another nail into it. I would not believe that anyone could have that much of a profound effect on another person unless it had happened to me. I am now ashamed of my reaction to Irene's words. It couldn't happen at this stage of my life. However, I have preached against that type of psychological abuse ever since.

WE MOVED TO PENNSYLVANIA

All during the 1950's the paper mill I was working in was going through a process called automation. As each department was revamped men would be laid off. Production was going up and the number of employees continued to decrease. Because of my skills I was able to avoid a layoff by shifting departments a few times. However, late in 1956 it became my turn to go. It was a difficult position to be in because if a person didn't work in the paper mill, or if he wasn't in business for himself, he could not earn a living wage in the area. I began to think of the advantages of moving to a big city. By then the threat of an atomic attack was definitely over and I wasn't interested in my house any more. We put our place on the market and moved to Philadelphia, Pennsylvania because I had heard that they had paper mills there. It took over three years to sell my property in Maine, and although we made some money on it, it wasn't much compared to the bills we had accumulated by then.

We rented an apartment in Coatesville, PA and I started looking for work. After almost three months, in March of 1957, I began working for the Downingtown Paper Company located in Downingtown, PA, just seven miles from Coatesville. I had been hired to work in the printing department where they manufactured folded cartons. I became a printer on a high-speed press and stayed with that company for over seventeen years.

Even before I had a job I contacted a local group of A.A. and became a regular member of that group. Through those people I got to know the folks in the Intergroup Office of A.A. in Philadelphia. Not long after that I was asked to serve on the Public Information Committee. As a member of that team I went into high schools, hospitals, colleges and rehabilitation centers sharing our knowledge of alcoholism and the program of Alcoholics Anonymous with anyone who would listen.

During the next ten years in the paper mill, I became active in the local union. At first I served on the grievance committee and on the safety committee. I enjoyed the involvement both of those positions made possible. Within two years I was elected their Shop Steward and served in that position off and on for years. From the very first day of my employment, my superiors knew that I was a recovering alcoholic and a member of A.A.. Quietly they called on me many times when an employee was in trouble because of his/her drinking. Of course it was understood that the employee in question was always asked if I could be called in before I was. I insisted on that one condition. I understand that today an employer may not be that considerate.

Things were going good for me at work and I was

390

enjoying my activities in Alcoholics Anonymous, but at home things were getting bad. Our oldest son Keith was beginning to give us serious problems. He would not stay in school and was openly defying my efforts to discipline him. In November of 1962, when he turned seventeen he enlisted in the army and we signed the papers for him gladly.

In the meantime my wife Irene was constantly under the care of one doctor or another. She was in and out of hospitals on a regular basis. I lost count of the number of times and the reasons for her hospitalizations. Regardless of what was done for Irene she didn't seem able to stay well for any length of time.

Arline, our next to the oldest daughter, had been bringing home failing report cards throughout her school life. Every report card would cause a scene in the house with me adding my ignorant comments to everyone else's. Arline was always devastated by those encounters. I never expected her to be promoted but every year she was. When she entered the eighth grade a knowledgeable teacher suspected that Arline's problems stemmed from dyslexia and testing proved her right. By then Arline was so far behind her classmates she felt out of place. As a result, when she turned seventeen in 1964, she refused to go to school one more day and I could not get myself to demand otherwise. I knew by then that she had been going through her own private hell for a long time. The very next year she got married to a young man she had known for only a few months. The year after that, 1966, our oldest daughter, Regina got married. Three of our children had left home in rapid succession and I felt the losses deeply.

Although I was having mixed feelings about the changes that were taking place in my family, 1966 was a good year for me in other areas of my life. That was the year the company offered to pay for my high school education through the International Correspondence Schools. That accomplishment took five years and led to a promotion. I became a front-line supervisor in charge of shipping and receiving. Unfortunately I had to leave that company in 1973 shortly after it was sold to a conglomerate. That was because my future with them became too uncertain.

Right in the middle of my high school course, when I really needed the time to study, I was forced to put everything on hold for a while and pay attention to Irene. That time she had withdrawn into her own world again and had become deeply depressed. So off to the doctor we went to keep an appointment I didn't know she had made. By then I was frantic. My mind was recalling the hours I had spent waiting in doctor's offices ... the additional hours visiting Irene in hospitals. I knew then that I was not the cause of her problems through my sexual needs.

After waiting the usual hour to see the doctor Irene was called in. I think I surprised everyone by marching right into the doctor's examination room with her. As soon as the doctor came into the room I blurted,

"Look, doctor, for the past twenty years I have taken this woman to doctor after doctor, year after year, without any relief. Would you please tell me today if there is anything wrong with her and if there is can you fix it! If there is nothing wrong with her I want you to tell me that too so I can act accordingly!"

I regretted my words the minute they were out of my mouth. Although the outburst had relieved my own frustration for the moment the shocked expression on both Irene's face and the doctor's let me know I had hurt them.

Rather sheepishly the doctor said,

"Well, Mr. Carpenter, we'll do our best to find out what's wrong. You are welcome to stay while I examine your wife if you like."

Wanting to take the sting out of the things I had just

said, I now added,

"No thank you doctor, you know what you're doing. I'll wait in the waiting room until you finish."

I figured if this doctor could help at all I didn't need to make an enemy out of him. It was my turn to feel sheepish as I slipped out the door.

Fifteen minutes later Irene was out of the doctor's examining room. She came up to me and said,

"The doctor wants to see you."

When I stepped into the doctor's office he said,

"Mr. Carpenter, I have given your wife a mild antidepressant and I have suggested she become more involved in the world around her. What she really needs," the doctor said, "is some close friends and something to take her interest."

When we got home I encouraged her to come to some open A.A. meetings with me but she didn't want to. Next I suggested, rather strongly, that she join Al-Anon but she refused. Then I insisted that she come to a marriage counselor with me. I even made an appointment for us for the following week.

The very next day, after I had gone to work, Irene withdrew our small savings from the bank, took the baby Andrea out of school and went home to her mother in Maine. Our youngest son, Freeman, refused to go with her or she would have taken him out of school also.

I was really at my wit's end that time. I could see that as long as we had children living at home where she could use them as pawns I couldn't force her to do anything. I resigned myself to living in an unhappy environment, at least for the moment. I had also decided not to react to her rash behavior. I reasoned that the only thing I could do was to wait awhile to see what she would do next. For the moment I could enjoy the peace her absence made possible.

Two weeks later she phoned one night and asked if she could come home. Not being able to think of anything else to say I said, "This is your home --- this is where you belong."

However, I was so angry over what she had done that it took me two full months before I could trust myself to speak to her about it without losing my temper. When I was sure I had my rage under control I took her for a ride one evening so we could talk without the children hearing us. We parked along the river where it was peaceful and quiet. In a very calm, matter of fact voice I said,

"Irene, whatever happens between you and me from now on, don't you dare interfere with our children's education. If you do something like that again I can't be sure of what I will do but you won't like it."

I was surprised to find myself getting angry again in spite of my efforts to remain cool. I was trembling it was that intense. Irene didn't answer me, I hadn't expected her too. She never did in situations like that. However, I think she knew how deadly serious I was. Even at that though, I didn't give her any reason to be afraid of me any longer. I stopped talking about a marriage counselor and everything else. From then on we just tolerated each other but it was killing me spiritually. I was fortunate to have my studies to return to; they helped to keep me sane and stable.

When I finished my high school course and received my diploma I was fifty-two years old. I was able then to increase my activities in Alcoholics Anonymous and to get involved in community projects.

All during the 1960's whatever time I could spare was spent with a group of people who were trying

394

to establish a certification board for alcoholics and drug abuse counselors in Pennsylvania. We wanted to bring professionalism and integrity into the field. When we finally had a board firmly in place I was "grandfathered in" as a certified addiction counselor and soon became one of their oral examiners. During that same time, with another small group, I helped to create The Chester County Council on Addictive Diseases. It has been exciting and rewarding for me to be a part of a pioneering profession.

I write about these accomplishments because I believe it is vital that recovering people become knowledgeable about their condition. In doing so they insure their own recovery and they can be much more helpful to others who are looking for answers.

While these changes were taking place in the community, changes were taking place at home too. In August of 1967 our youngest son, Freeman, voluntarily went into the service. Just after his basic training he married his girlfriend and was shipped out to Vietnam. He was only there six months when he was severely burned while repairing army tanks in the field. He was flown to a burn center in Japan and a few months later he was sent back to the United States where he finished out his three-year hitch. His burns left no permanent scars.

Then in 1971 our youngest daughter Andrea got married. She was nineteen and the last child to leave home. I had promised myself years before that I would leave Irene when the children were grown. I should have left her then. We were still hardly talking to each other, but I was afraid to. You see, some years before, when Irene was accusing me of seeing another woman, she had said,

"Freeman, if you ever leave me I will kill myself."

I had taken her words seriously and didn't dare leave even when I had the opportunity to. I didn't want her death on my conscience.

One year after another went by --- five of them since Andrea left. Irene was overweight and depressed and I was angry and sullen. I was still active in A.A. and in the community but my actions were more automatic than spontaneous. I was living in a spiritual blackout. My mind didn't realize how sick I was but my body did.

In March of 1976 I had a heart attack that almost killed me. I was rushed in a police ambulance to the nearest hospital. When they got me stabilized in the emergency room, a doctor whom I had never seen before, leaned over my bed and said,

"Mr. Carpenter, what is there in your life that is making you so unhappy that you decided to have a heart attack?"

I was shocked.

"Do you mean to tell me that I'm doing this to myself?" I asked.

"Certainly," the doctor said, "at one time it used to be fashionable for people to have a nervous breakdown, now it's fashionable to have a heart attack."

He left me then, as quietly as he had come in, but he left me with an awful lot to think about.

A few hours later the verdict was in --- open-heart surgery was absolutely necessary. There was only one problem the doctor told me. They may not be able to save my life even with the surgery.

"We are afraid you will have another heart attack while on the operating table," the doctor said.

At first I was angry at God for doing this to me. That brought on a depression and my companion, self-pity, who had been absent for so long, returned in full force. I indulged myself that way for only about twelve hours before my A.A. training came to my rescue. My thoughts turned to the many years of sobriety God had blessed me with. As I looked around the hospital and saw all the professional people who were going to try to save my life, I became grateful. I realized that none of that would have been available to me if I was dying drunk somewhere in a dark alley.

I prayed. That time I didn't ask God to spare my life. I believed that He knew I wanted to live. I prayed for Him just to be with me during surgery and whatever His will was for me, I was ready.

I can not describe the peace that flooded through me. All my fears dissolved and I felt warm from my head to my feet. I had the sensation that no matter what was going to happen to me I was going to be all right because I was in God's hands. I signed the papers for the surgery and turned my life over to God and to those men in white.

Early in the morning of the day surgery was scheduled, the surgeon came into my room and said,

"Freeman, I understand that today is your birthday."

"Yes, it is doctor," I answered.

"Would you like me to delay the surgery until tomorrow?" he asked.

"No sir," I said, "if you can do this for me today it would be the best birthday present I ever had."

He smiled then, patted me on the shoulder and said, "See you in the operating room in a few minutes." A nurse gave me a shot of something in my right arm and soon I began to drift off.

The next thing I knew, eight hours had gone by, and I came-to in the recovery room. I had made it through a triple by-pass operation. I had been briefed earlier about not moving because of all the tubes I would have sticking in me. The most uncomfortable was the one down my throat. However, although I couldn't move, I could think.

"If I only have a short time left on this earth I had better make the best of it. I'm going to tell Irene that I can't live with her any longer", I thought. I had already decided that if she did kill herself I would probably cry for her. I had promised myself I would bury her even if we were divorced. But I would not blame myself even if our children pointed a guilty finger at me. However, I was not foolhardy; I knew I had to get on my feet again before I could do anything else.

The road back was very slow and painful but I had a joy in my heart that wasn't there before and it was comforting. It took me over six months to recover enough to leave Irene, but I did get a divorce. She did not fight it and she didn't even attempt to commit suicide. I was as mad as hell that she hadn't even tried. Not that I wanted her dead by any means. I was angry that she had kept me at her side for such a long time with a threat she had no intention of carrying out. Later though, when I could laugh at my own foolishness, I thanked God for her inability to carry through even if she had wanted to.

When I walked away from Irene that day, knowing I was finished with that relationship, my spirits soared. I felt open and clean. The lie was over. But, there were days when I would feel terrible over the break up. On many a damp rainy day I felt the loneliness deeply and thinking about my childhood I would think, "I don't belong anywhere. Nobody wants me". I swore then that I would never marry again. I wasn't going to let another woman hurt me like that ever again. I also knew that I had not been the easiest man to live with. Not knowing anything about passive aggressive behavior, and still less about people suffering from depression, I probably did a lot of harm to Irene by the way I responded to her. I was not devastated by that realization but I did not want to harm another woman because of my ignorance of intimacy. So I had two very good reasons for vowing to stay away from women.

As my private life was being overhauled in 1976 the Governor's office on Drug and Alcohol Programs sponsored me into an intensive training course for alcohol and drug abuse counselors. The didactic portion of the training was held at Johns Hopkins University in Baltimore, Maryland, and I did my field practicum at the Veteran's Hospital in Coatesville, PA. In order to teach me what therapy was, and how to apply it, the instructors practiced therapy on me. What a valuable gift that was! I proved to be a receptive subject and the result was dramatic. I felt rejuvenated and alive as never before. When graduation time arrived, I was proud that my youngest son, Freeman, was in the audience to share in my accomplishment.

Then, right after my training I became the Executive Director of a halfway house for male recovering alcoholics and drug addicts. The house could accommodate sixteen men at a time and we always had a waiting list. For three years I lived with those men and for over two of those years I was the only staff member on duty. When I finally insisted that the Board of Directors get me some help, they hired a man with a college degree and gave him my title. I became the house manager. After seeing two hundred and twenty-five men go through that house, many of them still sober, I knew that I had to move on. The house needed different leadership and I could not be just a house manager. I began to look for another challenge. Seventeen years have passed since we opened that halfway house; at this writing, and it is still open today. I thank God for the privilege of being a part of it's beginning.

The support we received from the local A.A. members was outstanding right from the start. They really made the difference between success and failure for many of the men. With their help and continuing support we started two A.A. meetings in the house, one on Monday evenings and the other on Fridays at noon. Those meetings are still active today.

I MET MEGAN

It was during the last three months of my involvement in the halfway house that I began to wish for the companionship of a woman. That surprised and frightened me. I had thought that women were out of my life for good. I began to include my desires and my concerns in my daily prayers and as usual things began to happen.

In less than a month, at one of our Monday evening meetings, I met Megan. Megan was a forty-eight year old, divorced, professional woman who looked younger than her age. She was a college-educated physical therapist with a substantial income and very independent. She had been a member of our fellowship for five years by the time I met her.

At first I didn't look at Megan as a romantic possibility. To me she seemed too young and too pretty to be interested in someone like me. I thought she was paying attention to me only because I was the manager of the house and therefore an interesting character. However, when she called one day and invited me to the theater, I had to take another look. We began to date frequently then, and I found I enjoyed being with her, especially after a hectic day with the men. It was not long before I was taking her to the theater and many other places of interest. I was captured by her professionalism, her quietness and her warmth.

Meantime, knowing my mission at the halfway house was nearing an end, I began sending out resumes looking for another job. Ten interviews and three months later, in May of 1982, I accepted a position as a therapist in a prestigious psychiatric hospital. They had a long-term substance abuse/recovery program,

400

and I fit in right from the start. I rented an apartment near the hospital and Megan helped me pick out the furniture for it. From then on our relationship became a bit more intimate. We were together almost every evening and I began to feel as if I had known her all my life.

As our relationship deepened and finally grew into a love affair we were able to be quite open with each other. Walking along the riverbank on quiet evenings I told Megan more about myself than I had ever told anyone. She in turn told me all about herself, including her drinking, her involvement in Alcoholics Anonymous and even about her divorce. As we shared our stories with each other I found Megan's to be as unique as any I had ever heard. She has given me permission to share it with you.

MEGAN'S STORY

Megan told me that she had been a teetotaler until she was thirty-six years old, and she said she had felt very sanctimonious about that. She went on to tell me that she and her husband Dennis had married late in life. She was twenty-nine and Dennis was near forty. It was the first marriage for both. Because of their ages they both wanted a child as soon as possible, but try as they might it wasn't happening for them. The doctors could find nothing wrong with either of them even though they were sent to experts. And so they kept on trying --- for five years they tried.

Then, late in 1962, new symptoms appeared that were unrelated to childbearing. Megan began to experience periods of dizziness and confusion. At times she would lose her train of thought right in the middle of a sentence and her speech would become slurred. Those symptoms were often accompanied by transient feelings of numbness all down her right side. It was especially frightening for her when she went to brake her car because her reactions were slow and cumbersome. Her handwriting became illegible.

Eventually the situation became so bad she was admitted into the hospital. There, tests discovered a blood clot on the left side of her brain. It was decided that surgery was necessary to save her life. The delicate twelve-hour operation was a complete success, and Megan was on her feet and back home within two months. Four months later she was as good as ever.

After the surgery she and Dennis began talking seriously about adopting a baby. The proceedings were put in motion, and eleven months later they had a beautiful nine-month old baby girl. They called her Samantha. Megan and Dennis were thrilled, and as so often happens in cases such as theirs, Megan found herself pregnant ten months after the adoption.

Although Megan and Dennis were pleased about this new turn of events, her doctor was not. In fact he was concerned. The source of Megan's blood clot almost two years before had never been conclusively determined. He was apprehensive over any major changes in Megan such as a pregnancy. He was concerned about her developing another clot which could prove fatal. So he recommended, "No more children after this baby".

Then when their son Whitney was born in July of 1965, Megan was as happy as any mother could be, but she had her tubes tied just the same in order to comply with her doctor's recommendation.

Everything went well for Megan and her family for over a year after her son was born. Then the confusion and the slurred speech she had experienced before the surgery reappeared sporadically. She said she found herself crying a lot with no sensible explanation for the tears. After a thorough examination they found no reason to be alarmed. Her doctor told Megan to learn to live with it. He said,

"Go home, forget it and take care of your

children."

Megan said she was crushed, she felt as though her complaints had not been taken seriously. However, she tried to follow the doctor's suggestion. She tried to ignore her mood swings. The symptoms did not go away though and as time went by Megan felt overwhelmed by her mounting responsibilities. It got so bad that one night Megan called her doctor and asked if he could prescribe something so she could get a night's sleep. After listening to her complaints for a few minutes her doctor asked,

"Do you have any wine in the house, Megan?"

"Yes we do," she replied.

"Well, take a small glass of wine before you go to bed tonight and I think you will be all right," the doctor said.

Megan took a four-ounce glass of wine and in her own words, she said, "I felt warm and well all over." She slept soundly that night and without realizing it she was hooked! From then on she could not go to bed without her wine. Within six months her four-ounce glass became a tumbler-full and bedtime began to get a little earlier.

One day, out of curiosity, Megan tasted some creme sherry. She loved it. Then Megan found that if she took a glass of wine before she went out to meet friends her social life became more enjoyable.

Along with many other interests, Megan was a service unit director for thirty Girl Scout troops in her area. As such, she would often find herself in charge of a meeting for the thirty to forty Girl Scout troop leaders. Regardless of her position though, Megan said she had always felt alone and different. As a part of her self-made defense system, she would go to those meetings with her agenda well laid out. During the meeting she would be stoic, serious and in charge. But after she began to drink, she found that a little wine changed all that in an instant. She said she felt at one with the women for the first time. She was relaxed as never before and she found she could talk and joke with the women as if they were her close friends. For a few moments of her life Megan said she found she could forget that feeling of loneliness and it was marvelous.

For almost three years alcohol was good to Megan, but her drinking was slowly increasing without her being aware of it. Then one day Dennis began to complain about her bad breath. In an effort to get around his complaints Megan changed her daytime drinking from wine to vodka because somewhere she had heard you couldn't smell that!

She was drinking from the time she got up in the morning until she went to bed, and of course she would have to have her nightly glass of wine. She knew Dennis couldn't say anything about that because she was only "following the doctor's orders".

By that time Megan was buying so much liquor that she was ashamed of her consumption. Because of that she began to visit several liquor stores in the area where she was not known and she would only buy a little alcohol from each. She began to be concerned about her supply then, constantly worried she would run out at a time when she couldn't get more. She had bottles hidden all over the house but it was her basement that became her favorite hiding place. She said she could go down there and take a slug right out of the bottle anytime she felt like it. And she said, she felt like it often. As no one else ever went into the cellar she said she felt safe there.

Megan told me that as her drinking progressed she began spending a lot of time in the bathroom throwing up everything she had eaten. She knew she was in trouble but felt helpless and alone. To make matters worse, somehow she had gotten hold of some valium and began to add that to her daily intake. By that time her husband was aware of her drinking but may not have realized how bad it really had become.

He complained about her lack of interest in everything including sex. Megan thought that she was going insane but kept her thoughts and her fears to herself.

Then in 1977 two events took place in rapid succession that changed Megan's life completely. The first was a family fishing trip in the middle of February. Dennis wanted to teach the two children about ice fishing and they were eager to learn. Early that morning Megan got the picnic baskets ready but she was drinking a bit more than usual as she was doing so. Then, in order to have enough alcohol for the day, without being caught, Megan took a large thermos of home-made vegetable soup and laced it liberally with vodka.

Megan had her first blackout that day. She said she remembers getting to the picnic site all right, but that was about all she could recall when she woke up in her own bed the next morning. She became terrified that she had said or done something stupid or harmful the day before. Nevertheless, as frightening as that experience had been, Megan could not stop her drinking even though she tried. She knew a blackout was one of the beginning symptoms of alcoholism. The realization that she was an alcoholic became very clear to her and she felt doomed.

Then, on Mother's Day, just three months after her blackout, Megan had her last drink.

The family had planned a special picnic for that day. Megan was up early and drinking before anyone else was up. She said she didn't take any liquor on the picnic that time, partly because of what happened in February and partly because Dennis was watching her a little closer than before. She felt she could go six or eight hours without a drink at least once. Besides, she had a couple of valiums in her purse just in case.

They arrived at Valley Forge National Park early that morning, but even at that hour it was getting crowded. There were so many children running all over

the park that one would think it was kids day! Megan
found an empty picnic table and staked her claim.
Samantha and Whitney were off playing with the other
children even before Megan had spread out the
blankets.

In less than an hour Dennis and Megan had found
something to argue about. As the morning wore on the
atmosphere between them became strained. At lunchtime
the two children were excited and happy, but Megan and
Dennis were sullen and silent. The youthful joy of
the children seemed to aggravate Megan and Dennis
because right after lunch they decided to call it a
day. The children were disappointed and hurt for
being pulled away from so much fun. Megan and Dennis
were both angry and they were not speaking to each
other. The twenty-five mile drive home was anything
but comfortable. By the time they reached home even
the kids were glad.

As soon as Megan could get away from Dennis she
went right down into the cellar to her bottle. When
the two stiff drinks didn't seem to do what Megan was
looking for she downed eight valiums on top of them.
By dinnertime she was asleep (passed out?) on the
living room sofa. She said she had no idea how long
she had slept but when she became conscious again the
house was deadly quiet. However, Megan sensed that
she was not alone in the room. Slowly she opened her
eyes and the sight that greeted her almost broke her
heart. Standing at the foot of the sofa was her
twelve-year old son and his sister Samantha. Whitney
had found one of the half-empty bottles of vodka Megan
had hidden somewhere. He didn't say a word, he just
held the bottle in front of him in both his small
hands, one on the neck of the bottle and the other
under its bottom. The look of disgust on the
children's faces and the hurt in their eyes stabbed
Megan right in the heart. For a fraction of a moment
the children stared at Megan, then Whitney threw the
bottle onto the sofa at Megan's feet and ran from the
room with Samantha right behind him.

With a strong feeling of self-loathing Megan

slowly got up from the sofa and began to prepare a late dinner. Her actions were automatic, her brain was almost numb. When dinner was ready and the children came in for a bite, Megan couldn't look them in the eyes and they didn't want to look at her. Megan said she couldn't remember what she had made for dinner nor if anyone ate anything. She went to bed very early and for the first time in seven years she did not take any wine.

But, Megan could not go to sleep. She missed the soothing effects the wine had always given her. The aftereffects of the valium made her skin crawl. The images of her son holding her bottle and the expression of disgust on the children's faces were clearly etched in her mind. Her guilt was monumental, her self-esteem nonexistent. She was surely at her bottom, and she knew this had to end. When Dennis slid into bed hours later Megan pretended to be asleep. She was jealous over how fast he dropped off to sleep and resented his apparent lack of concern.

To this day Megan says she doesn't know how she got through the night without losing her mind. And when Dennis began to stir early in the morning Megan doesn't think that she was responsible for what happened next. It seemed as though a force outside of herself moved her body, she can't remember having anything to do with it. Impulsively she got out of bed, walked around to Dennis' side, and threw herself on her knees. With genuine tears streaming down her face she cried,

"Dennis, I need help. God I have to do something about my drinking."

Dennis, of course, was awake immediately.

"What's wrong, Megan?" Dennis asked, "what do you want me to do?"

Megan says she didn't hear Dennis clearly because she was listening to a small voice in her own head, the voice said, "Call Alcoholics Anonymous ---

407

you should have called them a long time ago."
Immediately in her own head she heard another voice
counter, "I don't know their telephone number." "Yes
you do," came back the small voice, "it's in the phone
book." And so, Megan looked up at Dennis and said,
"I'm going to call Alcoholics Anonymous today Dennis,
I need their help."

Dennis was skeptical, but he was willing to help
Megan do anything if it would help her to stop
drinking.

"Do what you have to do Megan," he grumbled, as
if he was tired of the whole thing.

At eight o'clock sharp Megan called a club house
of A.A. in the area.

"Good morning, this is A.A.. How can we help
you?" a male voice came through the wire. The man
sounded pleasant and friendly.

"I want to talk to someone about joining A.A.,"
Megan said.

"Well, there is a meeting here at eight o'clock
tonight," the voice said, "we would be pleased to see
you at the meeting."

"I'll be there," Megan said and hung up. It was
done --- she had gotten through the hardest part. She
was now committed. There was a feeling of relief, as
though a weight had been lifted from her shoulders.

At the meeting that night Megan met a young
woman who really took an interest in her. Megan said
she didn't remember much that went on during the
meeting. It was all too new to her. However, after
the meeting the girl asked Megan,

"What time of the day is the toughest for you?"

"Four o'clock in the afternoon," Megan answered.
"That's when the kids come home from school and I have

to think of getting dinner ready."

"I'll call you," the girl said. And sure enough, every day at four o'clock sharp, Megan got a call from that young woman wanting to know how Megan was doing. That routine lasted for more than thirty days, plenty of time for Megan to find a sponsor she could relate to.

Megan's emotional roller-coaster ride into sobriety began in earnest. Two years later, still sober and off of all tranquilizers, and after trying everything --- including marriage counseling --- Megan and Dennis were divorced. Three years later I became an important part of Megan's life and she became a wonderful part of mine.

OUR MARRIAGE

It took me the better part of a four-year courtship to learn all I did about Megan. By then I felt that I had healed enough myself to make a decent husband and so I proposed. To my fearful delight Megan accepted.

The wedding was beautiful. It was in Megan's church with her minister presiding. We had a friend sing for us who had a magnificent tenor voice. He sang the Ave Maria, Oh Promise Me and The Lord's Prayer. His singing sent shivers up and down my spine.

All five of my children were there as were Megan's son and daughter. Samantha was maid of honor and Whitney gave her away. My two sons, Keith and Freeman, acted as ushers and helped the activities run smooth. Our friends from the program, our friends from the church and the members and guests from both families crowded the sanctuary. Then, when Megan and I exchanged vows I felt the presence of the spirit of God and knew that He had blessed our relationship. I promised God, Megan and myself that I would be a better husband to Megan than I had been to Irene.

LIFE GOES ON

Megan and I had been married for over two years when my second open-heart surgery became necessary. That too was a close call. However, I had been blessed with Megan and every time I opened my eyes I could see her through the haze of my medication. The doctors saved my life with their surgery but it was Megan who mended my heart with her love.

Ten happy years have gone by since Megan and I married. She has nursed me through a couple of bad times with my heart problems and I have helped her through a few of hers. We all seem to have our personal cross to bear and Megan is no exception.

The surgery that saved her life in 1962 left scar tissue where the clot had been. Megan had no noticeable problems because of the scar tissue except that her handwriting, gradually became worse. Then in 1988 she began to have mild seizures on the right side of her face that would pull the corner of her mouth up just a little. Those seizures only lasted for fifteen or twenty seconds but they interrupted her thought process and made communication difficult. She was placed on Dilantin then, and the seizures were controlled for a while. Megan was able to function very well for a long time without anyone knowing about the problem except her children and myself. However, it took stronger medication to keep the seizures down and the medication brought on side effects.

Her ability to recall ordinary words in everyday conversation decreased rapidly until it became obvious to everybody and a daily burden to her. Because of that, in June of 1993, she was forced to retire on disability from her physical therapy profession. However, she has some bad days every now and then. But she has learned to laugh at herself and she goes on day-by-day, one day at a time.

Many of our friends comment on our obvious happiness and ask us what our secret is. We tell them that it is no secret that we have the A.A. program as a guide. And of course we have pledged to love, honor and respect each other with the help of God.

One thing more about Megan before we leave her. The book you are now reading was started when I was recovering from my first open-heart surgery in 1977. Within two years I had it over half written but then I set it aside and left it alone. But ever since we married, Megan gently but persistently kept at me to get it out of mothballs and finish it. Today as I write my closing pages I can say,

"Thank you Megan, for this book. I am sure that if it weren't for you it would still be in the cellar in a box."

As for me, I am retired now. After my second heart surgery I left the psychiatric hospital. No longer would it be wise for me to work forty hours a week. Shortly thereafter I was hired as a therapist in a detoxification unit in a local hospital. Sixteen to twenty hours a week was ideal. That job was so rewarding I kept it for four years. I only left then because they closed the unit for lack of funding.

I do some volunteer work at a local council and speak in schools and colleges from time to time. I still go to meetings regularly. I can always find ways to do twelve step work.

Throughout my lifetime I have gradually learned how to honor the fellowship of A.A., work the program into my daily life, live up to the principles A.A. teaches and uphold the traditions.

Today I consider myself to be a fairly well-adjusted individual. Self-pity and resentments, once constant companions, are now unwelcome strangers. The migraine headaches I used to get are now just bad memories from a distant past. Periodic bouts of depression became less frequent, and eventually disappeared. My attitude toward God, once intensely agnostic, changed to one of acknowledgment and then to acceptance. The courage I had taken from a bottle I now get from prayer and meditation. Today I enjoy peace of mind, self-respect and a new self-confidence. In other words my mind and my heart have mended tremendously since I began my journey into health.

In the beginning my personal recovery was a direct challenge. A challenge to develop poise, increase my knowledge, strengthen my courage, and to learn how to love myself and others. Now it has become a new and greater challenge --- to grow old gracefully and to die with dignity when my time comes. And so, my recovery from alcoholism, ignorance, boredom and fear continues to this day. Because of my alcoholism and my desperate need to remain sober, my life has been an exciting adventure.

Over the years I have had many a scary day with Megan, watching her deal with her physical problems and not knowing how to be helpful. And there have been a few frightening days with my bad heart acting up on me. But never again have I railed about my fate. The peace I had felt just before my first heart surgery has stayed with me and is quietly present in my heart even today. That peace, I believe, is a gift from God.

I will end this book appropriately with a thank you and a prayer.

> "Thank you God, for Alcoholics Anonymous. Thank you Alcoholics Anonymous for helping me through the toughest battle of my life. It has been exhilarating and rewarding. Although there are many skirmishes ahead I have been taught how to handle them, or if I can't, where to get the help I need. Slowly I have come to believe that which so many people had been trying to tell me for years - People <u>can</u> be trusted, God <u>does</u> love me, and <u>life</u> <u>is</u> <u>good</u>. May God be as good to you as He has been to Megan and me".

Your friend in recovery.

Freeman Carpenter - A pseudonym of course

For years I thought my alcoholism
was a curse. Today I know it was
a blessing in disguise because it
forced me to think and to learn.

Recovery is not an event - - -
it is a life long process.

Would you like to send a copy of this book to a friend? Then just send $ 17.95 plus $3.50 for shipping and handling for each copy using the order form below and mail to:

The Unique Educational Services
P.O. Box 341
Newtown, PA 18940

BOOK ORDER FORM

NAME_____ NUMBER OF BOOKS @_____

STREET ADDRESS_____ APT.#_____

CITY_____ STATE_____ ZIP_____

TOTAL AMOUNT ENCLOSED_____

BOOK ORDER FORM

NAME_____ NUMBER OF BOOKS @_____

STREET ADDRESS_____ APT.#_____

CITY_____ STATE_____ ZIP_____

TOTAL AMOUNT ENCLOSED_____

The Unique Educational Services
P.O. Box 341
Newtown, PA 18940